LIBRARY

Gift of

The Bush
Foundation

AUTHORIAL CONQUESTS

AUTHORIAL CONQUESTS

Essays on Genre
in the Writings
of Margaret Cavendish

Edited by
Line Cottegnies and Nancy Weitz

Madison • Teaneck
Fairleigh Dickinson University Press
London: Associated University Presses

Associated University Presses
2010 Eastpark Boulevard
Cranbury, NJ 08512

Associated University Presses
Unit 304, The Chandlery
50 Westminster Bridge Road
London SE1 7QY, England

Associated University Presses
P.O. Box 338, Port Credit
Mississauga, Ontario
Canada L5G 4L8

The paper used in this publication meets the requirements of the American National Standard for Permanence of Paper for Printed Library Materials Z39.48-1984.

Library of Congress Cataloging-in-Publication Data

Authorial conquests : essays on genre in the writings of Margaret Cavendish / edited by Line Cottegnies and Nancy Weitz.
    p. cm.
Includes bibliographical references and index.
ISBN 0-8386-3983-6 (alk. paper)
    1. Newcastle, Margaret Cavendish, Duchess of, 1624?–1674—Criticism and interpretation. 2. Women and literature—England—History—17th century. 3. Literary form. I. Cottegnies, Line. II. Weitz, Nancy, 1961–
PR3605.N2 A94 2003
828'.409—dc21   2002152747

Contents

Introduction

LINE COTTEGNIES AND NANCY WEITZ

I dedicate this Book to Fortune, for I believe she is a powerfull
Princess; . . . Wherefore if Fortune please, with her helping
hand, she may place my Book in Fames high Tow'r, where
every word, like a Cymball, shall make a Tinkling Noise; and
the whole Volume, like a Cannon Bullet, shall Eccho from Side
to Side of Fames large Brasen Walls, and make so loud a
Report, that all the World shall hear it.

Margaret Cavendish, *The Worlds Olio*
(London, 1655), fol. A1–A1v

MARGARET LUCAS CAVENDISH, DUCHESS OF NEWCASTLE (1623?–
1673), and her voluminous literary and philosophical works still
conjure up for many the image of "Mad Madge," the sometimes
lovable and vaguely improper woman scribbling away at a writing desk or riding through Hyde Park in her carriage in fanciful
costume, as immortalized by Samuel Pepys, the Evelyns, Dorothy Osborne, and, more recently, Virginia Woolf.[1] Her full and
rich biography, and the many historical figures who discuss her
in their own better-known writings, effectively prevented Cavendish's works from receiving concerted, serious attention for centuries: whenever the writings were mentioned, the same few poetic passages with their "eccentric" images were trotted out as
proof of her madness and thus gave license to disregard her work
as frivolous, fanciful, unstructured, uneducated. In the 1980s,
feminist critics wishing to retrieve Cavendish from oblivion not
surprisingly found the contradictions in her work infuriating and
often responded with a half-disappointed, half-defensive attitude
toward her. Due to the importance and influence of these studies,
this reaction lingers, despite the fact that her works are now
widely studied by scholars of English literature, philosophy, history, the history of science and women's studies alike.[2]

The intent of this book has been to encourage scholars and critics to find new ways to approach and account for the enigma of Cavendish's poetics and to offer a contribution to the recent Cavendish Renaissance[3]: it strives to approach her writings as a whole instead of atomizing them to make them fit critical agendas. Our contention is that the various works, precisely because of their puzzling, challenging nature, deserve full attention as original literary productions entering into dialogue with a tradition. Our aim has therefore been to explore the reverberations that emerge between her works and those of her contemporaries in carefully contextualized, theoretically informed studies. The contributions to this volume are international and interdisciplinary; they represent a range of modern critical approaches and offer a variety of responses and opinions— sometimes at odds with one another—about Cavendish's status within literary, intellectual, and cultural history. But as will be apparent, they are all, in their several ways, attempts to overcome the theory/history divide by harmoniously integrating these approaches. Cavendish's works, more than any others', it seems, require a hybrid perspective, and it bears evidence to their complexity and modernity that they still challenge their readers' responses and reading practices three-and-a-half centuries after they were first written.

That Cavendish thought of her works as contributing to a whole is apparent in the extraordinary variety of genres and forms she practiced. Although she may not have set out on this great literary project with Aristotelian generic categories in mind, the thoroughness of her long-term, systematic endeavor is indubitable.[4] Paying tribute to her husband's influence, in *The Worlds Olio* (1655), she clearly defines her enterprise:

> The reason why I have not dedicated any of my particular Books to your Lordship, is, that when I have writ all I mean to print, I intend, if I live, to Dedicate the whole Summe of my Works unto you, and not by Parcells: for indeed you are my Wits Patron.[5]

She refers again to this intention in her 1662 *Orations upon Divers Sorts,* which testifies to the adamancy of her resolve.[6] She wrote poetry and prose, didactic and lyrical works, and experimented with poetry, miscellania, prose fiction (tales and a 'novel'), philosophical treatises and orations, a biography and an autobiographical narrative, familiar letters and moral essays, and finally two collections of plays. This carefully planned "conquest," as her favourite metaphor of world exploration suggests, fits perfectly with her self-designation as "Margaret the First," which appears in her preface to *The Blazing World,* a creative exploration and reforming of new worlds.[7] Elsewhere, she is the self-crowned "Authoress," and also describes herself in "A True Relation of my Birth, Breeding and Life" as a General sending her works out marching "on the ground of white paper."[8]

In spite of this encyclopedic, comprehensive literary project, many critics have until recently taken her claim to ignorance and lack of education at face value, very likely as a reaction to her stylistic idiosyncrasies and tendency toward repetitiveness. The essays in this book make apparent the extent of reading, absorbing, and reshaping behind her writing practice; they demonstrate that we should peer beyond what appears largely as a self-protective strategy of *captatio benevolentiae* from an author eager to defuse accusations of excessive ambition. Due to the sheer bulk of her writings (sixteen folios totaling well over eight thousand pages), most studies have had to limit themselves to just one aspect of her production, generally focusing closely on a single work. Although valuable in themselves, the danger of such studies has been that many works and even whole genres have been left untouched. Consequently, the coherence of her thought has often been overstressed when in fact her corpus is replete with—even, in some respects, dependent upon—contradictions. Cavendish's literary practice is, in fact, highly sophisticated. This is not to say that each time she put pen to paper, she was in absolute control of the results, but she seems to have conceived her literary project as a conscious and deliberate exploration of the various forms and genres available to her at the time.

No single critical or rhetorical study could have given Cavendish a comprehensive knowledge of genres since, in a period when theory was nonexistent, genres were largely implicit notions, materialized by sets of tacit rather than formalized conventions.[9] Indeed, the essays in this book all recognize that no work of literature can exist in isolation: as Jean-Marie Schaeffer points out, each work necessarily defines itself, implicitly or explicitly, through the relations it establishes with other works,

when the author endorses or departs from widely shared, prescriptive practices.[10] As Alastair Fowler also reminds us, these
obey, often implicitly, a kind of codification, although the system
itself is constantly in transformation. The relationship literary
works entertain with "the genres they embody is not one of passive membership but of active modulation."[11] Thus, the complex
relationship to convention also determines the reader's response
to it. According to Tzvetan Todorov:

> [I]ndividual texts are produced and perceived in relation to the norm
> constituted by that codification. A genre, whether literary or not, is
> nothing other than the codification of discursive properties. . . . It is
> because genres exist in an institution that they function as "horizons
> of expectation" for readers and models for writing for authors.[12]

Even though Cavendish's works have often been described as
unclassifiable, in the wake of her own claim to absolute "singularity," an investigation into her own intercourse with generic
conventions proves that she did write in recognizable forms, implicitly inserting herself in a lineage and reshaping discursive
regimes through her own creative *bricolage*. Some of these are
relatively easy to decode: the moral *Orations* remind us of Bacon's essays, while her "romance," *Blazing World,* contains clear
echoes of his *New Atlantis;* her philosophical letters borrow a
form popularized by Descartes; her drama seems to echo Jonson
as well as Shakespeare, and so forth. But beyond isolated references to individuals, our claim is here that Cavendish takes up
generic categories as a conscious strategy to integrate herself
within a literary tradition and construct her fame as a "complete
author"—an enterprise never before attempted. "I am not covet-
ous, but as ambitious as ever any of my sex was, is, or can be," she
wrote in *The Blazing World* (124).

This book tries to render justice to this extraordinary literary
ambition by examining the way she patiently and systematically
appropriates genre after genre. As is apparent in the variety of
essays that follows, her creativity never lags: espousing common
forms, she then breaks away from servility to the tradition, sometimes turning those forms into something intensely idiosyncratic
and personal, but always with a flair for literary originality. This
is perhaps one of the major discoveries of this book—that Caven-

dish's works constitute the oeuvre of a literary author whose conception of originality is radically modern. Or rather, that the kind of poetics Cavendish practiced were in place three centuries before we have come to expect them from "modernism."[13] For her, authorship has little to do with the humanistic tradition's rhetorical spinning of variations on topoi derived from the authorities; it is principally concerned with establishing a personal voice and legitimizing the self as the authority of a necessarily subjective discourse.[14]

That a consistent poetics emerges from each work might well escape a casual reader, for this poetics is not based on humanistic ideals of order and symmetry: indeed, Cavendish evinces a predilection, both thematically and formally, for the fragmentary rather than the unified, incompleteness rather than definitiveness, proliferation rather than "singleness of purpose," paradox and juxtaposition rather than rational dialectic and transcendent meaning. This profoundly baroque oeuvre, "delighting" according to Kate Lilley, "in the subversive potential of generic and intellectual hybridization" nevertheless obeys its own aesthetic rules, while being the materialization of an ambitious literary programme.[15] When faced with literary works that don't fit our own expectations, we must, as critics, be ready to reevaluate those expectations. As Kenshur notes, we still tend to rely upon humanistic ideals of completeness in our approach to historic literature:

> Positive value resides in coherent unified knowledge—whether of the natural world or the spiritual one—and fragmentation of knowledge is valued negatively. Fragmentary knowledge, sometimes remediable, sometimes not, is always defective knowledge.[16]

Cavendish's literary fragmentation seems both consistent with and in contradiction to her grand project: although she sets out to gain as much generic ground as possible in her lifetime, she remains relatively unconcerned about perfecting her craft and filling in the specific gaps left by missing elements of subgenres and modal shifts. This attitude leads her to real innovation and modification of generic categories.

This collection of essays generally follows Cavendish's model by attempting to represent the whole by pieces, entering into a kind of conversation, sometimes at variance and sometimes in harmony; we offer here an insight into the generic swaths of Cavendish's work and attempt to account for the tremendous variety of her literary endeavors. The book is divided into two large sections: Part I, "Non-Fictional Writings," deals with the non-imaginative, didactic works; and Part II, "Imaginative Writings," treats the nominal literary genres. Each essay focuses on one or more works associated with a specific genre, allowing for comparison with other works by Cavendish and also with those by contemporary authors.

Emma Rees offers an investigation into Cavendish's relationship to genres mainly through her prefatory material, which can sometimes reach formidable proportions. She shows that Cavendish's prefatory material evinces a complex understanding of genre: in a truly unique way, she used the prefaces to manipulate her readers' expectations and links her highly conscious use of peritext with her position as an exile, both politically and symbolically. Genre, Rees claims, was for her a malleable, organic notion rather than a prescriptive norm. Lisa Sarasohn and Brandie Siegfried explore how Cavendish's philosophy was shaped and determined by her espousal of and departure from the philosophical genres to which she could refer. Sarasohn focuses on the genre of the philosophical letters as a medium for Margaret Cavendish to enter into dialogue with other thinkers also engaged in epistolary forms, mainly Descartes and Hobbes. It allows her to re-evaluate Cavendish's importance as a philosopher and to show that her materialism can be interpreted as an alternative to Hobbes's. Siegfried shows how complex is in fact Cavendish's attitude toward notions of philosophical genres. Her 1666 philosophical treatise entitled *Observations Upon Experimental Philosophy* thus reveals a conscious reliance on three different modes of writing: the satire or polemic as practiced in contemporary treatises she had read, modes specific to cabalistic writings, and the Cartesian deployment of personal anecdote in the service of philosophy. This essay demonstrates how agility with literary forms goes together with intellectual adaptability: she argues that Cavendish shows an awareness of how alternative and rival philosophical systems could yield mutually incompatible accounts of natural phenomena.

James Fitzmaurice and Line Cottegnies both offer a reconsideration of Cavendish's contributions to life writing, respectively through a study of her life of her husband and through her own autobiographical narrative. The *Life of William Cavendish, First Duke of Newcastle* (1667) is probably one of her better-known works, although it has often been dismissed as disjointed and repetitive. Contrary to received opinion, Fitzmaurice shows that, when read in context, Cavendish's life was not more "faulty" than those written by her contemporaries and questions our approach to the genre. Like Izaak Walton, she contributed, in her own way, to the gradual legitimizing of the emergent genre of biography; in doing so, she exhibits her debt to Plutarch. Her key innovation is the hybridity she brings to the text by welding together narrative, scrapbook, household accounts and even maxims in the final section that offers a sample of the Duke of Newcastle's wit. Her autobiographical text, published at the age of thirty-three as the concluding section of a collection of fictional miscellanea, *Natures Pictures* (1656), is an even more extraordinary text: with no direct precedent as such, it starts by breaking away from any subservience to history by questioning the rhetorical emphasis on memory. Cavendish thus frees her narrative from the dependence on historical truth to place it on the side of fiction. This allows her to write herself into the figure of the authoress manipulating her text and creating her own legend for posterity's sake.

In the first of the essays on the imaginative forms, Hero Chalmers offers a study of Cavendish's poetical miscellanea *Poems and Fancies* (1653) that contextualizes her invocation of variety and her rejection of rule and method. She shows how Cavendish appropriates a Royalist poetic such as had for instance been practiced by Robert Herrick in his *Hesperides* (1648), with his alternation of poems on miscellaneous modes, but goes beyond her predecessors to create a unique blend of philosophical and "fantastical" poetry. Nancy Weitz and Sarah Hutton offer two complementary essays on Cavendish's prose fiction. In the first, Weitz explores Cavendish's uses of "romance" and focuses on a tale published in the 1656 collection *Natures Pictures* and entitled "Assaulted and Pursued Chastity." Although distinctly belonging to the genre of the romantic adventure, it participates, she claims, in the tradition of conduct literature in its overt delineation of moral and social codes. She shows that by adhering to both the conventions of the chastity mandate and the aims of romance, the text is at odds with itself. Sarah Hutton offers a study of Cavendish's longer and better-known fiction, *The Blazing World* (1666), and places it in the tradition of the great Renaissance travel utopias or dystopias. In particular, she shows it stands in a similar relation to her treatise, *Observations upon Experimental Philosophy,* to the one Francis Bacon's *New Atlantis* entertains with his *Sylva Sylvarum:* both fictional works were intended as illustrations for the philosophy of their authors. But differently from Bacon, Cavendish intended her scientific "romance" as a satirical medium to express her critique of contemporary natural philosophy. The essay claims that the model for this particular brand of comic and serious elements is to be found in the scientific fiction of Lucian of Samosata.

The last three essays all study various aspects of Cavendish's drama—which, with two folios published successively in 1662 and 1664, represents the bulk of her literary production. All start from the paradox that Cavendish's plays have widely been interpreted as undramatic and even incoherent, because they did not follow the stylistic and generic conventions of the day. Through a study of, in particular, *Bell in Campo,* Alexandra Bennett shows that far from being ignorant of these rules, Cavendish in fact chooses to exploit the jarring, disjunctive mimetic possibilities that theater provides for ideological and aesthetic purposes of her own, as the only true mirror to a disjunctive reality. Similarly, Sara Mendelson describes how Cavendish conceived her plays both as educational artefacts—in a Humanist tradition—and as a mode of "self-fashioning." Mendelson then focuses more particularly on the dramatization of her autobiographical memoir ("A True Relation . . .") in *The Presence,* studied in conjunction with other plays that include semi-autobiographical characters. She shows that through autobiographical self-fashioning and gender games, Cavendish conceived of drama as a flexible medium to question natural and social identities and as a locus for experimentation with genre as well as gender. In conclusion, Gisèle Venet studies several of Cavendish's plays for their contribution to a baroque aesthetics, in that they manifest the loss of centered and unified perspectives. Framing idealizing models (pastoral, epic, heroic, etc.) within incomplete and fragmentary plots, Cavendish illustrates their obsolescence as cultural codes. Through the recurrent celebration of the idealized monarchical female self, Venet also sees an anticipation of the modern insular self or the "Monad" that was to become the thinking subject of eighteenth-century literature and philosophy.

Although some of these essays present differing interpretations of the range and exact nature of Cavendish's oeuvre, they all demonstrate her importance as an original author engaged in a comprehensive literary project which implies positioning herself towards the tradition in a way that has largely gone unnoticed heretofore. This book also proves, through its very kaleidoscopic variety, the need to take Cavendish seriously as a thinker in her own right, a meaningful mediator between the learned culture and an amateur, virtuoso culture, who, with her faith in reason, already adumbrates the Enlightenment.

The idea for this collection emerged in 1999 during the International Margaret Cavendish Conference in Paris, France. While an exhaustive study of Cavendish's total production proved impossible, it appeared that a concerted, collective study of as large a sample as possible of her writings was needed. A few of the contributions herein began as papers delivered at the conference, and other contributors responded with enthusiasm to our project to complete the picture. However, there were far more excellent papers at the Paris Conference alone than we could possibly include in a single volume on genre and poetics. We would like to thank all of the participants and indeed everyone who continues to work on Cavendish for their larger contribution to the field and their influence on the work in this volume. Many thanks to Susan Wiseman, whose careful and perceptive comments helped bring this volume to fruition.

NOTES

1. *The Diary of Samuel Pepys,* ed. Robert Latham and William Matthews, 11 vols. (London: G. Bell, 1970–1983), 26 April 1667 (8: 186), 1 May 1667 (8: 196), 10 May, 1667 (8: 209), 18 March 1668 (9: 123); *The Letters of Dorothy Osborne to William Temple, 1652–1654,* ed. Kingsley Hart (London: Folio Society, 1968), 58; John Evelyn's *Diary* 30 May 1667 (3: 482–83); Mary Evelyn's "Letters" to Ralph Bohun, c. 1667; Virginia Woolf, "The Duchess of Newcastle," in *The Common Reader* (London: Harcourt Brace-Harvest, 1925), 69–77.

2. For example: Mary Ann McGuire, "Margaret Cavendish, Duchess of Newcastle, on the Nature and Status of Women," *International Journal of Women's Studies* 1 (1978): 193–206; Dolores Paloma, "Margaret Cavendish:

Defining the Female Self," *Women's Studies* 7 (1980): 55–66; Sophia B. Blaydes, "The Poetry of the Duchess of Newcastle: A Pyramid of Praise," *The Bulletin of the West Virginia Association of College English Teachers* 6 (1981): 26–34. Hilda L. Smith, *Reason's Disciples: Seventeenth Century English Feminists* (Urbana: University of Illinois Press, 1982), 12–13, passim.

3. There have been many essays published on Cavendish to date, a steady stream of new editions of her works and no fewer than three biographies. There has, however, been only one critical book to this date: Anna Battigelli, *Margaret Cavendish and the Exiles of the Mind* (Lexington: University Press of Kentucky, 1998). See also a special issue of *Women's Writing* devoted to Cavendish, *Women's Writing* 4.3 (1997), ed. Emma L. E. Rees. The principal biographies are: Richard Ten Eyck Perry, *The First Duchess of Newcastle and Her Husband as Figures in Literary History* (Boston and London: Ginn and Co., 1918); Douglas Grant, *Margaret the First* (London: Rupert Hart-Davis, 1957); and Kathleen Jones, *A Glorious Fame* (London: Bloomsbury, 1988).

4. Aristotle and classical writers after him distinguished between lyrical, epic, and dramatic genres (cf. *Poetic,* 1447a, b; 1456–1462 a, b), although according to Genette, the Aristotelian theory of genres stems from a miscomprehension of his thought. Cf. Gérard Genette, *The Architext, an Introduction,* trans. Jane E. Lewin (Berkeley: University of California Press, 1992), 3–4. Emma L. E. Rees, who appears in this volume, has been working on issues of genre and argues that in *Natures Pictures* Cavendish deliberately reworked Platonic categories in *"Heavens Library* and *Natures Pictures:* Platonic Paradigms and Trial by Genre," in *Women's Writing* 4.3 (1997): 369–81.

5. *Worlds Olio,* fol. A2.

6. *Divers Orations* (1662), fol. a: "I have mentioned in my other Books, that I think it not fit I should Dedicate unto your Lordship the Single parts of my Works, before I dedicate all the parts in the Whole." Karen Raber also remarks on this, in "'Our wits joined as in matrimony': Margaret Cavendish's *Playes* and the Drama of Authority," *ELR* 28.3 (1998): 464–93, see 492.

7. *The Blazing World and Other Writings,* ed. Kate Lilley (Harmondsworth: Penguin, 1992) 124. Mary Baine Campbell showed that in Cavendish's works, the thematic of the new world coalesces with that of the discovery of other worlds. Cf. Campbell, *Wonder and Science; Imagining Worlds in Early Modern Europe* (Ithaca and London: Cornell University Press, 1999), 202–18.

8. "A True Relation . . .", in *The Life of William Cavendish, First Duke of Newcastle, to which is added A True Relation of My Birth, Breeding and Life by Margaret, Duchess of Newcastle,* ed. C. H. Firth (London: George Routledge and Sons, 1907), 172.

9. In the first essay in this collection, Emma Rees offers a complementary perspective on Cavendish's use of genres.

10. "Genres littéraires," *Dictionnaire des Genres et notions littéraires, Encyclopaedia Universalis* (Paris: Albin Michel, 1997): 339–44, see 339. See also (for a useful discussion of notions of genres, among others) M. M. Bakhtin, *The Dialogic Imagination* (Austin: University of Texas Press, 1981); Alastair Fowler, *Kinds of Literature: An Introduction to the Theory of Genres and Modes* (Oxford: Clarendon Press, 1982); Claudio Guillén, *Literature as System, Essays*

toward the Theory of Literary History (Princeton: Princeton University Press, 1971); Jean-Marie Schaeffer, *Qu'est-ce qu'un genre littéraire?* (Paris: Editions du Seuil, 1989) and Joseph P. Strelka, ed., *Theories of Literary Genre: Yearbook of Comparative Criticism* (University Park and London: Pennsylvania State University Press, 1978).

11. Fowler, *Kinds of Literature,* 12–13, 20.

12. *Genres in Discourse,* trans. Catherine Porter (Cambridge: Cambridge University Press, 1990) 17–18. The phrase "horizon of expectation" was borrowed from Hans Robert Jauss and his reception theory. See "Literary History as a Challenge to Literary Theory," in *Toward an Aesthetic of Reception,* trans. Timothy Bahti (Brighton: Harvester Press, 1982) 3–45.

13. As Oscar Kenshur asserts:

Most scholars, and particularly those concerned with modern literature, apparently continue to adhere to the belief that discontinuous literary works—works whose gaps, whether logical, narrative, grammatical or typographical, prevent the separate parts from combining into unified wholes—constitute a distinctly modern phenomenon that somehow reflects modern views about the world.

See *Open Form and the Shape of Ideas: Literary Structures as Representations of Philosophical Concepts in the Seventeenth and Eighteenth Centuries* (Lewisburg, Pa.: Bucknell University Press; London: Associated University Presses, 1986), 13.

14. Patricia Phillips, *The Adventurous Muse: Theories of Originality in English Poetics 1650–1760* (Stockholm and Uppsala: Almqvist and Wiksell International, 1984), especially 1–7. Cavendish clearly heralds Edward Young's *Conjectures on Original Composition* (1759). See also David Quint, *Origin and Originality in Renaissance Literary Versions of the Source* (New Haven and London: Yale University Press, 1983), esp. 217–20.

15. "Introduction", *The Blazing World,* xiv.

16. Kenshur, *Open Form,* 71.

AUTHORIAL
CONQUESTS

Part I
Non-Fictional Writings

Triply Bound:
Genre and the Exilic Self

EMMA L. E. REES

DESPITE HER PROTESTATIONS TO THE CONTRARY, MARGARET CAV-
endish had a wily and clearly developed understanding of the
possibilities of genre. This is in evidence in different ways in
all of her publications. It is in her texts of the 1650s, however, that genre is pragmatically and ingeniously conflated with
exile. These texts themselves register—in spatial and material
terms—the political impetus underlying their intratextual generic play. They record the kind of exile Cavendish endured—
a potentially debilitating set of circumstances which threatened to bind the writer in no fewer than three ways: legisla-
tively, politically, and along gender lines. In Cavendish's case,
to play with genre was to resist this situation of being triply
bound.

Understanding how such resistance was registered in Cavendish's texts necessitates an evaluation of her understanding of
contemporary ideas about genre. Cavendish's idiosyncratic take
on these ideas facilitated both political comment and self-definition. Using the genre of "autobiography," for example, enabled
her to publicize political ideas, as did her use of—to use the
language of Gérard Genette—*peritextual* material. Once Cavendish established a degree of understanding with her readers, she
could make these political points *intratextually* too, by manipulating contemporary generic expectations. In this way she arguably wrote her way out of exile.

How, then, did Cavendish regard theories of genre? In the preface to her *Life* of her husband, William, she suggestively offers an
indication of the stage her perception of genre had reached by
1667, almost the end of her writing career. "When I first Intended
to write this History," she declares,

[I was] no Scholar, and as ignorant of the Rules of writing Histories, as I have in my other Works acknowledg'd my self to be of the Names and Terms of Art . . . Many Learned Men, I know, have published Rules and Directions concerning the Method and Style of Histories.[1]

A theory of genre comprises just such "Rules and Directions." However, in terms of Cavendish's oeuvre, the idea of "genre" is, characteristically, not straightforward. Instead, "genre" becomes an interpretative, and not merely a classificatory, notion. To return to the preface, Cavendish's professed ignorance—she is "no Scholar"—does not stop her from proceeding to enter into a little taxonomic play of her own. She establishes a trinity of classifications, in this instance, of history, identifying general, national, and particular sorts of historical account, and at once politicizing them by comparing them with "the three sorts of Governments, Democracy, Aristocracy, and Monarchy" (*Life,* unnumbered prefatory material). These kinds of distinctions and classifications continue throughout the volume, as when she discusses her husband's literary works. She claims that William is "the best *Lyrick* and *Dramatick* Poet of this Age," going on to praise the mimetic and didactic qualities of his comedies, "for they are composed of these three Ingredients, viz. *Wit, Humour,* and *Satyr*" (*Life,* 146). Even though the rulebooks of the "Many Learned Men" are *represented* as being unread, Cavendish evidently is not without her own sense of taxonomic divisions and literary classifications.

It is clear, then, that Cavendish was aware of wider cultural connections between genre and hierarchy. The primacy accorded in the period to an heroic mode may be attributable in part to a blurring of the disciplines of history and poetry—and this is a blurring Cavendish articulates in her preface to her biography of her husband. It was a generic elision that had prompted Lorenzo Valla, in his 1520 work, *Historiae Ferdinandi Regis Aragoniae,* to ask:

Why should poets who are worthy of the name of philosophers be thought inferior to philosophers, seeing that poets originated philosophy, and secondly that where they differ from philosophers is in philosophizing better?[2]

When Cavendish declares in her preface to *Poems, and Fancies* that she chose to explicate her atomist theory in verse, "because I thought *Errours* might better pass there, then in *Prose,*" she is recalling an older set of generic theories and assumptions, echoing Philip Sidney's description in *An Apology for Poetry* of the poet: "he nothing affirms, and therefore never lieth."[3]

Significantly, in the same work, Sidney articulates an awareness of the same potential of genre for disguise that, as will become apparent, Cavendish exploits in her own works. He argues, for example, that Aesop's fables are "pretty allegories, stealing under the formal tales of beasts" (Sidney, 109). A Bakhtinian understanding of genre may go some way towards shedding light on what it is Cavendish is trying to do with genre. In such terms, then, genre in the 1650s still possessed a potentiality and open-endedness. The generic skeleton of Cavendish's work, far from being fossilized and immovable, was not even fully constituted. Indeed, Cavendish treats all genres as having organic potential and adaptability, recalling Bakhtin's "hardened and no longer flexible skeleton" of "already completed genres."[4] That Cavendish's readers may expect to encounter a fossil rather than a living, developing creature, can only work to her advantage. The readers' very expectations, if they are rigid, ossified, Bakhtinian expectations, allow Cavendish license to take old genres in new directions.

In the case of *Natures Pictures,* then (more specifically, in the case of "Assaulted and Pursued Chastity"), the reader expects to encounter a Bakhtinian epic "dinosaur." What actually happens is that the reader may discover that, for very specific political reasons, Cavendish has reinvented or rediscovered the romance genre's plastic potential. If, as Bakhtin argues, "studying other genres is analogous to studying dead languages," then what Cavendish does in her use of genre is to find an idiolect informed by the peculiar personal and political circumstances of her life in the 1650s.[5] In Cavendish's work, genre is not ossified, but is both the mould and the content; it is both a category and a technique. The structurally closed form that Bakhtin proposes, for example for the epic, positively precludes the sort of personal political commentary that it contains in Cavendish's work.

To continue for a moment to use Bakhtin's vocabulary of genre, Cavendish's own treatment of genre undergoes a transformation during and because of the civil wars. These, on some significant level, spelled the end of a royalist epic past. In royalist literary sensibilities, the civil wars were a cusp marking a move from flexibility to ossification; from epic to novelistic discourse. Read in the light of this, then, passages of Cavendish's work such as the first book of *Natures Pictures* can be understood as novelistic adaptations of Socratic discourses. They can therefore focus and comment on contemporary reality without the bounded, closed-off distance associated with the epic. So, elements of this first book serve to emphasize the "low" nature of the seriocomical genre, just as the archetypally low characters found in William's *Beggars Marriage* do.[6]

"Genre," it would seem, is an inherently unstable and mutable category, particularly so in the unsettled years of the mid-seventeenth century. As Alastair Fowler makes clear, generic parameters are constantly changing, and over time, an inverse relationship often emerges between a text's utility, and its literariness.[7] Early modern scientific theories, for example, may since have been entirely discredited on scientific grounds, but retain a poetic or literary quality. As far as literary works are concerned, their "relation to the genres they embody is not one of passive membership but of active modulation."[8] Such a flexible skeleton is the antithesis of Bakhtin's fossilized dinosaur, and his repeated recourse to a notion of the "novelistic" as describing almost any innovative literary work is persuasively critiqued by Fowler:

> to expect fixed forms, immune to change yet permanently corresponding to literature, is to misunderstand what genre theory undertakes . . . The sequel must be dismay, when real genres are found to change and old account of their earlier states to be remote from newer literature.[9]

Genre is less a prescriptive force than a modulation which alters the generic code from which it is a departure, or of which it is a version. Fowler goes so far as to suggest that the changeable form of genres means that satisfactory definitions are impossible, since once a genre operates within literature it is subtly changed. The fleeting nature of genre led the Renaissance theorist, Scaliger, to identify more than a hundred different ones, since he was operating under what Fowler terms the "delusion," shared by Bakhtin, that "generic rules were fixed."[10]

Key to this present discussion is the paradox that a culture which views genre as fixed or prescriptive actually encourages precisely the kind of innovative generic play that is manifested repeatedly in Cavendish's writings. In other words, in order to write beyond the parameters of the genres that interest her, and in order to reinvent them to accommodate her own political agenda, Cavendish had first to be utterly *au fait* with the genres of her contemporary literary culture. If it is the case that, in terms of literary communication, generic assumptions color the reader's interpretation of or presumptions about, or responses to, a work of literature, then consistently throughout Cavendish's work, to question genre is to access—as far as can ever be possible—authorial intention. When approaching a work of literature, the reader engages in a hermeneutic task made possible by the generic indicators which permeate a work. These, in turn, direct the reader to think about and approach the text in a specific way, with a specific set of assumptions operating upon it. What Cavendish does in her work is to exploit these assumptions, frustrate and reverse them, precisely by appearing to make them work in and for her texts.

This highly complex literary and generic play is produced by—and is itself a product of—the very particular set of circumstances under which Cavendish was writing in the 1650s. Without doubt the literary implications of what I have already termed a "triple exile" are far-reaching. The writer is exiled not only in a legislative sense (by being married to a man who was politically designated a delinquent and banished), but in two other interrelated senses, too. She is analogously exiled firstly, as a woman trying to write at a time when this was seen as promiscuously transgressive, and secondly she is exiled as a royalist maintaining and promoting the prohibited aesthetic of theatricality in various forms in her writing. The central importance placed upon exile that this formulation of the triple exile suggests is evident not only in Cavendish's generic play but in the material and spatial configuration of the publications themselves.

During her sixteen years in exile, Cavendish sent five volumes into London to be published.[11] Despite the fact of her being, politically speaking, persona non grata, Cavendish appears to have encountered little resistance to having her large, opulent volumes distributed. Whether they were simply considered harmless, even faintly ridiculous, whereas in fact, when carefully read, they demonstrate an incisive political awareness, remains in part the object of this essay. It is to some degree the case that the self that Cavendish articulates in her prefatory material is carefully constructed so as to appear unthreateningly conventional in its multiple professions of humility. What this construction creates is the opportunity for the writer to seize the potential of the liminal status of this material for seducing a readership—a readership she needs, in order for the polemical goals of her *intratextual*, generic, manipulations to succeed, to be alert to the possibility that appearances can be deceptive.

In her 1656 publication, *Natures Pictures*, Cavendish's comprehensive title can only be designed to influence the mindset of her reader:

NATURES PICTURES DRAWN BY FANCIES PENCIL TO THE LIFE. *In this Volume there are several feigned Stories of Natural Descriptions, as Comical, Tragical, and Tragi-Comical, Poetical, Romancical, Philosophical, and Historical, both in Prose and Verse, some all Verse, some all Prose, some mixt, partly Prose, and partly Verse. Also, there are some Morals, and some Dialogues; but they are as the Advantage Loaves of Bread to a Bakers dozen; and a true Story at the latter end, wherein there is no Feignings.* (*Natures Pictures*, title page)

As Douglas Grant writes, "A more specific and inclusive title could hardly have been devised."[12] Gérard Genette provides some informative ways of theorizing such "paratextual" material. As the French title of his work suggests, *Seuils* is a study of the "thresholds" of a publication—that is, its prefatory, dedicatory and titular components—and in his formulation, the paratextual threshold comprises two parts: the epitext and the peritext.[13] It is with the latter of these two that I am most closely concerned here.

Genette analyzes how the form of a title can be connected to a function such as genre indication. The synopsis-title of *Natures Pictures* may be understood as a way of delimiting the possible interpretations a reader might—to use Genette's terms—transport over the peritextual threshold into the text. A title is open to multiple interpretations. Its ultimately extrinsic relationship to the text it designates is a problem that Cavendish here tries wittily to confront. Indeed, *Natures Pictures* marks a change in

Cavendish's choice from the non-synoptic rhematic titles of her earlier works to the more (although not solely) thematic inclusivity of the title of the 1656 work, in which she continues to play with thematic conventions and classifications in the title's juxtaposition of "Nature," "Fancy," and "Life." A connection thus begins to emerge between peritext and genre. Cavendish experiments with both in full awareness of the quasi-official status they grant to a text. As Genette writes of this status, "no reader can justifiably be unaware of or disregard this attribution, even if he does not feel bound to agree with it."[14]

In differentiating between "kinds" and "modes," Fowler indicates how modal transformation may produce precisely these apparently hybrid genres Cavendish advertises in this title to *Natures Pictures*—"*Comical, Tragical, and Tragi-Comical, Poetical, Romancical.*" *Genera mista* result from a mode, for example, the heroic, operating on a kind, for example, a romance, and thus producing an heroic romance. Modal transformation, suggests Fowler, is typified by a dominance of one of the constituent modes.[15] When this imbalance is less pronounced, however, "hybridity" may be a more fitting description, and may be more informative in a discussion of Cavendish's work.[16]

Cavendish used genre in her writings of the 1650s, then, as a means of articulating her powerlessness in the face of the "triple exile." In the relationship between peritext and main text, the material organization of Cavendish's very publications registers her exile. Despite, indeed, precisely on account of this triple exile, Cavendish produced publications that I read as intensely and articulately polemical. In the production of these publications, genre is the key to unlocking how Cavendish makes her political commentary. In other words, Margaret Cavendish, a woman writer at a time when print culture was almost exclusively male; a royalist when the dominant political ideologies were Puritan; married to an aristocrat but dependent on the goodwill of creditors, and an Englishwoman unable to live in England, manipulated existent literary genres as a way of articulating and negotiating her contrary, triply debarred situation.

So, an examination of the paratextual, or more precisely, peritextual, material of Cavendish's exilic publications, *Poems, and Fancies, Philosophicall Fancies, The Worlds Olio, The Philosophical and Physical Opinions,* and *Natures Pictures,* suggests that their very form is informed by and may be read as a response to her experience of exile. In other words, the physical organization of Cavendish's texts is politicized in ways directly related to the triple exile already identified.

Cavendish is as manipulative of her readership or, perhaps more precisely, her public, in her peritextual material as she is in her intratextual use of genre. In this liminal zone of contact, Cavendish endeavors to generate in her readers a mind-set conducive to receiving the main body of the text in a quite intentional way, and to be in some degree alert to the possibility that all may not be as it seems, that is, that the author is capable of ingenious literary or generic operations. Further, in her peritexts, Cavendish's presence and voice are explicitly present. What is more, in her intratextual generic interventions Cavendish does not altogether exile this peritextual voice. There is a slippage over the threshold, the effect of which is analogous to the inroads Cavendish attempts to make in her act of publishing out of exile. Her voice does not remain in the liminal, confined space of the peritext, but seeps into the main body of each publication. Cavendish will not succumb to the triple exile, and in the very structuring of her texts, this refusal is reiterated. This peritextual, literary contestation of the condition of exile is another attempt by the exiled to seize an element of discursive power. The multiplicity and intimacy of Cavendish's peritexts, and her explicit self-presentation within them, register the anxiety behind her appeal to be heard. She goes to great lengths to reach the public poised on the thresholds of her texts, perhaps acutely aware that, to quote Genette, "no one is required to read a preface (even if such freedom is not always opportune for the author)."[17]

An examination of Cavendish's exilic peritextual material suggests that it is not only the content, but also the very physical presence of her works that registers the triple exile. Before any part of a publication is read, its size and shape make an impression. Most of Cavendish's volumes are quarto or folio, thereby immediately making a visual impact. Even this has a political element to it—in their very ostentation, their impudent presence, her texts declare that her writing will not be exiled. This presentation also has a generic implication, since, as Genette writes of seventeenth-century French texts, such large sizes

"were reserved for serious works (that is, works that were religious or philosophical rather than literary)."[18] The very format,
then, is suggestive of an audacious and ostentatious response to
those authorities which would have Cavendish triply exiled. Similarly pertinacious is Cavendish's delight in "onymity," a status
that, opposing as it does anonymity and pseudonymity, constitutes her legalistic assumption of responsibility for her work.
Further, her emphasis of her nobiliary status could be read as a
deliberate refusal to acknowledge as anything other than temporary and illegitimate her social and political exclusion. *Poems,
and Fancies* is advertised as being "WRITTEN *By the Right
HONOURABLE, the Lady* MARGARET Countesse of NEWCAS-
TLE."[19] In *The Philosophical and Physical Opinions,* she is described as a marchioness, her status and degree reaching a peak
in her last exilic publication, *Natures Pictures,* which is *"Written
by the thrice Noble, Illustrious, and Excellent Princess, the Lady
Marchioness of* NEWCASTLE" (*Natures Pictures,* title page).

The titles of Cavendish's publications of the 1650s differ one
from another in length and complexity. Before departing for England in 1651, she had started to compose *The Worlds Olio,* which
was published in 1655, when *Philosophicall Fancies* was revised
and reissued as *The Philosophical and Physical Opinions.* This
new nomenclature arguably marks a growing sense of confidence
in Cavendish's publishing activities. The titles of her works began to shift from suggesting the purely imaginative, to asserting
the rational or scientific. Gone, then, were the "Fancies," the
more emphatic "Opinions" replacing them; generic expectations
were being indicated or suggested by the works' titles.[20] The
ramifications of this for *Natures Pictures* have already been
discussed.

On occasion, the apparent anxiety of the writer's peritextual
voice is carried over into the text without the use of intertitles.
Her interventions do not remain exiled on the far side of the
textual threshold. In an exposition entitled *"The sympathies and
antipathies of sound to the minde and actions,"* for example, Cavendish's voice is intrusive as she again attempts to define her
project and defy her (textual and political) marginality. "If I have
not matched my strains and notes, with words and thoughts
properly," she begins:

[L]et those that understand musick, and Rhetorick mend it, for I understand neither, having neither fed at the full table, nor drank at the full head of learning, but lived alwayes upon scattered crums, which I pick up here and there, and like a poor lasie begger, that had rather feed on scraps then work, or be industrious to get wealth, so I had rather write by guesse, then take the pains to learn every nice distinction.

And if my book will not please the learned, yet it may please the vulgar, whose capacity can onely dig in the earth, being not able to reach the celestial Orbs by speculation.[21]

This characteristic move to flatter the reader and simultaneously to promote her own natural wit is unusual in its utter incorporation into a wholly unrelated text, unannounced by any form of intertitle. Such authorial interventions emphasize the degree of intimacy and rapport Cavendish attempts repeatedly to assume with her reader. Unlike a work's main title or designated peritextual material, such interventions are only stumbled upon in the course of the text being thoroughly read. Genette allows that a preface may be situated other than at the opening of a work. What a preface essentially is, he stresses, is "a discourse produced on the subject of the text that follows or precedes it."[22] This formulation provocatively suggests another way of reading those authorial interventions such as the one quoted above from *The Philosophical and Physical Opinions*. If Genette's argument is logically pursued, then Cavendish may be seen as transforming herself into her text. That is, much of her prefatory material—preludial or otherwise—is about herself, her humility, natural wit, professions of ignorance, and so on.

Such deliberate conflation of self and text, such explicitly transliminal interventions, suggests once more that, as I have been arguing, the material and spatial arrangement of Cavendish's texts is psychologically motivated and specifically a response to her condition of triple exile. However, it is important that the "sender" of a preface is not automatically assumed to be its "actual writer . . . whose identity is sometimes less well known to us than we suppose."[23] That is, the reader must be alert to the possibility that the peritextual material of Cavendish's publications may constitute her deliberate presentation of a persona that may or may not correspond exactly to "Margaret Cavendish," but rather to a political or literary point that she is attempting to convey.

More brazen paratextual material comes in the form of the elaborate frontispieces of Cavendish's exilic publications. The function of such illustrations exceeds the purely decorative; they participate in the paratextual project of, to quote Genette once again, ensuring "for the text a destiny consistent with the author's purpose."[24] Cavendish's frontispieces are engravings taken from paintings by the Dutch artist Abraham van Diepenbeke. One shows Cavendish in a classical pose, draped with a togalike gown and looking, as James Fitzmaurice expresses it, "very much like a statue of a Greek goddess."[25] Another shows the author in a library or study whose shelves are empty, two putti with a crown of laurels hovering over her head, and a third frontispiece shows a group of people gathered around a fire, Cavendish and William seated next to each other. The frontispieces appeared attached to different volumes, bound next to their title pages, and each served to portray its author in a confident pose. This confidence is at once astonishing and yet curiously characteristic when viewed in the context of the triple exile of their author. Her paratexts at once register and are a response to this exile, an exile that she refuses to impose structurally, by refraining from banishing her voice to the peritextual margins of her own texts.

Cavendish's polemic stems, then, from her experiences of exile. In *A True Relation,* Cavendish defines her relationship with the men closest to her in terms of exile and dispossession, telling how her father, after killing a man in a duel, had to flee, his exile lasting "from the time of his misfortune to Queen *Elizabeths* death."[26] Some pages later, she talks of her husband's own exile. Her use of the term "exile" in talking of her father's case, and her preferred expression of William's exile as a "banishment" may be deliberate, the former implying a necessitous and pragmatic self-removal, the latter being indicative of an involuntary, enforced experience.[27] "Though my Lord hath lost his Estate," she writes,

and banish'd out of his Country for his Loyalty to his King and Country, yet neither despised Poverty, nor pinching Necessity could make him break the Bonds of Friendship, or weaken his Loyal Duty to his King or Country. (*Natures Pictures,* 376)

It is in her *Life* of William, written, significantly, after their return from exile (and the starting point of this essay), that Cavendish differentiates between William's initial departure—"he went voluntarily out of his Native Country"—and his subsequent official banishment (*Life,* unnumbered prefatory material). The specific nuances to "exile" in Cavendish's discussion echo the specific nuances it had in her life, and serve to underline the importance of dealing with it, in a project like this, not only as an abstract concept, but also as an actual set of historical events. The milieux Cavendish inhabited in the 1650s provided her with a clear impetus to write, and her writing, in turn, served as both an escape from and a critique of, that particular period in her life.

Those historical circumstances meant that literary forms other than drama were also being appropriated by vying political sides. Further, as Steven Zwicker has observed:

[W]hen such literary systems as epic and pastoral were carried through the force field of civil war, they emerged brilliantly charged, freighted with convictions and urgencies quite different from those that animated literary forms before the civil wars and after the wars had passed from living memory.[28]

Other "literary systems" such as the "ballad and the emblem," as Lois Potter writes, "because of their associations with the popular sentiment," were hotly contested.[29] To adopt a genre, then, was to make a political commitment, and drama was not the only genre that the Puritan administration tried to control. Cavendish's apparent political subversion was staged in the face of various Acts that had been passed to control the circulation of literature and ideas. In March 1642, it was deemed compulsory to license newsbooks, and on 14 June 1643, a Parliamentary Ordinance was passed controlling all book and pamphlet publication. By September 1647, the army had press control, and, in October 1649, an Act of Parliament led to the control of the press until the Restoration, and the suppression of blatantly subversive literature. The placatory tones of parts of the 1652 Act of Oblivion extended to anti-government literature, too, which, for the sake of avoiding a royalist rebellion, might have a parliamentary blind eye turned towards it. The answer to such authority, then, was to make sure, as Cavendish did in her manipulation of generic conventions and expectations, that one's work did not appear blatantly subversive.[30] Her clever generic play acted like a code, without drawing to itself the attention that might have led to its interception either at the ports or in London.[31] Like allegory or fable, genre functioned as a literary cipher, arousing certain readerly expectations that, while being fulfilled on some levels, were profoundly challenged on others.

To conclude, I should like briefly to discuss Cavendish's *CCXI Sociable Letters*. In this semi-autobiographical account of much of her life in Antwerp in the 1650s, Cavendish records her delight in the dramatics of an Italian mountebank troupe, going so far as to hire a room overlooking the stage in order to watch them daily.[32] While this may or may not be an authentic autobiographical detail—*CCXI Sociable Letters* occupies an anomalous generic position between fiction and autobiography—the passion expressed for the exiled genre, "drama," shows how clearly politicized such an activity could be, since acting and public performance of this kind were specifically banished from Puritan England. The mountebank troupe's performance thus becomes royalist by association, and, despite its uncertain status as autobiographical fact, Sophie Tomlinson has identified the incident as constituting a key moment in Cavendish's self-creation as a writer whose plays were to feature a "use of performance as a metaphor of possibility for women."[33] The continued enjoyment of public performance becomes, then, an expressly royalist, exilic act. Although the royalists were in exile from their native land, and exiled from dominant discourses and power, associated practices or activities continued unabated, becoming in themselves charged with a political significance.

It has been seen how permutations of Cavendish's presentation of the autobiographical are significant in peritextual material, or in sections, for example, such as the first book of *Natures Pictures,* where there is no one single "heroine" to be identified with, but where autobiographically motivated political comment is present in a generically disguised way. Cavendish's actual autobiography, her *True Relation,* like her *Life* of William, is in itself an example of how an established genre could become highly politicized to the point of subversion. The overall impres-

sion given by the autobiography is of a woman with a fantastic-
ally busy creative mind, a singularity in dress, and, in counter-
point, a delight in the quiet, passive life of the country, and a
natural tendency towards melancholy—"not crabbed or pee-
vishly melancholy, but soft melting solitary, and contemplating
melancholy"—and bashfulness (*Natures Pictures,* 388). She exploits the vehicle of autobiography to express vindications of her
own and her husband's wretchedness during the Civil War years,
and widens her focus to embrace a critique of the Interregnum.
Her explicit impetus for writing her autobiography is clearly conveyed in its concluding paragraph, where she ensures against the
eventual effacement of her identity, and vindicates herself in the
face of imputations of vanity, emphasizing the work's function
not as entertainment, but as historical document:

> I hope my Readers, will not think me vain for writing my life . . . I
> write it for my own sake, not theirs; neither did I intend this piece for
> to delight, but to divulge; not to please the fancy, but to tell the truth,
> lest after-Ages should mistake, in not knowing I was daughter to one
> Master *Lucas* of *St. Johns* neer *Colchester* in *Essex,* second Wife to
> the Lord Marquiss of *Newcastle,* for my Lord having had two Wives, I
> might easily have been mistaken, especially if I should dye, and my
> Lord Marry again.[34]

This assertion conflicts with her declaration some few lines before, that she is "so vain, if it be a Vanity, as to endeavor to be
worshipt, rather than not to be regarded" (*Natures Pictures,* 390).
Such hyperbolic language is immediately and paradoxically def-
lated by its apparently unaffected frankness.

The opening words of her autobiography—"My Father was a
Gentleman"—are echoed in its concluding preoccupations with
the possibilities that William might remarry should she die. Her
self-definition is ultimately in terms of her relation to her father
and husband. Implicit in the work's last paragraph is the assumption that Cavendish will be remembered not for her oeuvre,
but for her familial (and specifically male) connections. However,
when such self-presentation is not labeled with, and consequently confined by, the generic signifier of a "True Relation,"
with all the cultural expectations of a woman which that entails,
but rather is present elsewhere in Cavendish's works, in her
prefaces and fictions, it is more audacious and experimental. In

portraying her life, as in all else she does, Cavendish is a wily manipulator of generic codes, making them work for, and not on, her writings.

Cavendish's person and her voice were both exiled in the 1650s, then, and whole aspects of royalist culture were also sent into exile on the Continent. Objections to drama, therefore, were not simply objections to immorality, but had complex religio-political bases. Performance, ceremony, and spectacle were constructed and perceived as inherently royalist activities that had explicitly to demonstrate parliamentarian sympathies before being acceptable. They were activities that the royalists took into exile with them, this continuity between royalism and performance being underscored after the Restoration with the almost immediate granting of permission to establish theater companies to Davenant and Killigrew.[35] The motivation behind Cavendish's construction of a text with multigeneric meanings was—unsurprisingly, perhaps, given its inception in this particular climate—also primarily political, and directly informed by her experience of the triple exile. Her literary maneuvers, both peritextual and intratextual, registered this experience as she utilized genre not only to facilitate her initial movement into print, but also to negotiate others of the triple binds of exile.

NOTES

1. Margaret Cavendish, *The Life of the thrice Noble, High and Puissant Prince William Cavendishe* (London, 1667), unnumbered prefatory material. Significantly, to Cavendish there is no formal division between "history" and "biography." This serves to underline the importance of an historically contextualized approach to genre, which treats it as a flexible and contingent phenomenon.

2. Lorenzo Valla, cited in Philip Sidney, *An Apology for Poetry or The Defence of Poesy,* ed. Geoffrey Shepherd (Manchester: Manchester University Press, 1984), 37.

3. Cavendish, "To Naturall Philosophers," *Poems, and Fancies* (London, 1653), n.p.; Sidney, op. cit., 123.

4. M. M. Bakhtin, "Epic and Novel: Toward a Methodology for the Study of the Novel," in *The Dialogic Imagination: Four Essays by M. M. Bakhtin,* ed. Michael Holquist (Austin: University of Texas Press, 1981), 3.

5. Ibid., 3.

6. Margaret Cavendish, *Natures Pictures drawn by Fancies Pencil to the Life* (London, 1656), 94–96.

7. Alastair Fowler, *Kinds of Literature: An Introduction to the Theory of Genres and Modes* (Oxford: Clarendon Press, 1982), 12–13.

8. Ibid., 20.

9. Ibid., 24.

10. Ibid., 27.

11. At least one other text was sent into England for publication, but was lost when the ship conveying the manuscript from Antwerp was sunk. See Douglas Grant, *Margaret the First: A Biography of Margaret Cavendish, Duchess of Newcastle, 1623–1673* (London: Rupert Hart-Davis, 1957), 159.

12. Ibid., 151.

13. Gérard Genette, *Paratexts: Thresholds of Interpretation,* trans. Jane E. Lewin (Cambridge: Cambridge University Press, 1997). Genette defines the peritext as the "spatial category" composed of "such elements as the title or the preface and sometimes elements inserted into the interstices of the text, such as chapter titles or certain notes." The epitext comprises "distanced elements . . . interviews, conversations . . . private communications" about a text. As Genette summarizes, "for those who are keen on formulae, *paratext = peritext + epitext*" (4–5).

14. Ibid., 94.

15. Fowler, *Kinds of Literature,* 167.

16. Ibid., 191.

17. Genette, *Paratexts,* 4.

18. Ibid., 17.

19. Cavendish, *Poems, and Fancies,* title page.

20. Grant suggests how the change from "Fancies" to "Opinions" marks "the greater seriousness of her intentions" (*Margaret the First,* 143). What I am identifying, which is implicit to Grant's assertion, is a concomitant and enabling change in Cavendish's confidence. She has the ability and right to project herself into the world as a writer with just those opinions which deserve to be taken seriously.

21. Cavendish, *The Philosophical and Physical Opinions* (London, 1655), 168–69.

22. Genette, *Paratexts,* 161.

23. Ibid., 178.

24. Ibid., 407.

25. James Fitzmaurice, "Front Matter and the Physical Make-up of *Natures Pictures,*" *Women's Writing* 4 (1997): 354.

26. Cavendish, *Natures Pictures,* 368–69. When writing of the Cavendishes' "dispossession," it should be remembered that all things are relative, and that a court, even in exile, is nonetheless still a court with a degree of the social advantage which that implies. William Cavendish appears repeatedly to have utilized this fact in his negotiations with creditors.

27. As though to emphasize this distinction between advisable exile and enforced banishment, Cavendish elsewhere talks of William's "necessitated Condition" in exile. See *A True Relation,* in *Natures Pictures,* 383.

28. Stephen N. Zwicker, *Lines of Authority: Politics and English Literary Culture, 1649–1689* (Ithaca: Cornell University Press, 1993), 201.

29. Lois Potter, *Secret Rites and Secret Writings: Royalist Literature, 1641–1660* (Cambridge: Cambridge University Press, 1989), 73.

30. The dates in this paragraph are from Potter, *Secret Rites,* 4. Potter makes the important point that, since Royalists did not recognize Parliamentary authority, they could characterize themselves less as being subversive than as in fact maintaining an assumed right (*Secret Rites,* 6). This idea is also Potter's concluding caveat, as she emphasizes that for a reader to share a writer's point of view, and to understand a writer's allusions, leads to an interpretation of the text in question as rather supportive—because it accords with the reader's perspective—than subversive. See Potter, *Secret Rites,* 209–10.

31. On such interceptions, see Potter, *Secret Rites,* 39.

32. Cavendish, *CCXI Sociable Letters* (London, 1664), letter CXCV, 405–8. The mountebank show was soon closed down by the magistrates "for fear of the Plague . . . although some said, the Physicians through Envy to the Mountebank, Bribed them out" (Ibid., 407).

33. Sophie Tomlinson, "'My Brain the Stage': Margaret Cavendish and the Fantasy of Female Performance," in *Women, Texts and Histories 1575–1760,* eds. Clare Brant and Diane Purkiss (London: Routledge, 1992), 137.

34. *A True Relation,* 390–91. Such confusions between the Duke's two wives indeed appear to have arisen: "This mistake, as Brydges points out, was actually made. In *The Loungers Common Place Book,* vol. ii. p. 398, there is a notice of the Duchess wherein this passage occurs. 'This lady, the first of characters, a good wife, as well as a sensible and accomplished woman, was the daughter of William Basset, Esquire, of an ancient family in the county of Stafford.'" *The Cavalier and his Lady: Selections from the works of the First Duke and Duchess of Newcastle,* ed. Edward Jenkins (London: Macmillan, 1872), 77.

35. Charles II arrived in London on 29 May 1660. Killigrew got his grant to set up a theatrical company on 9 July, just six weeks later.

Leviathan and the Lady: Cavendish's Critique of Hobbes in the Philosophical Letters

LISA T. SARASOHN

IN HER 1664 *PHILOSOPHICAL LETTERS,* MARGARET CAVENDISH, the first woman to publish extensively on scientific subjects, critiqued several of the most important natural philosophers of her time, including René Descartes, Henry More, J. B. Van Helmont, and especially Thomas Hobbes, the English philosopher most famous for the political treatise *Leviathan.*[1] By joining the discursive community of natural philosophers, Cavendish hoped to force an acknowledgment of her own parity with other investigators of nature. Cavendish used the genre of the philosophic letter, an increasingly common form of intellectual exchange, both to attack other philosophical systems and to articulate the content of her own natural philosophy. In her letters, Cavendish challenged Hobbesian mechanistic materialism, Cartesian realism, Paracelsianism, and Cambridge Platonism, and emphasized the uniqueness—and validity—of her own vitalistic materialism. In both her ideas and choice of form, Cavendish proclaimed her status as a natural philosopher and her unique insights from a female sensibility.

In the Preface to *Philosophical Letters,* Cavendish proclaimed:

> I took the liberty to declare my own opinions, as other Philosophers do, and to that purpose I have here set down several famous and learned Authors opinions, and my answers to them in the form of Letters, which was the easiest way for me to write; and by so doing, I have done that, which I would have done unto me; for I am as willing to have my opinions contradicted, as I do contradict others.[2]

Cavendish's letters contradicting Hobbes's mechanistic materialism were crucial to the development and implications of her own
vitalist materialism. Cavendish and Hobbes were linked by both
intellectual and personal ties. Both thinkers shared an antipathy
to Cartesian philosophy and experimental science, and both believed the universe was composed of matter in motion. William
Cavendish, the Earl (1628), Marquis (1643), and then Duke of
Newcastle (1665), was Hobbes's patron and Cavendish's husband. His protection shielded both his client and his wife from
the scandal their views generated among traditionalists and proponents of the new science.[3] Margaret Cavendish and Hobbes
demonstrate the different routes materialism could take in the
mid-seventeenth century, and how divergent concepts of matter
resulted in a different understanding of animal and human nature, and the extent to which matter and mankind may be described as free, either to move or to chose.[4]

Cavendish and the Genre of the Philosophic Letter

Cavendish was familiar with the use of the letter as both a polemical tool to undercut other philosophers and a textual testimony
to the worthiness of both protagonist and antagonist.[5] She had
become acquainted with the letter-writing community of natural
philosophers while in exile in France during the English Civil
War. Her husband, William Cavendish, and his brother, Sir
Charles Cavendish, were patrons of the leading French philosophic thinkers of the age. Pierre Gassendi, Descartes, and
Hobbes all dined with the Newcastles, and Sir Charles had an
extensive correspondence with Marin Mersenne, who functioned
as the epistolary facilitator of the intellectual community.

Within the context of the emerging natural philosophic community, letters on scientific subjects could function in two different ways. On the one hand, they could be relatively informal,
serving as a kind of newsletter for what was going on within the
community, containing pleas for jobs, reports of experiments and
encouragements for further exploration of a particular program
or experiment.[6] Thus, through letters, Mersenne had urged the
development and publication of Hobbes's political and scientific
ideas, Gassendi's philosophic rehabilitation of Epicurean atom-

ism and Descartes' system of philosophy. In the 1640s, an important correspondence between Sir Charles Cavendish and the mathematician John Pell connected the philosophic communities of Holland, France, and England.[7]

Cavendish herself was in epistolary correspondence with several of the prominent natural philosophers of her time, including Walter Charleton, Joseph Glanvill, and Henry More, whom she later attacked for his idea of immaterial spirits.[8] Many of these letters are adulatory in content; for example, in 1663 Walter Charleton thanked Cavendish for the gift of her treatises on natural philosophy, and proclaimed, "Your Wit, Madam, is beyond all Commendations; your Industry above Belief; your Labours, in Writing, above humane patience; your Curiosity above Imitation; your Notions above any, but your own Subtlety; and all above your Sex."[9] Charleton, and most of her other correspondents, were attempting to gain Cavendish's patronage, but Charleton and Glanvill did engage her in discussions about natural philosophy, vitalism, and the mechanistic worldview.[10]

Cavendish's *Philosophical Letters,* however, were closer to the more formal and polemical epistolary discourses, which play a major part in articulating the divisions within natural philosophy in the seventeenth century. As early as 1615, Galileo had defended the Copernican system in the "Letter to the Grand Duchess Christina." In the 1640s, Gassendi's and Hobbes's refutation of Descartes' *Meditations* appeared in the form of letters or *Objections* appended to his work and answered by Descartes. Gassendi also used formal letters to present his scientific ideas, including the first accurate formulation of the Law of Inertia.[11]

Indeed, when Gassendi's *Opera Omnia* was published in 1658, it contained a volume of letters defending his own ideas and questioning others. Gassendi's *Opera* was shepherded through publication by the French physician Samuel Sorbière, who in 1660 published his own epistolary polemic *Lettres et Discours.* Sorbière visited the Newcastles in 1663, and his presence may have precipitated Cavendish's decision to publish the *Philosophical Letters.*[12]

While Cavendish could not have read the letters or works of Mersenne, Descartes, Gassendi, or Sorbière—they were in Latin and French, which she did not understand—she would have been very familiar with Hobbes's use of the polemical natural philosophical letter. Sometime in 1645, in Newcastle's presence and under his protection, Hobbes and the Bishop of Derry, John Bramhall (1594–1663), engaged in a discussion of free will and determinism that eventually found its way into print, leading to a bitter dispute between the philosopher and the theologian.[13] Hobbes had recast his oral objections in a letter to Newcastle, which the nobleman had promised not to publish, but which nevertheless appeared in print in 1654. In this letter, Hobbes explained his philosophy of voluntary behavior and his interpretation of animal and human rationality. This letter, together with Hobbes's earliest written book, the 1640 *Elements of Law,* dedicated to Newcastle, and the 1651 *Leviathan,* were the targets of Cavendish's critique of Hobbes's thought in the *Philosophical Letters.*[14]

Cavendish's *Philosophical Letters* belongs most closely to the genre of the formal epistolary polemic, but it deviated from the genre in matters of presentation, style, and methodology. Almost all formal letters in the scientific tradition are addressed to a particular person, either a patron or a fellow natural philosopher or friend. Thus, Hobbes's 1654 treatise "Of Liberty and Necessity" was addressed to Newcastle, who therefore explicitly became the arbiter of the disagreement between Hobbes and Bramhall.[15] Paradoxically, Cavendish's letters were addressed to a unidentified "Madam," rather than an actual person; this lack of specificity allowed Cavendish an untrammeled discourse, where she could ignore the possible response of a critical recipient, but claim parity with other natural philosophers. This independence was clearly a self-conscious strategy, which she reinforced in "A Preface to the Reader," which served as a apologia for her former and present work. In it, Cavendish openly separated herself from the discursive community she was seeking to join, proclaiming,

> As for School-learning, had I applied my self to it, yet I am confident I should never have arrived to any; . . . wherefore I do not repent that I spent not my time in Learning, for I consider, it is better to write wittily then learnedly; nevertheless, I love and esteem Learning, although I am not capable of it.[16]

By embracing ignorance as a defense, Cavendish justified her unfocused and diffuse argumentative style, because it allowed her to ignore the conventions of the genre she was using, and to escape the possible reaction of the (non)person to whom she was writing. This stance should be contrasted with Hobbes's evaluation of his own style and work in the Dedication to Newcastle of his early treatise, the 1640 *Elements of Law:*

> For the style, it is therefore the worse, because, whilst I was writing, I consulted more with logic than with rhetoric: but for the doctrine, it is not slightly proved; and the conclusions thereof of such nature, as, for want of them, government and peace have been nothing else, to this day, but mutual fears.[17]

All of Hobbes's works were rhetorically sophisticated and methodologically punctilious.[18] He is rightfully famous for his use of the deductive method in explicating the intricacies and coherence of his philosophic views. His methodology was particularly important in his theories of matter and motion, and in how these ontological principles were related to human psychology. Nothing could be further from Cavendish's own method; she proclaimed,

> [F]or at first, as my Conceptions were new and my own, so my Judgment was young, and my Experience little, so that I had not so much knowledge as to declare them artificially and methodically. . . . But although they may be defective for want of Terms of Art, and artificial expressions, yet I am sure they are not defective for want of Sense and Reason.[19]

"Sense and Reason" served as the methodological justification for Cavendish's natural philosophy, but these principles subsumed under their rubric a largely undisciplined, imaginative consideration of topics that were being scrutinized with great exactitude by the great metaphysicians and chemists of the early seventeenth century, and later by the experimenters of the Royal Society—whose Baconian methodology Cavendish also rejected in her 1666 *Observations upon Experimental Philosophy.* Cavendish expressly rejected metaphysics and experimentation because she preferred to rely on a kind of philosophic probabilism, which precluded the possibility of absolute and demonstrative knowledge or the discovery of concrete experimental facts.[20] During a time when philosophers and investigators of nature sought physical and philosophic truths, this stance relegated her to the margins of the natural philosophic community. It did, however, allow her to claim membership in that community, because in her opinion, all doctrines were open to question, and all thinkers entitled to challenge the ideas of others:

> Wherefore to find out a Truth, at least a Probability in Natural Philosophy by a new and different way from other Writers . . . I was in a manner forced to write this Book; for I have not contradicted those Authors in any thing, but what concerns and is opposite to my opinions; neither do I any thing, but what they have done themselves, as being common amongst them to contradict each other.[21]

Cavendish planned to explicate her own philosophy in an epistolary dialogue with other authors, whom she considered her peers, even while acknowledging the limitations of her knowledge and abilities. Repetition of her themes became the vehicle for conveying her own ideas, while rejecting the conceptions of others. Her focus was on the implications of the new mechanistic universe, which was most forcefully presented by Hobbes, and which, in his hands, became a justification for determinism for both material interactions and human actions. Such a stance offended everything Cavendish was or wanted to be: a natural philosopher, who was at liberty to develop a material philosophy without the constraints of method or metaphysics, whose universe itself contained a principle of freedom in its very constitution.

THE MATERIALISM OF CAVENDISH AND HOBBES

Both Cavendish and Hobbes were materialists; they both believed that the universe consisted primarily of matter in motion. Both were also ridiculed and rejected by the philosophic and scientific establishments of the late seventeenth century. As we have seen, both also shared ties to the Duke of Newcastle: Cavendish was married to him, while he was Hobbes's patron. They had met as exiles in France during the English Civil War. Cavendish was famous for her eccentricities of behavior and deportment; she was even called "Mad Madge." Hobbes was called an atheist and devil. Their common materialism offended and intrigued;

their work demonstrated the profound implications of material-ism for both science and ethics.

According to Hobbes's materialism, which preceded Caven-dish's, the universe is composed of bits of moving matter.[22] These particles are inert and all physical causation happens because they hit each other. Even human beings are determined in their actions by external factors, and in fact "all action is the effect of motion." Hobbes did not hesitate in drawing what he considered the evident consequence of his ontology of motion, that the hu-man understanding is determined by the last antecedent motion that strikes it, which in turn determines the will.[23]

For Hobbes, even the human striving for self-preservation is basically physiological and necessary because the organism must continue in motion to survive. External objects stimulate the senses by "mechanistic pushes," and the vital, circulatory motion of the heart is either helped or hindered. When the vital motion of the heart is increased, one feels pleasure; when it is diminished one feels pain. Human reason, which only differs in degree from that of other animals, is directly related to our perception of what will cause pleasure and pain, or good and evil. Appetite and fear, stimulated by external causes, alternate during deliberation, which ends in an act of will, either the will to yield (appetite), or the will to abstain (fear).[24] Freedom, or "voluntary action," is merely the ability to act in response to appetite and fear. In other words, one is free whenever there is an absence of impediments to voluntary action; although causally necessitated in one's ac-tions, nothing hinders one's acting.[25] Thus, in Hobbes's rendition of mechanistic materialism, the actions of all created beings, from beasts to human beings, are determined by the action of matter in motion.[26]

When Cavendish first started to develop her scientific ideas in the 1653 *Poems and Fancies,* she had also advocated a mechanis-tic materialism. In one of her shorter poems, she argued, "If atomes all are of the selfe same matter; / As Fire, Aire, Earth, and Water: / Then must their severall Figures make all Change / By Motions helpe, which orders as they range."[27] Thus, matter is distinguished by shape or figure—there are square, long, round, and sharp atoms. The various concatenations and motions of these atoms produce all the forms and changes we see in the physical world. In "A World made by Atomes," Cavendish argued:

> Small Atomes of themselves a World may make,
> As being subtle, and of every shape:
> And as they dance about, fit places finde,
> Such Formes as best agree, make every kinde. . . .
> And thus, by chance, may a New World create:
> Or else predestinated to worke my Fate.[28]

While this form of mechanistic materialism seems more fanciful than Hobbes's, it shares a common materialism, and seems equally deterministic. In another poem, Cavendish proclaimed, "Thus Vegetables, Minerals do grow, / According as the severall atomes go, / In Animals, all Figures do agree; / But in Mankinde, the best of Atomes be.[29]

But even at this early stage, a profound sense of sympathy with the animal world indicates that Cavendish was discomfited by a world devoid of soul. In a series of poems, she looks at hunting from the perspective of the hunted animal, and concludes

> As if that God made Creatures for Mans meat,
> To give them Life, and Sense, for Man to eat
> Or else for Sport, or Recreations sake,
> Destroy those Lifes that God saw good to make.[30]

Here Cavendish seemed at least open to the notion that animals possess some kind of spirit or soul, given by God, which makes it inappropriate to use them for food or sport. This spiritualized understanding of nature ultimately came to dominate Cavendish's materialism, and she extended its scope not only to animals and humans but also to matter itself. In the scientific works she wrote in the 1660s, she explicitly rejected mechanistic materialism, and implicitly repudiated Hobbesian determinism: "the actions of nature are not forced by one part, driving, pushing or shoving another, as a man doth a wheel-barrow, or whip a horse; not by reactions, as if men were at football or cuffs."[31]

Instead of mechanistic materialism, Cavendish endorsed a vitalist materialism. The two most recent commentators on Cavendish's vitalist natural philosophy, and her attack on the mechanistic worldview, link her to what John Rogers, in *The Matter of Revolution,* calls "the Vitalist Movement" of the 1650s in England. Proponents of vitalism, inspired by Paracelsian natural philosophy, envisioned a spiritualized and living matter, which possessed attributes of self-movement and internalized free-dom.[32] Rogers argues that Cavendish knew of this philosophy through her connections with the physician Walter Charleton and her reading of John Milton. It does seem clear that some of these ideas may have encouraged her break with mechanistic materialism, although it seems more likely she became acquainted with Paracelsian philosophy while in France—where her husband patronized the chemical physician William Davisson, and even wrote chemical recipes himself.[33] Pierre Gassendi's theory of the infused motion of matter could also be interpreted in a hylozoic manner and France in the midcentury buzzed with animist ideas drawn from natural magic, the Cabbala and hermeticism.[34] Cavendish herself expressly repudiated the direct influence of the Paracelsian Van Helmont in the *Philosophical Letters,* mainly because she could not understand his "strange terms and unusual explanations."[35]

Cavendish's own natural philosophy posits a hierarchy of matter, integrated into an organic whole, which composes the entire natural world. As before, the principle of her system is matter in motion, but now she distinguished three different kinds of matter: rational matter, which is the most excellent, is self-moving, the seat of conception, and the director of the rest of matter; sensible matter, which carries out the commands of rational matter and is the vehicle for sense perception; and inanimate matter, which lacks perception and is the material substratum of all being. These three kinds of matter are inextricably integrated in composed forms of matter, so at the most basic level, the universe can be conceived of as both material and animate.

This animate nature is also free; freedom is located in the capacity of matter to move itself, unlike Hobbes's matter, which can move only in response to an external stimuli. In the 1666 *Observations upon Natural Philosophy,* in what seems to be a direct reaction to Hobbes, Cavendish argued,

> self-motion is the onely cause of the various parts and changes of figures; and that when parts move or separate themselves from parts, they move and joyn to other parts at the same point of time; I do not mean that parts do drive or press upon each other, for those are forced and constraint actions, when as natural self-motions are free and voluntary.[36]

The all-encompassing internalized freedom of self-motion re-sults in a continuum of spirituality or soul from the smallest piece of matter to the rational soul of man. In fact, when Caven-dish explicitly challenged Hobbes in the *Philosophical Letters,* her reformulated materialism echoed the traditional great chain of being, where all material being is arranged hierarchically along a continuous ladder. Using the metaphors of the new sci-ence, Cavendish described a holistic and diffuse natural world:

> [N]ature is one continued Body, for there is no such Vacuum in Na-ture, . . . nor can any of her Parts subsist single and by it self, but all the Parts of Infinite Nature, although they are in one continued Piece, yet are they several and discerned from each other by their several Figures.[37]

Ultimately such unity and continuity results in Cavendish's ar-ticulation of an entirely living and sentient natural world:

> [T]here is not any Creature or part of nature without this Life and Soul; and that not onely Animals, but also Vegetables, Minerals and Elements . . . are endued with this Life and Soul, Sense and Reason.[38]

Hobbes had also postulated a resemblance between human nature and material nature, but with him this continuity con-sisted of a similar mechanical reactive capacity to external stim-ulation. For both Cavendish and Hobbes, human beings are like stones: But Cavendish stones live, while for Hobbes humans act like stones. Hobbes argued,

> For every man is desirous of what is good for him, and shuns what is evil, but chiefly the chiefest of natural evils, which is death; and this he does by a certain natural impulsion of nature, no less than that whereby a stone moves downward.[39]

Explicitly repudiating Hobbes, Cavendish argued stones "have motion, and consequently sense and reason, according to the na-ture and propriety of their figure, as well as man has according to his."[40] This animistic vitalism was the most extraordinary pic-ture of a living nature that the seventeenth century produced. Cavendish's continual claim of originality and singularity was not misplaced.[41] Not surprisingly, Cavendish believed that animals shared the animized spirituality of all natural being, but in their own fashion:

> Man denies, they [animals] can do it [reason] at all; which is very hard; for what man knows, whether Fish do not Know more of the nature of Water, and ebbing and flowing, and the saltness of the Sea, or whether Birds do not know more of the nature and degrees of Air, or the cause of Tempests; or whether Worms do not know more of the nature of Earth, and how Plants are produced?[42]

Cavendish's argument for the rationality of animals, it should be noted, was also an attack on Descartes' separation of mind and matter, and his subsequent belief that animals are merely automatons. In attacking Cartesian presumption in limiting reason only to man, Cavendish once again proclaimed the principles of her natural philosophy, and concluded,

> Wherefore though other Creatures have not the speech, nor Mathematical rules and demonstrations, with other Arts and Sciences, as Men; yet may their perceptions and observations be as wise as Men's, and they may have as much intelligence and commerce betwixt each other, after their own manner and way, as men have after theirs.[43]

Both Cavendish and Hobbes believed that humans and animals possess reason, but Cavendish's analysis exalted animals, while Hobbes's thinking lowered man. In "Of Liberty and Necessity," dedicated to Newcastle, Hobbes explicitly equated the determined and mechanical actions of animals and humans:

> [Y]our Lordship's own experience furnishes you with proof enough, that horses, dogs, and other brute beasts, do demur oftentimes upon the way they are to take, the horse retiring from some strange figure that he sees, and coming on again to avoid the spur. And what else doth a man deliberateth, but one while proceed toward action, another while retire from it, as the hope of the greater good draws him, or the fear of greater evil drives him away.[44]

According to Hobbes, such motion on the part of an animal or a human was "voluntary." If one is unimpeded in responding to a stimulus, which creates an impression in the imagination, one's actions are willing and voluntary.[45] Cavendish questioned Hobbes's entire doctrine of voluntary motion:

I think, by your Authors leave, it doth imply a contradiction, to call them Voluntary Motions, and yet to say they are caused and depend upon our Imagination; for if the Imagination draws them this way, or that way, how can they be voluntary motions, being in a manner forced and necessitated to move according to Fancy or Imagination?[46]

For Cavendish, the original freedom of all being lay in the ability of matter to move according to its own will, independent of any necessitating factors. An element of indeterminacy, built into the very matter of the universe, produces the fundamental liberty of all creatures.[47] Cavendish argued most forcefully for the autonomy and freedom of all nature, insisting that such freedom was rooted in a self-moving principle of matter itself. She argued, "Nature hath a natural Free-will and power of self-moving, and is not necessitated; but yet that this Free-will proceeds from God, who hath given her both will and power to act freely."[48]

For Hobbes, the mechanistic similarities between humans and animals had political consequences. The analysis of human ability and action in *Leviathan* begins by equating human and animal understanding. According to Hobbes,

The Understanding which is raysed in man (or any other creature indued with the faculty of imagining) by words, or other voluntary signes, is that we generally call Understanding, and is common to Man and Beast. For a dogge by custome will understand the call, or the rating of his Master; and so will many other Beasts.[49]

In fact, humans and beasts both possess the ability to anticipate what will be the consequence of a particular course of action. They are both capable of prudent actions. They are also both capable of understanding the causes of particular effects; according to Hobbes, "The Trayne of regulated thoughts is of two kinds; One, when of an effect imagined, wee seek the causes, or means that produce it: and this is common to Man and Beast." It is the capacity for speech, and particularly the ability to name and to understand the connections between names, that elevates humans above animals. Without this ability, according to Hobbes, there would be "neither Common-wealth, nor Society, nor Contract, nor Peace, no more than amongst Lyons, Bears, and Wolves."[50]

In fact, in the most famous line in *Leviathan,* Hobbes contended that in the state of nature, before the establishment of the state, human life was "solitary, poore, nasty, brutish, and short."[51] Natural man is essentially a beast. The means humans take to overcome their animal fate is the establishment of, in Hobbes's words, "an Artificial Animal," the state, which functions in every way like an automaton, and is conceived mechanistically, just as man was in Hobbes's psychological theory. Hobbes's understanding of animals allowed him to construct a revolutionary political theory, and to characterize the nature of human rationality and society.

Cavendish rejected Hobbes's view of animal and human rationality completely, and though not specified, this rejection encompassed Hobbes's political theories also. She argued,

> But certainly, it is not local motion or speech that makes sense and reason, but sense and reason makes them; neither is sense or reason bound onely to the actions of Man; but it is free to the actions, forms, figures and proprieties of all Creatures; for if none but Man had reason, and none but Animals sense, the World could not be so exact, and so well in order as it is.[52]

For Cavendish, the ordering principle of the world is internalized. Just as the material substratum of nature also contains its own self-regulating principles, beasts possess the capacity to live in harmony and order. Since the world of nature is not a chaotic congress of irrational creatures, by implication the state of nature does not consist of bestial human anarchy. Human beings, even before the establishment of the state, are also capable of order and organization.

Margaret Cavendish also used animal imagery to expand her thought. As we have seen, every particle of matter composing her universe is animate, and every creature, from worms to human beings, possesses some kind of rationality, and consequently the ability to choose. Her analysis allowed her to envision a political and social universe, just as Hobbes had led him to imagine the great *Leviathan.* Her universe, the New Blazing World, is presented as a fantasy, but it is published in the same volume as one of her densest philosophical treatises, the *Observations upon Ex-*

perimental Philosophy. Both Hobbes and Cavendish constructed imaginary worlds, which allowed them to link their materialist philosophies with speculative social and political thought.

The *New Blazing World* tells the story of a beautiful young maiden who escapes the lascivious advances of a merchant by transversing the poles between her world and the Blazing World. There she meets its strange inhabitants, all sorts of anthropomorphic beasts, including bear-men, fox-men, bird-men, ape-men, and fish-men. The maiden is at first is "extreamly strucken with fear," but much to her amazement, the bear-men "shewed her all civility and kindness imaginable."[53] She might have been amazed, but we are not, because Cavendish's philosophical works have taught us that all creatures, including animals, possess reason. In fact, they demonstrate their intellectual prowess by debating every current theory of natural philosophy in her presence. Ultimately, the maiden, now Empress of the New Blazing World, decides that the worm-men have made the best case; not surprisingly, their philosophy resembles nothing so much as Margaret Cavendish's vitalist materialism.[54]

Cavendish's fascination with hybrid creatures in the *New Blazing World* demonstrates the power animal imagery had in her thought. Her fantasy represents the ultimate conclusion of her philosophy. There is a continuum of being from the first vitalist bits of matter to the rational human being. Self-moving matter animates the natural world, and consequently, in a world where nature operates freely, all being is free.

But the actual world Cavendish lived in was not free and natural. It resembled more closely Thomas Hobbes's artificial state where motion, and freedom, is constrained.[55] In fact, vitalistic materialism allowed Cavendish to speculate on the fate of women in the social and political world of the seventeenth century. In *The World's Olio* (London, 1653), written early in her career, Cavendish had argued,

> True it is, our sex makes great complaints, that men from the first creation usurped a supremacy to themselves, although we were made equal by nature: which tyrannical government they have kept ever since; so that we could never come to be free, but rather more and more enslaved. . . . Which slavery has so dejected our spirits,

that we are become so stupid, that beasts being but a degree below us, men use us but a degree above beasts.[56]

Beasts and women share the same fate: They are both enslaved by masculine tyranny. If the innate rationality of both were recognized, presumably their freedom would also be acknowledged and respected. By emphasizing the rationality that characterizes stones, beasts and women, Cavendish's universe became both animate and free, and the existence of a female natural philosopher possible.[57]

CONCLUSION: A WOMAN NATURAL PHILOSOPHER

Margaret Cavendish knew that her gender marginalized her within the community of natural philosophers. Most would only view her within the context of her sex, as a reproach to masculine ability. The ironic response of Thomas Barlow, an Oxonian professor, was typical:

Your Works will be a just foundation of a lasting and immortal Honour to your self; (but I fear) a reproach to our Sex and us, when Posterity shall consider, how little we have done with all our Reading and industry, and how much your Excellency without them.[58]

And Joseph Glanvill, her most sympathetic correspondent, could only comment, "You are the First Lady, that ever Wrote so much and so much of your own: and, for ought we can divine, you will also be the Last."[59]

It is no wonder that Cavendish, when she decided to write her own philosophical letters, wrote them to an anonymous Lady, rather than one of the natural philosophers she knew. It was, perhaps, the only way she could receive the hearing she desired from a masculine community that refused to take her seriously. "I have been informed," she tells the reader in her Preface to *Philosophical Letters,* "that if I should be answered in my Writings, it would be done rather under the name and cover of a Woman, then of a Man, the reason is, because no man dare or will set his name to the contradiction of a Lady." Cavendish would not accept this as an excuse for natural philosophers refusing to engage her in debate, which would therefore validate her equality and membership in the community of letters. Rather, she insisted,

> But I cannot conceive why it should be a disgrace to any man to maintain his own or others opinions against a woman, so it be done with respect and civility. . . , and then I shall be ready to defend my opinions the best I can, whilest I live, and after I am dead, I hope those who are just and honorable will also defend me from all sophistry, malice, spight and envy.[60]

The genre of the philosophical letter allowed Cavendish the ability—and liberty—to choose to be a natural philosopher who was also a woman. She seized the field by critiquing the major thinkers of her time. With their consent or without, she would leave the margins and place herself in the middle of the fray. She would wrench from them the respect and participation they refused to grant.

Just as matter was active, vital, and free, Margaret Cavendish became, through her own self-movement, an actor in the natural philosophic community of her time. While Hobbes's mechanistic worldview, if not his determinist morality, would eventually become the primary principle of the science of the seventeenth and eighteenth century, it did not succeed without disputation. Cavendish imagined a natural philosophy which made both herself and nature viable and self-determining. In doing so, she perhaps better than he, forecast the future of science and women.

NOTES

1. Margaret Cavendish, *Philosophical Letters: or Modest Reflections Upon some Opinions in Natural Philosophy By several Famous and Learned Authors of this Age, Expressed by way of Letters* (London, 1664).

2. Ibid., "A Preface to the Reader."

3. On Hobbes and Newcastle, see Lisa T. Sarasohn, "Thomas Hobbes and the Duke of Newcastle," *Isis* 90 (1999): 715–37.

4. The most recent works on Cavendish and Hobbes are the following: Jay Stevenson, "The Mechanist-Vitalist Soul of Margaret Cavendish," *Studies in English Literature* 36 (1996): 527–43; John Rogers, *The Matter or Revolution* (Ithaca: Cornell University Press, 1996); Sarah Hutton, "In Dialogue with Thomas Hobbes: Margaret Cavendish's Natural Philosophy," *Women's Writing* 4 (1997): 421–31; and Anna Battigelli, *Margaret Cavendish and the Exiles of the Mind* (Lexington: University Press of Kentucky, 1998).

5. For a discussion of the use of rhetorical and literary devices in signifying status and position, see Lisa T. Sarasohn, "Margaret Cavendish and Patronage," *Endeavour* 23 (1999): 130–32.

6. There are several collections of these kinds of letters, some published in the mid-seventeenth century and other only published recently. Even unpublished letters had a wide circulation among the members of the national philosophic community. The most important epistolary collections of the mid-century are the following: Pierre Gassendi, *Opera Omnia*, 6 vols. (Lyons, 1658; rpt. Stuttgart–Bad Cannstatt: Friedrich Fromman Verlag, 1964), volume 6; Thomas Hobbes, *The Correspondence of Thomas Hobbes*, ed. Noel Malcolm, 2 vols. (Oxford: Oxford University Press, 1994); Marin Mersenne, *Correspondance du P. Marin Mersenne, religieux minime,* ed. Cornelis de Waard, R. Pintard, B. Rochot, A. Beaulieu, 17 vols. to date (Paris: CNRS, 1932–); and Henry Oldenburg, *The Correspondence of Henry Oldenburg,* ed. A. Rupert Hall and Marie Boas Hall, 11 vols. (Madison and London: University of Wisconsin Press, 1965–1977).

7. Some of these letters have been published in J. O. Halliwell-Phillips, *A Collection of Letters Illustrative of the Progress of Science in England from the Reign of Queen Elizabeth to that of Charles II* (London, 1841). See also Helen Hervey, "Hobbes and Descartes in the Light of some Unpublished Letters of the Correspondence between Sir Charles Cavendish and John Pell," *Osiris* 10 (1952): 69–90; and Jean Jacquot, "Sir Charles Cavendish and his Learned Friends," *Annals of Science* 8 (1952): 13–27.

8. Cavendish, *Philosophical Letters,* 194–97.

9. *A Collection of Letters and Poems: Written by Several Persons of Honour and Learning, Upon divers Important Subjects, to the Late Duke and Dutchess of Newcastle* (London, 1676), 92.

10. Ibid., 85, 92–93, 99–100, 102–3, 105, 108, 111–12.

11. Pierre Gassendi, *Opera Omnia,* III: 271–662.

12. Sorbière's visit to England is described in Samuel Sorbière, *Relation d'un voyage en Angleterre, où sont touchées plusieurs choses, qui regardent l'estat des sciences, et de la religion, & autres matières curieuses* (Paris, 1664).

13. Thomas Hobbes, *The Questions concerning Liberty, Necessity, and Chance, clearly stated and debated between Dr. Bramhall, Bishop of Derry, and Thomas Hobbes of Malmesbury,* in Thomas Hobbes, *The English Works of Thomas Hobbes of Malmesbury,* ed. William Molesworth (London, 1839–1845), V:1–455.

14. Thomas Hobbes, "Of Liberty and Necessity," in *English Works,* 239–78.

15. Ibid.

16. Cavendish, *Philosophical Letters,* "The Preface."

17. Hobbes, *Elements of Law (Human Nature, or the Fundamental Elements of Policy),* in *English Works,* IV: xiv.

18. On Hobbes's style and method, see Quentin Skinner, *Reason and Rhetoric in the Philosophy of Hobbes* (Cambridge: Cambridge University Press, 1996).

19. Cavendish, *Philosophical Letters,* "A Preface to the Reader."

20. On Margaret Cavendish's natural philosophy, see Lisa T. Sarasohn, "A Science Turned Upside Down: Feminism and the Natural Philosophy of Margaret Cavendish," *Huntington Library Quarterly* 47 (1984): 289–307. On the concept of experimental fact, see Steven Shapin and Simon Schaffer, *Leviathan and the Air-Pump: Hobbes, Boyle, and the Experimental Life* (Princeton: Princeton University Press, 1985).

21. Cavendish, *Philosophical Letters,* "To His Excellency The Lord Marquis of Newcastle."

22. On Hobbes's mechanistic materialism, see Frithiof Brandt, *Thomas Hobbes' Mechanical Conception of Nature* (Copenhagen: Levin and Musksgaard, 1927).

23. Hobbes, *The Questions Concerning Liberty, Necessity and Chance,* V:305; 323–24.

24. Hobbes, *The Elements of Law Natural and Political,* ed. Ferdinand Tönnies (Cambridge: Cambridge University Press, 1928), 63.

25. *Ibid.*

26. Hobbes, "Of Liberty and Necessity", 242–45.

27. Margaret Cavendish, *Poems and Fancies* (London, 1653), 10.

28. Ibid., 5–6.

29. Ibid., 12.

30. Ibid., 112.

31. Margaret Cavendish, *Philosophical and Physical Opinions* (London, 1663), 289–307.

32. Rogers, *The Matter of Revolution,* 8–14, 177–211, and Battigelli, *Margaret Cavendish and the Exiles of the Mind,* 98–102.

33. B. L. Harley 6491 contains the correspondence between Davisson and Newcastle and some chemical recipes in Newcastle's hand.

34. Lisa T. Sarasohn, *Gassendi's Ethics: Freedom in a Mechanistic Universe* (Ithaca: Cornell University Press, 1996), 59–60. Brian Easlea, *Witch-hunting, Magic and the New Philosophy: An Introduction to the Debates of the Scientific Revolution 1450–1750* (Brighton: Harvester Press, 1980).

35. Cavendish, *Philosophical Letters,* 234. This did not stop her from devoting almost two hundred pages to his refutation. Walter Charleton recognized both Cavendish's affinity with prior natural philosophy, but also her originality: "And those obscure Hints delivered to you in the Discourses of others, by passing through your lightsome Imagination, are turned into bright and full Discoveries. You solve Problems with more ease than others have proposed them" (*A Collection of Letters and Poems: Written by several Persons of Honour and Learning,* 92–93).

36. Margaret Cavendish, *Observations upon Experimental Philosophy* (London, 1666), 138.

37. Cavendish, *Philosophical Letters,* 7.

38. Cavendish, *Philosophical Letters,* "A Preface to the Reader."

39. Thomas Hobbes, *Philosophical Rudiments Concerning Government and Society in English Works,* in *English Works,* II:8.

40. Cavendish, *Philosophical Letters,* 193.

41. Sarasohn, "A Science Turned Upside Down," 293–94.

42. Cavendish, *Philosophical Letters,* 40.

43. Ibid., 114.

44. Hobbes, "Of Liberty and Necessity," II:244.

45. For a more detailed analysis of Hobbes's theory of voluntary motion, see Lisa T. Sarasohn, "Motion and Morality: Pierre Gassendi, Thomas Hobbes and the Mechanical World-View," *Journal of the History of Ideas* 46 (1985): 363–79.

46. Cavendish, *Philosophical Letters,* 45–46.

47. Rogers, *The Matter of Revolution,* 204–11, argues that much against her own will, Cavendish at least unconsciously adopted Hobbes's theory of voluntary or forced action. Her ambivalent position as an intellectual woman, forced to be subservient by the gendered patriarchy to which she belonged, made her recognize the role impact or force played in the mechanistic universe. I think this interpretation is very interesting, but I am hesitant about reinterpreting Cavendish's natural philosophy to support a theory she consciously repudiated. However, gender certainly played a part in the articulation of her philosophy, as I have discussed in my article, "A World Turned Upside Down," and affected her positive reappraisal of the freedom and rationality of all creatures, as I will discuss later in this piece.

48. Cavendish, *Philosophical Letters,* 225.

49. Thomas Hobbes, *Leviathan,* ed. Richard Tuck (Cambridge: Cambridge University Press, 1991), 21.

50. Ibid., 24.

51. Ibid., 89. Rod Preece, *Animals and Nature: Cultural Myths, Cultural Realities* (Vancouver: University of British Columbia Press, 1999), 30, discusses this idea, and is also very insightful about Cavendish's position in the tradition that honored animals (151–52).

52. Cavendish, *Philosophical Letters,* 43–44.

53. Margaret Cavendish, *The Description of a New Blazing World, called The Blazing World,* second section of *Observations upon Experimental Philosophy,* 5.

54. Ibid., 33–43.

55. Rogers, *The Matter of Revolution,* 204–11, also emphasizes the disparity between Cavendish's philosophy and the social world to which she belonged.

56. Margaret Cavendish, *The World's Olio* (London, 1653), "The preface."

57. Rogers, *The Matter of Revolution,* 204–11, also connects Cavendish's vitalism and her feminism, but concludes that Cavendish eventually was driven to adopt Hobbes's theory of voluntary motion, a conclusion that I think is questionable.

58. *A Collection of Letters and Poems,* 69.

59. Ibid., 118.

60. Cavendish, *Philosophical Letters,* "A Preface to the Reader."

Anecdotal and Cabalistic Forms in *Observations upon Experimental Philosophy*

BRANDIE R. SIEGFRIED

> It is probable, some will say, that my much writing is a disease; but what disease they will judg [*sic*] it to be, I cannot tell . . . but to be infected with the same disease, which the devoutest, wisest, wittiest, subtilest, most learned and eloquent men have been troubled withal, is not disgrace, but the greatest honour, even to the most ambitious person in the world.
>
> Margaret Cavendish, *Observations upon Experimental Philosophy* (London, 1666), c.

I$_N$ CONTRAST TO THE OPENING LINES TO THE PREFACE OF HER *Observations upon Experimental Philosophy,* in which a certain passive receptivity is figured as the defining characteristic of her philosophical endeavors (writing as disease), Margaret Cavendish concludes the passage with a decidedly contrapuntal vision of the intellectual force driving her written expressions. "It may be the World will judg [*sic*] it a fault in me, that I oppose so many eminent and ingenious Writers, but I do it not out of a contradicting or wrangling nature, but out of an endeavor to find out truth,"[1] she writes, seeming to hark back to her first metaphor in which—in the company of the likes of Aristotle, Cicero, and Tacitus—she languished with the fevers of the disease of "much writing."[2] As it turns out, though, this passive *state* is invoked as a teasing contrast to what she considers the real character of her writing persona, the daring *act:*

> I have heard my Noble Lord say, that in the Art of Riding and Fencing, there is but one Truth, but many Falshoods and Fallacies: So it may be said of Natural Philosophy and Divinity; for there is but one

Fundamental Truth in each, and I am as ambitious of finding out the truth of Nature, as an honourable Dueller is of gaining fame and repute; for as he will fight with none but an honourable and valiant opposite, so am I resolved to argue with none but those which have the renown of being famous and subtil Philosophers. (Preface, d 1–2).

The bravado of her rhetorical stance is characteristically Cavendish. Yet the pugilistic overtones which often accompany Cavendish's extravagant metaphors are meant to be more than a throwing down of the intellectual gauntlet before her male peers.

Indeed, Cavendish expresses some doubt as to whether those peers will engage her at all. "They will perhaps think my self an inconsiderable opposite, because I am not of their sex," she writes, "and therefore strive to hit my Opinions with a side stroke, rather covertly, then openly and directly" (Preface, 6). Her stance is meant to figure an intellect that is self-consciously female, yet aggressively masculine in ambition and capability. Moreover, by contrasting the vision of a passel of diseased male icons declining into irresistible fits of writing with the gallant figure of Cavendish herself standing with her weapon *en garde* (while her contemporaries take unfair swipes from the side), Cavendish dramatizes the grounds for the kinds of literary experimentation that characterize her written works. When her peers refuse to allow her equal participation in the cut and thrust of philosophical inquiry, and when they seem to insist on subjecting her to behavior that clearly places her outside the parameters of the rules of the game, the appropriate response would seem to be clear: rewrite the rules. Or, for the purposes of this discussion, *challenge custom itself with assays into form.*[3]

This discussion considers three significant ventures in form in Margaret Cavendish's *Observations upon Experimental Philosophy.* Cavendish is particularly adept in her use of explicit parody, a formal means of side-stepping the politely dismissive tendencies of her male peers. In fact, Cavendish's judicious deployment of parody represents a telling engagement with similar scientific treatises, such as Kenelm Digby's *Observations upon Religio Medici* (London, 1643), Robert Hooke's *Micrographia: Or Some Physiological Descriptions of Minute Bodies Made by Magnifying Glasses* (London, 1665), and Joseph Glanvill's *Scepsis Scientifica* (London, 1665), all of which use extended metaphorical descriptions, often gendered, to advance their notions of the relationship between movement, matter, and organic systems in the natural world. Cavendish explicitly parodies such language, at once advancing a scathing critique yet maintaining an important element of epistemological decorum.

The second segment of this discussion moves from a consideration of the function of parody in her scientific writing to a delineation of Cavendish's employment of generic characteristics of cabalistic writing. Although to some extent writers such as Hooke and Boyle also borrowed from cabalistic literature for their more mechanistic notions of natural systems, Cavendish does something quite unique. Specifically, by dramatizing the essentially performative aspects of matter as elaborated by Severinus, Cavendish sets the stage for a theory of energy and matter that derives its metaphorical clout from cabalistic sources yet situates the particulars firmly within contemporary arguments about the natural world. Thus, to some extent, Cavendish's treatise relies on a particular mode of cabalistic theatricality for some of its theoretical impact.

Based on her experiments with form as described in the previous two sections, the last segment of this essay suggests that Cavendish's engagement with Descartes' *Discours de la Méthode* (1637) is more complex and sophisticated than we have previously been able to appreciate. By recuperating Descartes' penchant for linking personal anecdote to theoretical discourse, and by conserving critical aspects of Descartes' assertions regarding the relationship between reason and essence, between memory and imagination, Cavendish can re-sort key components of rationalist epistemological models by situating them within cabalistic theories of performative matter.

In short, by melding three modes of discourse—focused parody of particular metaphorical customs popular among those exploring natural philosophy, the cabalistic emphasis on theatricality borrowed from those whose work focused on essence and the possibility of fundamental transformations, and the Cartesian deployment of personal anecdote in the service of theoretical paradigms—Cavendish emphasizes the ways in which ontology precedes epistemology: *being* constitutes the grounds for *reason*. Although I will not examine *The Blazing World* in relation to this, I will suggest that this helps to explain the strategic enterprise that leads Cavendish to attach her fictional piece to her scientific treatise.

I

One of the most notable formal elements of Cavendish's scientific treatise is her frequent deployment of teasing sarcasm and outright parody, both of which hinge on clever analogies. One of the best examples is found in the first segment of the *Observations* when she chooses to critique what she considers a false confidence in both the tools and the usefulness of measurement as proposed and exercised by several prominent natural philosophers of the day. Such experimentalists are mistaken "and much more if they think they can measure all the several sorts of heat and cold in all Creatures by artificial experiments," she writes, momentarily eliding the specific arguments for the new technologies and preferring, instead, to address the logic driving such methods, "for as much as a Natural man differs from an artificial statue or picture of a man, so much differs a natural effect from an artificial, which can neither be so good, nor so lasting as a natural one" (101). To Cavendish's mind, the experimentalist's inductive practice relies on and produces artifice, and is thus more akin to painting (which captures and preserves surface phenomena with the assumption that it can reveal some aspect of interiority or core principle to the viewer) than reasoned exposition (which moves toward particulars based on principles which have ethical and logical grounds). In short, rather than simply dismissing the methods of her contemporaries in the Royal Society, Cavendish teasingly recategorizes their experiments as naive expressions of art.

This rhetorical stance allows Cavendish to dismiss opinions and practices she sees as too superficial—not concerned enough with essential characteristics of states of things (heat and cold, in this instance)—and prepares the ground for the incisive use of parody. Indeed, the parody is double, for she goes on to paint a portrait of nature that is both a critical exaggeration of the gendered metaphors found in the written work of her contemporaries, and a self-referential joke based on the criticism of superficial measurement she has just advanced:

Indeed artificial things are pretty toys to imploy idle time; nay, some are very useful for our conveniency, but yet they are but Natures bastards or changelings, if I may so call them; and though Nature takes so much delight in variety, that she is pleased with them, yet they are not to be compared to her wise and fundamental actions. (101)

Having dismissed the measuring devices of her peers as mere "toys" and "bastards," Cavendish goes on to develop a hyperbolic vignette that is part feminized stereotype and part veiled invective:

Nature, being a wise and provident Lady, governs her parts very wisely, methodically and orderly; also she is very industrious, and hates to be idle, which makes her imploy her time as a good Huswife doth, in Brewing, Baking, Churning, Spinning, Sowing, &c. as also in Preserving for those that love Sweet-meats, and in Distilling for those that take delight in Cordials; for she has numerous imployments, and being infinitely self-moving, never wants work, but her artificial works are her works of delight pleasure and pastime: Wherefore those that imploy their time in Artificial Experiments, consider onely Natures sporting or playing actions. (101–2)

In other words, the "toys" of contemporary scientific observation and measurement can only record the least meaningful of nature's processes and functions.

The hyperbolic description of nature as "Huswife" is a humorous exaggeration and distortion of the female figure male writers typically employed to represent nature in their own work. The point of such parody can be glimpsed in the work of Kenelm Digby who, in *Observations upon Religio Medici* (1643), rhapsodized that:

the sweetest companion and entertainment of a well tempered mind, is to converse familiarly with the naked and bewitching beauties of those Mistresses, those Verities, and Sciences, which by faire courting of them, they gaine and enjoy; and every day bring new fresh ones to their Seraglio; where the ancientest never grow old or stale. Is there anything so pleasing or so profitable as this? (37)

Even the ever-sober Hooke managed to personify natural phenomena as possessing both coquettish and feral qualities, and in

Micrographia: Or Some Physiological Descriptions of Minute Bodies Made by Magnifying Glasses (1665), the process of observation becomes a sexualized hunt echoing the Petrarchan commonplaces of early English Renaissance poets such as Thomas Wyatt, Henry Howard, and Philip Sidney: "[T]he footsteps of Nature are to be trac'd, not only in her ordinary course, but when she seems to be put to her shifts, to make many doublings and turnings, and to use some kind of art in endeavoring to avoid our discovery" (Preface, 6).

In fact, experimentation itself begins to smack somewhat of sadistic pleasure in the writing of Joseph Glanvill whose *Scepsis Scientifica* (1665) urges that "'tis (however) a pleasant spectacle to behold these shifts, windings and unexpected capriccios of distressed Nature, when pursued by a close and well-managed experiment" (b 3). The imagery of implied rape, while a means of expressing the desire of the male observer for an intellectual consummation of some sort, no doubt had a hollow ring for a social critic such as Cavendish who, with witty insight, treated issues of female vulnerability and male predation in several of her plays and epistolary fictions. In fact, a later tribute to the poet (signed by the "Master and Fellows of the Colledge of St. John . . . University of Cambridge") conscientiously notes—although not without some irony—precisely this correction in the works of Cavendish:

> [Y]ou render all things clear and genuine, indeed nature truly natural: So difficult to men is nature and truth. Alas how do they vex and pursue her fleeing from them; others suppose her to be swallowed in Whirlpools . . . others grope for her in a vain Vacuity with the like success; yea, some there are which seek her among ghosts and Goblins, as if she were some Witch, or Sorceress, some offer violence to her, and put her to the rack, and make her rather Lie than Confess. To your Grace she doth freely open and unbowel her self fearing to be branded with incivility if she should deny.[4]

Although rendered with a certain salaciousness that must give us pause (even this tribute slips back into the habit of subjecting the female figure of Nature to images of violence), the author was nevertheless at pains to suggest that Cavendish was proposing theories of observation that were less oriented toward intellectual contortions and perversions than those of her contemporaries.

Along similar lines, and as a humorous flourish to her extended parody, Cavendish suggests that the prurient tendencies of male observers make them less fit for philosophical inquiry. Women, being less likely to fall into the perceptual distortions that the gendering of nature entails for men, would make the better natural philosophers—especially since women seem to regularly engage in tasks more analogous to the actions of nature:

> But if any one would take delight in such things, my opinion is, that our female sex would be the fittest for it, for they most comonly take pleasure in making of Sweet-meats, Possets, several sorts of pyes, Puddings, and the like; not so much for their own eating, as to imploy their idle time; and it may be, they would prove good Experimental Philosophers, and inform the world how to make artificial snow by their Creams or Possets beaten into froth, and Ice by their clear, candied or crusted quiddinies or conserves of fruits; and Frost by their candied herbs and flowers; and Hail by their small comfits made of water and sugar with whites of Eggs. (102)

The tongue-in-cheek is a natural extension of the parodic portrait of nature advanced on the previous page. Moreover, the ironical tone with which Cavendish handles women's relationship to a feminized nature allows her to come back to a favorite theme: "for who knows but Women might be more happy in finding it out [the philosopher's stone], then Men, and then would Men have reason to imploy their time in more profitable studies, then in useless Experiments" (103). Illustrating her thesis with this humorous depiction of men fussing with experiments like women in the kitchen, Cavendish somewhat alleviates the culturally perceived perils of a woman engaging in the speculative art of natural philosophy by making it an extension of traditional women's roles. By collapsing the archetype of male intellection (the Experimental Philosopher) into common concerns with "making of Sweet-meats," she deflates the traditional reverence for masculine privilege—and invites her audience to smile as she does so, thus sweetening the sting of social critique.

Parody is especially useful to Cavendish since on the one hand it offers incisive though indirect criticism of specific theoretical propositions, and on the other hand, it may be taken to imply a flattering tribute to the original writer. She is thus able to cross blades with her intellectual rivals without breaking epistemological decorum. In fact, as Steven Shapin points out, in the world of late seventeenth-century England, such decorum was understood as being fundamental to the process of intellection;[5] no surprise that Cavendish enthusiastically critiques contemporary theorists who dismiss ancient philosophers without giving due recognition to the influences of the past: "In this present age those are thought the greatest Wits that rail most against the ancient Philosophers, especially Aristotle, who is beaten by all; but whether he deserve such punishment, others may judg" (*Further Observations,* 1).[6] By caricaturing her male contemporaries as impertinent young thugs mauling a venerable old Aristotle, Cavendish places her critics in the awkward position of having broken epistemological decorum.[7] In this manner, she challenges their fitness as professors of knowledge on the very grounds upon which the Royal Society had been founded: the understanding that there must be "particular stress upon the role of truthfulness in gentlemanly social relations and the cultural practices attending the practical handling of gentlemanly testimony."[8]

That she considers this a particularly effective rhetorical strategy may be seen in her return to the same stance, without the lens of parody, in the third segment of her treatise, *Observations upon the Opinions of Some Ancient Philosophers:*

> The Opinions of the Ancient, though they are not exempt from errors no more then our Modern, yet are they to be commended that their conceptions are their own, and the issue of their own wit and reason; when as most of the opinions of our Modern Philosophers, are patched up with theirs. . . . and what is worst, after all this, instead of thanks, they reward them with scorn, and rail at them; when as, perhaps, without their pains and industry, our age would hardly have arrived to that knowledg it has done . . . To which ungrateful and unconscionable act, I can no ways give my consent, but admire and honour both the ancient, and all those that are real Inventors of noble and profitable Arts and Sciences, before all those that are but botchers and brokers. (2–3)

For Cavendish, there is a distinct relation between the rapine imagery used by her male peers to discuss nature, and the ungentlemanly rhetorical "beating" of the ancients by intellectually unruly "botchers and brokers."

In contrast to discourse that figures scientific inquiry as amorous pursuit, and which roughly dismisses the relevance of past thinkers, Cavendish advances yet another gendered image meant both to bolster her own sense of decorum and to sharpen the edge of her on-going criticism. Indeed, Cavendish begins this satirical passage with a complaint similar to that with which she began the first segment of the *Observations:*

> But I, being a woman, do fear they would soon cast me out of their Schools; for though the muses, Graces and Sciences are all of the female gender, yet they were more esteemed in former ages, then they are now; nay, could it be done handsomely, they would now turn them all from Females into Males; so great is grown the self-conceit of the Masculine, and the disregard of the Female sex. (3.2)

Cavendish recuperates the classical notion of inspiration, figured by the imagined fruitful reciprocity which obtained between the ancient philosophers and the female muses from whom such thinkers received their wisdom, and with considerable fanfare lets it stand as foil to the vision of thinkers perversely engaged in attempts at changing women into men. In this manner, those who are concerned that Cavendish's own writing indicates a dangerous departure from appropriate womanly behavior are answered smartly with the authority of classical precedent.

II

The use of parody speaks to another issue central to Cavendish's criticism of methods and devices espoused by members of the Royal Society: optimistic attitudes toward technological devices tend to elide the issue of distortion in observation. While the manipulation of exaggeration may be useful in philosophical parody (a tool that can expose weaknesses in form and method, logic and exposition), what, wonders Cavendish, is the use of being on the butt-end of mechanical distortion? Concluding a long list of the failings of microscopes and other sorts of magnifying lenses, Cavendish quips, "In short, Magnifying glasses are like a high heel to a short legg, which if it be made too high, it is apt to make the wearer fall, and at the best, can do no more then represent exterior figures in a bigger, and so in a more deformed shape and posture then naturally they are" (1.12). Just as Hooke and others are the focus of her parody, so they are the butt of the unintentional distortions of a mindless technology; but while the former position is meant to provide a useful mirror by which their work may be carefully revised, the latter merely makes clowns of these naive natural philosophers.

After tossing out the image of the natural philosopher's microscope as a high-heeled shoe worn by a tottering, short-legged dandy, Cavendish immediately turns to the more serious issue implicit in her humorous analogy:

> but as for the interior form and motions of a Creature, as I said before, they can no more represent them, then Telescopes can the interior essence and nature of the Sun, and what matter it consists of; for if one that never had seen Milk before, should look upon it through a Microscope, he would never be able to discover the interior parts of Milk by that instrument, were it the best that is in the World . . . Wherefore the best . . . judge is Reason, and the best study is Rational Contemplation. (1.12)

Her repeated critique of knowledge based on superficial observations—and more especially, of epistemes dependent on devices (such as the microscope) which necessarily distort the viewing subject's observational capabilities as well as the observing subject's relationship to the object under scrutiny—echoes the premises of popular cabalistic writing. In this we should not be surprised, for as recent work on Robert Boyle and his contemporaries has demonstrated, occult philosophical traditions continued to flourish well into the early eighteenth century. John Henry, for instance, points out that "the mechanical philosophy as it was presented by English natural philosophers, had a strong tradition of active principles" and the "use of occult qualities or unexplained active principles in matter . . . was always a major feature of the mechanical philosophy in England."[9]

In fact, the mechanistic language of Hooke, Boyle, and others initially was gleaned both from thinkers influenced by and interested in extending cabalistic theory (such as Peter Severine, or Severinus as he was known in the literature), and moral philosophers struggling with mind-matter issues (such as Descartes). Interestingly, in her development of at least one cabalistic allusion, Cavendish makes use of the metaphorical potential of Severinus's notion of matter in a way that her more-respected contemporaries do not. By dramatizing the essentially performative aspects of matter as elaborated by Severinus, she sets the stage for a theory of order that accommodates her position on the active principle in all matter. In short, the natural world could be figured as theater—and all matter made up a company of lively actors engaged in various roles.[10]

The English translation of Severinus available to Cavendish was especially careful to emphasize the theatrical analogy. As Jole Shakelford explains,

> When Severinus wrote that species carry out the liturgy of the world comedy by means of generations, transplantations, and mixtures, the English translator wrote that they "doe by meanes of generations, transplantations, and mixtures *play their parts* in the worldly comedy," rendering lithurgia as "parts," as in the "parts" or "roles" that actors play on stage. [Severinus paints] nature as a worldly stage (*mundana scena*). This terminology reinforces the metaphor of the world as theater.[11]

Thus, Severinus espoused a "mechanical" view more akin to actors in their roles (agents) than machines in the sense which Cavendish's contemporaries seem to espouse. For Cavendish, the link between the order of a script and the improvisation of performance was the same as that which connected ideal and material natures: imagination. In this she shares significant ground with Descartes, a point we will explore in some detail later. For now, we may simply note that the allusion to cabalistic discourse invokes a well established model by which the natural world is understood in terms of the stage—a device that simultaneously conjures a kind of order and predictability (script and role) that is imbedded in chance (improvisation and the inherent variability of performance). The following, then, is a cursory glance at the intellectual ingenuity at work in a philosophical narrative that combines aspects of Cavendish's forays into drama with an epistemological framework that relies on images of costume, stage, actors, and roles for its persuasive impact and fluidity of formulation.

A brief consideration of the form she gives to "An Argumental Discourse Concerning Some Principal Subjects in Natural Philosophy" (which is a kind of postscript to the Preface of the *Observations)* illustrates the extent to which Cavendish borrows the theatrical metaphor from occult philosophical traditions to achieve a particular twist of theoretical insight. In fact, this section is proffered as a key to the subsequent treatise, as well as "all other Philosophical Works, hitherto written by the AUTHORESSE."[12] We are shortly introduced to a dramatic dialogue and given the setting for the theatrical moment:

> When I was setting forth this Book of *Experimental Observations,* a Dispute chanced to arise between the rational Parts of my Mind concerning some chief Points and Principles in Natural Philosophy; for some New Thoughts endeavouring to oppose and call in question the Truth of my former Conceptions, caused a war in my mind, which in time grew to that height, that they were hardly able to compose the differences between themselves. (h 1)

The dialogue between the characters of her "former Thoughts" and "latter Thoughts" is lively and full of direct quotations from writers such as Hooke, another parodic element deftly used to good effect. Cavendish is emphasizing a point that Shapin's study makes emphatically clear: "the making of knowledge in general takes place on a moral field and mobilizes particular appreciations of the virtues and characteristics of types of people."[13] In fact, by dramatizing the process of intellection, the theatrical attributes of this passage function as an ethnomethodological exploration and appreciation "of the ways in which knowledge of the world and knowledge of other people are drawn together in social interaction." Further, the theatricalization of cognitive processes suggests that "presuppositions about the nature of an objective external world are embedded within ordinary social interaction and within practices inquiring about that world."[14] In short, while on the one hand the dramatic dialogue gives an aesthetic form to an otherwise abstract vitalist premise about the nature of matter as shared by Cavendish and Severinus, on the other hand, it functions as a metaphorical shorthand for the complex manner in which social relationships intersect with the ways in which observers relate to phenomena in the natural world.

As formal elements meant to enhance theoretical propositions, it is worth noting that both parody and dramatic dialogue hinge on the concept of memory—both presuppose a recollection of particular works or social situations. Cavendish is intensely preoccupied with the nature of memory because knowledge itself is so intimately bound up with, and even disturbingly dependent on, the ability to give direction and meaning to recollection. Like Severinus, Cavendish finds that theatrical allusions are particularly instructive for exploring the relationship between matter and intellection, a relationship which is central to the act of memory. Later in the *Observations* Cavendish poses the question, "Whether there may be a Remembrance in Sense, as well as there is in Reason?" Echoing Severinus, she writes,

> I answer, Yes: for Remembrance is nothing else but a Repetition of the same figure, made by the same corporeal figurative motions; and as there is a rational remembrance, which is a repetition of the same figures, made by the rational, corporeal figurative motions, so there is also a sensitive remembrance, that is, a repetition of the same figures. (1.240)

In contrast to her earlier parody of the Royal Society, in which she seems to suggest an unflattering familial resemblance between observations made with a microscope and naïve aesthetic endeavors—which rely on superficial phenomena for the derivation of essential natures—Cavendish now suggests that there is an important aesthetic aspect (insofar as art is always imitation, as she had earlier insisted) to intellectual endeavors: sensory knowledge may be a necessary layer in a multilayered view of intellection, especially given that reason is always to some degree dependent on recollection.

This is literalized to good rhetorical effect when in the second segment she weaves the notion of imitation into a theory of how material objects might affect the behavior of other natural phenomena. Transformations in nature are a matter of "inherent figurative motions" and are an extension of the subject, not merely the result of outside forces acting upon otherwise passive objects:

> I will not deny, but there is as much variety in occasioning, as there is in acting; for the imitation is according to the object, but the object is not the immediate agent, but onely an occasional efficient . . . In the same manner does the Blood-Stone stop bleeding; not by imparting invisible Atomes or Rays to the affected parts . . . *but by being imitated by the corporeal figurative motions of the distempered parts.* Thus many other examples could be alledged to prove, that natural

motions work such or such effects within their own parts, without receiving any from without, that is, *by imitation, and not by reception of Motion.* (2.68, 70, emphasis mine).

In this respect, memory itself is an expression of the vitalist principle she espouses.

III

For Cavendish, matter bears the imprint of genius—and she is decisively influenced in this position by the work of Descartes. This may fly in the face of Anglo-American philosophy which has largely relied on the belief that the mind/body split defined Cartesian thinking. However, Descartes' work was far more complicated than this caricature suggests. As Timothy Reiss points out, "no more than others did he consider extended thought possible without information garnered by and through the body."[15] In fact, Descartes never doubted that

> the seat of thought was physically situated in the human body: focused, wrote Descartes, in the pineal gland, although he also came to assert that it was "really joined to the whole body," and not able to be conceived clearly in terms of any limiting dimension. There is actually much justification for seeing the 1649 *Passions de l'âme,* whence come these last remarks, as showing how mind and body work together through those passions.[16]

The problem for Descartes is that the body bears the marks of history—memory is imprinted in the flesh. Eventually, to his way of thinking, "either the mind had to be divided from body, or body placed somehow outside history".[17] Descartes fiddles with both possibilities, and the problem of memory ends up being his special focus, for memory is the aspect of knowing that is indelibly imprinted on the body. Cavendish's own dalliance with memory and imagination exhibits some of the same assumptions found in Descartes—but as we might expect, the Duchess adds a few significant flourishes of her own.

In *Discours de la Méthode* (1637),[18] Descartes begins the history of his own mind and its training with an account of his travels, and places special emphasis on his experience in the

Thirty Years' War. The aim of this work was to begin the process of building knowledge anew; the old models no longer seemed sufficient, and he sought to furnish himself with the makings of something that would more meaningfully account for the variety of the world's phenomena. In particular, the account of his experience of war served to demonstrate his point about the inevitable inaccuracy of historical accounts; but it also served to figure the conditions under which a new model of knowledge could be developed: memory must be invoked and then subjected to radical doubt, for reason and memory are ultimately at odds. Insofar as memory is filled with wrong ideas and false conceptions, intellection would always have to combat the inaccuracies of history. Accordingly, the anecdote was a narrative form that Descartes put to theoretical use.

Thus, in addition to parody and dramatic dialogue, Cavendish's *Observations* also relies on well-placed anecdotes for similar purposes. One of the best examples of this is found in her discussion of the "Generation of Butter-flies" in which she addresses various theories of reproduction. She decides that in this case, rather than determine which theory seems most apt, she will investigate the relationship of memory to reason by recounting her own experience through recollection: "When I lived beyond the Seas in Banishment with my Noble Lord, one of my Maids brought up an old piece of wood, or stone (which it was I cannot perfectly remember) something to me which seemed to grow out of that same piece; it was about the length of half an inch or less" (16). She goes on in this vein for two pages, providing a wealth of descriptive detail, and suggesting that a small experiment she did with a pupa may have fostered the generation of two butterflies which appear at the end of the account. She resists certainty even here, though, concluding that

> This is all I have observed of Butter-flies, but I have heard also that Caterpillars are transformed into Butter-flies; whether it be true or not, I will not dispute, onely this I dare say, that I have seen Caterpillars spin as Silk-worms do, an oval ball about their feed [*sic*], or rather about themselves. (1.26–28)

In short, when employing extended anecdotes, Cavendish is less interested in proving a particular hypothesis (in this case, that a

specific action with a pupa results in the generation of two butterflies), and more interested in exploring how the accumulation
and recollection of sensory details pertains to the act of intellection, to the creation of possible new knowledge. Already formally
emphasized through the use of parody and dramatic dialogue,
the importance of memory as a philosophical issue is bolstered
further through the theoretical use of the personal anecdote.

Indeed, Cavendish's frequent discussions of intelligent matter
merely refract the physicality of memory into the moment of
recall. In this sense, she is much like Descartes who suggests
that an external stimulus is like a seal leaving its impression in
wax. First, he writes, the senses operate "in the same way as wax
takes on its shape from the seal . . . we must think of the external
shape of the sentient body as being really changed by the object in
exactly the same way as the shape of the surface of the wax is
altered by the seal."[19] This imprint is "conveyed" immediately "to
another part of the body known as the "common" sense."[20] This
time, the analogy is to writing:

> In exactly the same way, I understand that while I am writing, at the
> very moment when individual letters are traced on the paper, not
> only does the point of the pen move, but the slightest motion of this
> part cannot but be transmitted simultaneously to the whole pen.[21]

Returning to the idea of imprinting, he goes on to explain that:

> the "common" sense functions like a seal, fashioning in the phan-
> tasy or imagination, as if in wax, the same figures or ideas which
> come, pure and bodiless, from the external senses. Phantasy is a
> genuine part of the body, and is large enough to let the different parts
> of it take on many different figures and generally to retain them for
> some time; in which case it is to be identified with what we call
> "memory."[22]

Thus, memory and imagination are linked in their relation to
body and the body's role in knowing. However, the model is complicated still further by another analogy. Descartes also likens
memory to the holes between the fibers of woven cloth, so that,

> when the soul wants to remember something, this volition makes the
> gland lean first to one side and then to another, thus driving the
> spirits towards different regions of the brain until they come upon

the one containing traces left by the object we want to remember. These traces consist simply in the fact that the pores of the brain through which the spirits previously made their way owing to the presence of this object have thereby become more apt than the other to be opened in the same way when the spirits again flow towards them. And so the spirits enter into these pores more easily when they come upon them, thereby producing in the gland that special move-ment which represents the same object to the soul, and makes it recognize the object as the one it wanted to remember.[23]

Writing is an important tool for Descartes because it makes the repeated re-impressions of memory on the body unnecessary, "thus allowing the imagination to devote itself freely and com-pletely to the idea immediately before it."[24] Imagination-as-intuition is seen as a means by which the prejudices of memory are overcome. However, while freedom from the grooves and folds of memory allows intuition to leap to new knowledge, order of some sort must be imposed to transform intuition into intellec-tion, otherwise intuition would be no better (and in some cases worse) than the perversions of false recollection. For Descartes, that order was the language of mathematics which directed the otherwise random jumble of human experience into the orderly paths of equational expression.

Cavendish shares Descartes' appreciation for the role of imag-ination in rational thought; however, unlike Descartes, she re-jects mathematical expression as the best route for reason. In-stead, Cavendish espouses a kind of narrative virtuosity meant to resist the very strictures Descartes sees as necessary to bridle memory's influence on imagination. Her critique of Aristotle develops this possibility more thoroughly:

Sense, says he, is in all Animals, but fancy is not, for Fancy is not Sense; Fancy acts in him that sleeps, Sense not. To which I answer, first, Fancy or Imagination is a voluntary action of Reason, or of the rational parts of Matter, and if reason be in all Animals, nay, in all Creatures, Fancy is there also; Next, it is evident that Sense acts as much asleep as awake . . . the sensitive motions, Work inwardly in sleep, and outwardly awake . . . If nature be material, as it cannot be proved otherwise, sense and reason are material also . . . *and all Fancies, Imaginations, Judgment, Memory, Remembrance, and the like, are nothing else but the actions of reason, or of the rational parts of Animate Matter.* (3.39–40, emphasis mine).

As we have seen, parody, dramatic dialogue, and personal anecdote all have serious theoretical possibility for Cavendish, and seem to be her means of urging form to reproduce the concrete experience of an abstract proposition.

Since for Cavendish the language of mathematics lacked the aesthetic fluidity required for the successful transition of imagination to intellection, it would have to be dismissed in favor of something far more elastic. Her alternative was the replacement of detached observation with the controlled variability of improvisational performance. For this reason, I wish to argue, the attachment of the *Blazing World* to her formal treatise is a further dramatization of the relationship between aesthetic sense and the process of knowledge-making. As Cavendish asserts, the natural philosopher is ultimately a virtuoso, one who expertly navigates between imagination and intellection for the sake of advancing human understanding.

Phyllis Gorfain describes virtuosity as the process in which "humans re-present reality to themselves in one imaginative substitution of experience after another," turning the flux of experience into narrative, "narrative into drama, plays into replays."[25] This intellectual agility uses "all these means of interpretation and reinterpretation to maintain and invent roles, generate power in spectacle and symbol, refashion expectations, and question the "givenness" of rules and institutions." Ultimately, it is through the fabrication of "openly artificial events, reflexive situations, liminal processes, reframings, deceptions, and fictions" that worlds are made (ibid.). Gorfain's definition of virtuosity in relation to knowledge-making does much to explain the epistemological relationship between *Observations* and *The Blazing World*. Cavendish's original treatise on speculative philosophy is transformed into narrative, the narrative into a threefold drama of romancical, philosophical, and fantastical parts.

Indeed, not only does Cavendish develop in practice a vision of virtuosity as fundamental to knowledge-making, she speculates *overtly* on the *value* of that virtuosity. Remember that at one point in the *Blazing World,* the character of the Emperor desires for the Blazing World "such a theatre as may make wise men" and consults the character of the Duchess, who disclaims any knowledge of stagecraft and stresses the unpopularity of her own dramatic efforts in her native land (another bit of self-parody in which Cavendish dramatizes the popular failure of her own work). We quickly learn, however, that this is no disparagement to the Duchess, since, according to her own words, "my plays may be acted in your Blazing World, when they cannot be acted in the Blinking World of Wit" (220). This is a particularly significant moment in the *Blazing World* since the long passages reiterating Cavendish's observations (as borrowed directly from *Observations*) have been funneled into a focused critique of England's (to be deplored) lack of quality imagination. Ignorance is not equated with false impressions in the waxy seal of memory, but with the whistling echo of emptiness in a mind lacking the rational part of *imagination.*

In the fictional narrative, the Duchess/Cavendish eventually agrees to help to establish a new national theater and even to write plays for it. In short, the philosophical has revealed its debt to the fantastical, and with the invocation of the theater, Cavendish collapses Descartes' desire for mathematical virtuosity into theatrical improvisation, the characteristic of dramatic virtuosity that makes each performance distinctly singular. She emphasizes this point again in the epilogue:

> [A]nd if any should like the world I have made, and be willing to be my subjects, they may imagine themselves such, and they are such, I mean, in their minds, fancies or imaginations; but if they cannot endure to be subjects, they may create worlds of their own, and govern themselves as they please. (225)

This imaginative substitution of experience—natural philosophy dramatized, made spectacle—dissolves the epistemological into the ontological. Or, to put it another way, the passive *state* of knowing is dismissed in favor of knowing as the daring *act.*

Ultimately, with *Observations* wed to the *Blazing World,* Cavendish can confidently assert that knowledge is always complicated and informed by "the uncloseable distance between behavior and its meanings, between the immediacy of experience and the shaping of experience into transmittable forms."[26] By melding three modes of discourse—focused parody of the gendered metaphors popular among members of the Royal Society, the theatrical form borrowed from those whose cabala-inflected work focused on essence and the possibility of fundamental transformations, and the Cartesian deployment of personal anecdote in the service of theoretical paradigms—Cavendish ultimately pits ontology against epistemology.

For Cavendish, the elasticity of being (potentiality) precedes knowing by setting up the conditions under which true thinking can take place. Cavendish's experiments with form suggest that a thinker may come to recognize the possibility of systematically different interpretations of the same set of natural phenomena, of the existence of alternative and rival schemata which yield mutually incompatible accounts of what is going on in the natural world. In this sense, her agility with literary form translates to a broader meditation on the very nature of knowledge as well as on the particular kinds of knowledge being advanced by her peers.

NOTES

1. Margaret Cavendish, *Observations upon Experimental Philosophy* (London, 1666), d. All subsequent citations refer to this edition.

2. Ibid., c.

3. Although I will not address the issue at any length here, note that *all* who published in natural philosophy were, to one extent or another, obliged to make character an issue in assertions regarding the natural world. Hooke, Boyle, Hobbes, Locke, and others understood that one's social identity influenced the reception of theoretical propositions: the making of a personal identity and the making of public knowledge were parallel enterprises. For a thorough study of this phenomenon, see Steven Shapin, *A Social History of Truth: Civility and Science in Seventeenth Century England* (Chicago: University of Chicago Press, 1994).

4. *Letters and Poems in Honour of the . . . Duchess of Newcastle* (Cambridge, 1676), 4–5.

5. Shapin, *A Social History of Truth,* 231–40.

6. For the sake of clarity and convenience, in subsequent citations, each main segment of the treatise will be numbered accordingly (each segment has separate pagination). Thus, page five of the first part of the *Observations* will be cited as 1.5; page eleven of the third segment will be cited as 3.11; etc.

7. The fact that Cavendish sometimes defends and sometimes dismisses both ancient and contemporary writers is less a mark of contradiction or inconsistency in her work than a persistent selectivity. We should expect this from a thinker whose ruminations on the philosophical underpinnings of particular methodologies consistently exhibit a predilection for a taxonomical approach to the works of others. Cavendish habitually sorts what she considers to be useful from what is not, sometimes from among the works of various writers (Hobbes

and Locke, for example) or from among various works by a single thinker (such as Aristotle). This is not to say that Cavendish is unfailingly consistent in her thought, but that she is as much so as her peers. To confuse her selectivity with polemical contradiction is to miss the fascination with classification at the heart of Cavendish's philosophical project.

8. Shapin, *A Social History of Truth,* 193.

9. John Henry, "Occult Qualities and the Experimental Philosophy: Active Principles in Pre-Newtonian Matter Theory," *History of Science* 24 (1986): 335–81. See also Antonio Clericuzio, "A Redefinition of Boyle's Chemistry and Corpuscular Philosophy," *Annals of Science* 47 (1990): 561–89.

10. As Anna Battigelli points out, Cavendish dismissed some aspects of Paracelsian theory and absorbed others into her own theoretical propositions. See *Margaret Cavendish and the Exiles of the Mind* (Lexington: University Press of Kentucky, 1998), 98–101. Cavendish had access to Paracelsian views through a variety of contemporary sources, some of which included translations of Severinus's treatments of a Paracelsian chemical world anatomy. See Jole Shakelford, "Early Reception of Paracelsian Theory: Severinus and Erastus," *Sixteenth Century Journal* 26:1 (1995): 123–35.

11. Jole Shakelford, "Seeds with a Mechanical Purpose: Severinus's Semina and Seventeenth-Century Matter Theory," in *Reading the Book of Nature: The Other Side of the Scientific Revolution,* ed. Allen G. Debus, and Michael T. Walton (Philadelphia: Thomas Jefferson University Press, 1998), 25.

12. Cavendish, *Observations,* h.

13. Shapin, *A Social History of Truth,* xxvi.

14. Ibid.

15. Timothy Reiss, "Denying the Body?: Memory and the Dilemmas of History in Descartes," *Journal of the History of Ideas* 57.4 (1996): 590.

16. Ibid.

17. Ibid., 591.

18. René Descartes, *Discours de la Méthode* (Discourse on Method), trans. Laurence J. Lafleur (New York: Liberal Arts Press, 1956).

19. Descartes, Regula 12, *The Philosophical Writings of Descartes,* trans. John Cottingham, Robert Stoothoff, and Dugald Murdoch (Cambridge: Cambridge University Press, 1984), vol. 1, 40.

20. Regula 12, *Philosophical Writings,* 41.

21. Ibid.

22. Ibid., 41.

23. Passions 42, *Philosophical Writings,* 343–44.

24. Regula 16, *Philosophical Writings,* 67.

25. Phyllis Gorfain, "Play and the Problem of Knowing in *Hamlet:* An Excursion into Interpretive Anthropology," in *The Anthropology of Experience,* ed. Victor W. Turner and Edward M. Bruner (Urbana and Chicago: University of Illinois Press, 1986), 211.

26. Gorfain, "Play and the Problem of Knowing," 207.

Margaret Cavendish's *Life of William,* Plutarch, and Mixed Genre

JAMES FITZMAURICE

FROM TIME TO TIME, MARGARET CAVENDISH CASUALLY MAKES reference to her reading of *The Lives of the Noble Grecians and Romans,* and she undoubtedly thought of herself as something of a literary descendent of Plutarch. Nevertheless, she only occasionally engages with him directly as a writer, and she makes no attempt to follow his or anyone else's model in her own life writing. Indeed, her narrative thread ends after the middle of Book II of *The Life of. . . William Cavendish, Duke of Newcastle* (London, 1667).[1] The remainder of this book details, mostly in spreadsheet form, the financial losses that resulted from Newcastle's involvement in the English Civil Wars. The third book lists his garrisons and their commanders, chronicles his pedigree and education, and provides information regarding discrete aspects of his daily life. This book dwells on his sufferings. It also, as if to maintain balance, includes a brief passage on his blessings. The fourth book is a collection of his and her observations about life along with pithy maxims. Modern readers are liable to be disappointed by the fact that Cavendish apparently makes no genuine effort to examine her husband's intimate feelings as such feelings were generated by stressful events or as they were associated with unpleasant situations. For the majority of us living today, there is likely to be the sense that much of *The Life* is no more than odds and ends mixed together in random fashion to create at best an ordinary, unrevealing family scrapbook.

PLUTARCH

Scholars like Paul Hunter have warned us not to apply the standards of the novel, a genre that originated in the eighteenth century, to earlier fiction.[2] It is foolish, for instance, to fault Thomas Nashe's *The Unfortunate Traveller* (1594) for having a loose and rambling structure. Attending to this admonition to avoid anachronism, one might say that Cavendish wrote "before biography" even as Nashe wrote "before novels." Thus we should not expect that Cavendish's *Life of William* necessarily would be marked by strong narrative line combined with discussion of its subject's intimate feelings. It would be a mistake, however, to attribute our sense of mixed genre found in *The Life* entirely to our experiences with modern biography. So too, the paucity of discussion of feelings. Plutarch, who also wrote before modern biography, pays far more attention to storytelling than does Cavendish, and Plutarch is far more given to examination of his subjects' feelings—or, perhaps, to moral judgments about their characters.[3] For instance, Plutarch asserts that Mark Anthony was unable to control feelings of despondency that derived from his love for Cleopatra. That inability, for Plutarch, marks a fatal flaw in Anthony's character as a man.

Cavendish, nevertheless, was by no means an inept follower of Plutarch. Rather, she simply continues in a pattern that she had established many years before with others of her books. Thus she mixes types of life writing in her volume on her husband in a way not so very different from the way in which she mixes types of fiction in *Nature's Pictures* (1656). The first third or so of *Nature's Pictures* is composed of tales in verse, while the remainder of the book is made up of stories in prose. The whole of the collection mixes the serious and comic, the idealistic and cynical. Cavendish, in a preface to *Nature's Pictures,* likens the situation to what is found in musical performance.

> I must intreat my Readers to take notice, that . . . I was forced to order my several Chapters, as Musicians doe their tunes, when they play upon Musicall instruments, who for the most part do mix light Aires with Solemn sounds.[4]

Cavendish undoubtedly is joking when she says that she was "forced" to create a mixture. Indeed, she already had mixed the comic and the serious, the idealistic and the cynical in brief her essays in *The World's Olio* (1655). In *Olio,* she also mixes discussions of science and medicine on the one hand with observations about classical myth and English history on the other. Her joke in the preface to *Nature's Pictures* in all likelihood makes use of mock deference to the Puritans' distaste for mixture in theology. Even Milton, who was a far cry from the most strict of Puritans, had contempt for "an Oglio or Medley of various Religions."[5] Cavendish, who had no love for Puritans, thought, to the contrary, that an "olio" was an artistic mixture that might be both entertaining and fashionable.[6] Her life of her husband was to be made up of such an entertaining mixture, though she is never so specific as to say so.[7]

Cavendish probably believed that it would have been impertinent for her to offer a view of her husband's intimate feelings in some sort of explicit statement intended for print. She does, of course, routinely praise his character as virtuous, loyal, courageous, and the like, but these assertions, while completely genuine on her part, are not rooted in detail of feeling and would have been expected of any other wife of a military commander of the time. Nevertheless, in working to achieve two unrelated goals, she, along the way, managed to suggest a good deal about her husband's feelings, albeit in a way that is implicit rather than explicit. Her primary goal in *The Life* was to defend her husband's reputation against charges that he should not have left England after the defeat of his army at the Battle of Marston Moor (2 July 1644). Edward Hyde, Earl of Clarendon and an old rival of Newcastle for political power, writes that Newcastle's army, while defeated, was not destroyed. Clarendon goes on to assert that Newcastle could have put together another army but was "so transported . . . with passion and despair, that he could not compose himself to think of beginning the work again."[8]

Cavendish, of course, was not responding to Clarendon's *History of the Great Rebellion* (1702–1704), which had yet to be published when *The Life of William* appeared, but she easily could have reacted against Clarendon's opinions and the opinions of likeminded others, which quite probably had been in circulation for some time before her life of her husband was printed. In her husband's life, Cavendish writes the following simply and without elaboration:

[Newcastle] having nothing left in his power to do his Majesty any further service in that kind [making war]; for he had neither Ammunition, nor Money to raise more Forces, to keep either York or any other Towns that were yet in His Majesty's Devotion . . . he took a Resolution, and that justly and honourably, to forsake the Kingdom.[9]

Cavendish does not directly discuss the details of her husband's intimate feelings but rather makes the question of his staying or leaving England one of economic prudence. She does, however, take up the topic of his feelings indirectly in her careful delineation of his mental makeup. Cavendish presents to her reader a man who, far from being consumed with "passion and despair" at any point in his life, was always able to deal with life's difficulties in a prudent way. He was, coincidentally, a man of considerable wit and gallantry, in sum a likeable sort of person. She does not, as some have suggested, always portray him as saint, but neither does she have any desire to treat him in a disinterested manner. Her willingness to mingle "objective truth and creative invention," to borrow the words of Judith Anderson, was not unusual for life writing of the time.[10] Her particular understanding of Newcastle, one might allege, is both her bias and her point of view.

Cavendish occasionally includes in *The Life* remarks about her husband that might seem to betray a man who we living today would find to be less than likeable.

For he, having but two sons, proposed to marry me, a young woman that might prove fruitful to him and increase his posterity by a masculine offspring. Nay, he was so desirous of male issue that I have heard him say he cared not (so God would be pleased to give him many sons) although they came to be persons of the meanest fortunes. (*Life,* 45)

I am quite certain that Cavendish is not taking this opportunity to offer a "warts and all" account of what we would see as her husband's irresponsible attitude regarding the fathering of illegitimate children. Nor is she guilty of what we would call a "Freudian slip." What she *is* doing is more difficult to ascertain exactly. It is quite possible that she is suggesting that Newcastle, like Charles II, would not have minded fathering a child or two out of wedlock. It is more likely, given the lack of any record of such children, that Cavendish is referring to a witty and jocular remark made by her husband rather than alluding to his habitual practice and is herself being arch.[11] She accedes, tongue in cheek, to the charge of irreverent fornicator that frequently was leveled against him in the Puritan press during the 1640s.[12] Those days were gone at the time of the publication of *The Life of William* but were by no means forgotten by her readers, who might have found a chuckle or two in the allusion. Less comic and less obvious is that Newcastle did not increase the number of his offspring in his marriage to Cavendish. What is also unexpressed in the passage is the possibility that his jokes on the subject would have reflected a genuine sense of disappointment and even sadness on his part. What Cavendish, herself, felt—inadequacy, irritation, or whatever— we can only imagine.

Cavendish's secondary goal in *The Life* was to establish herself as a serious historian, a historian of "some particular person" and what we would call a biographer or practitioner of life writing. In her general preface, she puts her view of her undertaking thus:

> Although, there be many sorts of histories, yet these three are the chiefest: (1) a general history; (2) a national history; (3) a particular history. Which three sorts may, not unfitly, be compared to the three sorts of governments, democracy, aristocracy, and monarchy. The first is the history of the known parts and people of the world; the second is the history of a particular nation, kingdom, or commonwealth. The third is the history of the life and actions of some particular person. (*Life,* xl)

Amiot, in his preface to *The Lives of the Noble Grecians and Romans,* had equated Plutarch's writing with the writing of history, and it was Amiot's edition of Plutarch that Cavendish undoubtedly read in the North translation:

> In respect whereof it may be reasonably avowed, that men [of historical importance] are more beholding to such good wits, as by their grave and wise writing have deserved the name of historiographers than they are to any other kind of writers. Because an history is an orderly register of notable things said, done, or happened in times past, to maintain the continual remembrance of them, and to serve for the instruction of them to come. (Plutarch, xxix)

Cavendish, then, might become her husband's Plutarch, even though her actual approach to life writing was much different from what is found in *The Lives of the Noble Grecians and Romans*. She was not unambitious, and she knew full well that Plutarch was highly regarded in his own right. If she were to be a Plutarch, then her husband, reasonably enough, might assume the role of her Julius Caesar:

> I have observed, that many, by flattering poets, have been compared to Caesar, without desert; but this I dare freely and without flattery say of my Lord, that though he had not Caesar's fortune, yet he wanted not Caesar's courage, nor his prudence, nor his good nature, nor his wit. Nay, in some particulars he did more than Caesar ever did; for though Caesar had a great army, yet he was first set out by the state or senators of Rome; when as my Lord raised his army (as before is mentioned) most upon his own interest [i.e., money] . . . at such a time when his gracious King and sovereign was then not master of his own kingdoms, he being overpowered by his rebellious subjects. (*Life,* 142–43)

In the process of making herself into a Plutarch, she works at achieving both of her goals. Most importantly in this passage, she reminds her reader that her husband's army was funded by himself, his friends, and his kin, not by the king. The implication here is that when Newcastle's money was gone, he had no choice but to retire into exile. The fact that the king found it difficult to collect taxes and pass the revenue along to his generals, leaves the monarch blameless but also Newcastle with no recourse but to sail for the Continent. As if by chance, Cavendish also slips in a few particulars of her understanding of her subject's character: Caesar was likeable, as was the case with Newcastle. Caesar and Newcastle were both prudent; both were gifted with wit. Newcastle's wit and his amiability, however, are more than incidental attributes, and Cavendish invokes them in the very last lines that she gives to Newcastle in *The Life:*

> [D]iscoursing one time merrily with his friends, [Newcastle] was pleased to say, that though his earthly king and master seemed to have forgot him, yet the King of Heaven had remembered him, for he had given him £2000 a year. (*Life,* 141)

What Cavendish does not say, though it is clearly implied, is that Newcastle had every reason to resent the ill treatment that he received from his "earthly king." Newcastle might have been bitter and angry but he was not. Astute readers could well surmise that Newcastle *did* feel anger and bitterness, particularly around the time of the restoration of the monarchy when he made his remarks about the £2000, but that he chose to deal with what was an unpleasant situation in a witty and amiable way.[13] The man who controlled his passions, or feelings, was, of course, much to be admired in seventeenth-century England, but Cavendish had no interest in making this claim directly.

The passage that compares Newcastle to Caesar drew derisive comment from Horace Walpole in the much-reprinted *Catalogue of the Royal and Noble Authors of England* (1759):

> It is equally amusing to hear her sometimes compare her Lord to Julius Caesar, and oftener to acquaint you with such anecdotes, as in what sort of coach he went to Amsterdam.[14]

Walpole's remarks, while frequently noted in the anthologies of women's writing that sprang up during the nineteenth century, did not alter the enormous popularity of *The Life of William* at the end of that century. Nor did they dissuade C. H. Firth, Regius Professor of Modern History at Oxford University, from undertaking his heavily annotated edition of it. If Newcastle was not a Caesar, he had been a military commander of considerable importance. Indeed, Walpole, some might say, was willful in ignoring the mountain of significant military history contained in *The Life of William*.

Cavendish only occasionally discusses her reading in detail or with reference to particular authors, but on two occasions in *Sociable Letters* (1664) she casually mentions that she read Plutarch:

> Yesterday, being not in the Humour of Writing, I took Plutarch's Lives, or as some call them, Plutarch's Lies, but Lives or Lies or a mixture of both, I read part of the day in that Book.[15]

Here, the joke "Plutarch's Lies" suggests that Cavendish is teasing a predecessor for whom she feels affection. She goes on to consider Plutarch's description of the life of Aspasia, a courtesan who married the Greek ruler Pericles. Plutarch is apologetic about discussing Aspasia, presumably because of her profession. However, since as she was the much-loved wife of his subject and because she was a rhetorician of considerable standing in her own right, Plutarch says that he could not pass over her in silence.[16] Plutarch's apologies are probably pro forma, for, while he writes that Aspasia was called a "whore" by Cratinus, he then offers a long passage in which he shows his admiration for a woman who "Socrates himself went to see [in order to discuss philosophy] . . . sometimes with his friends" (Plutarch, 360–61). Cavendish, as might be expected, is fascinated by a woman who was at once respected among the great thinkers of her time and, paradoxically, open to the insult "whore." Cavendish would have known that there were men in England who would call any woman who aspired to serious thought a "whore," and she may have known that one of them had suggested that she, herself, was both an atheist and "Welbeck's illustrious whore."[17] Her way of dealing with the problem of her own reputation as a woman is to distance herself from Plutarch at the end of her letter, in much the same way as she distanced herself from controversial situations that she discusses in other letters:

> It seems the Graecians were not like the Italians concerning their Wives, although they were like them concerning their Courtesans; but honest Women take not so much care to Speak well as to do that which is Virtuous. (*Sociable Letters*, letter 30)

Cavendish, of course, allows her reader to infer that she is herself one of the virtuous. This distancing does not work to put to rest her fascination with Aspasia, however, and only helps to make clear that Cavendish does not equate herself with this woman.

The second reference that Cavendish makes to *The Lives of Noble Grecians and Romans* in *Sociable Letters* also involves an engagement with what she found in Plutarch:

> My Imployment continues as yet, which is, to read Plutarch's Lives, and amongst the rest, I find Described the Life of Cato Uticensis, whose Story, if true, makes me love the Memory of . . . Cato. (*Sociable Letters*, letter 187)

While Cavendish begins by saying that she loves the memory of "this Cato," she goes on to call into question the Roman notion that suicide can be an honorable death:

> For [Cato] perceiving his Country was like to be Govern'd as a Monarchy, which was before a Republick, Kill'd himself, although he knew the old Government was so Corrupted, as it caused great Riots, Tumults, Seditions, Factions, and Slaughters, Killing and Murdering even in the Market-place, so as it could not be Worse what Chance soever came, but was Probable a Change of Government might make it more Peaceable and Safe; wherefore Cato did not Kill himself for the Peace and Safety of his Country, but for the Government, as choosing rather to have it Governed Ill by the Old way, than to have it Govern'd Well another way. (*Sociable Letters,* letter 187)

Cato was no more than a curmudgeon, a stick-in-the-mud. One might expect that Cavendish, in expressing her judgment so strongly, takes the opposite of Plutarch's view, but Plutarch does not pass judgment on Cato's suicide. Plutarch does not even take sides in the dispute that developed between Julius Caesar and Cicero over the posthumous reputation of Cato. According to Plutarch, there are two views, and different people support the one or the other:

> Cicero had written a book of praise of Cato, which he entitled *Cato.* . . . [Caesar] heaped up a number of accusations against Cato, and entitled the book *Anticaton.* Both these books have favorers unto this day, some defending the one for the love they bear to Caesar, and the other allowing the other for Cato's sake. (Plutarch, 1423)

Cavendish was not likely to have remained neutral in this dispute, and she sided with Julius Caesar not only because she saw him as being similar to her husband in character but also because the form of government that Caesar advocated most resembled the system to which she and her husband were famously committed, monarchy.[18] Cavendish also had little use for suicide, and without mentioning Plutarch, she is critical in *The World's Olio* of the suicide of Brutus's wife Portia. Portia, for Cavendish, was a coward rather than a heroine:

> For true Love will hope untill there is no ground to raise Hopes on, and Hope begets Courage, and Courage will give Assistance. [Though

Portia's] Husband run out of *Rome,* yet he had his Life, and an Army to defend it for a time.[19]

If, as is probably the case, Cavendish is responding Plutarch's *Lives* in this instance, then she simply goes further than he does, for he hints that Portia was the victim of mental illness:

> There was a letter of Brutus found written to his friends, complaining of their negligence—that his wife being sick, they would not help her, but suffered her to kill herself. (Plutarch, 1908–19)

Cavendish, simply put, was much more critical of suicide than was Plutarch.[20] Suicide, was, of course, a crime in seventeenth-century England, and the consequence of it was that the suicide's estate was forfeit to the crown. A wife's suicide might not damage a husband very much financially, since all of what she counted as her property was legally his. A husband's suicide, by contrast, meant that his widow's jointure became property of the crown, though the crown had the option of restoring it to her. Cavendish, as a woman living in early modern England, had more reason to dislike suicide than did Plutarch, a man living in classical antiquity.

The tidy package of Cavendish as Plutarch with the outlook of a seventeenth-century woman is, however, just a little too tidy. In *Sociable Letters,* Cavendish boldly states that she, herself, would have liked to have been Julius Caesar. The life writer would not have minded being a subject for life writing, herself:

> And of all the Men I read of, I Emulate Julius Caesar most, because he was a man that had all these Excellencies, as Courage, Prudence, Wit and Eloquence, in great Perfection, insomuch as when I read of Julius Caesar, I cannot but wish that Nature and Fate had made me such a one as he was; and sometimes I have that Courage, as to think I should not be afraid of his Destiny, so I might have as great a Fame. (*Sociable Letters,* letter 27)

Another letter in *Sociable Letters* seems to explain how Cavendish went on to transform such hopes and ambitions into something like hero worship for her husband:

> Remember, when we were very young Maids, one day we were Discoursing about Lovers, and we did injoyn each other to Confess

who Profess'd to Love us, and whom we Loved, and I Confess'd I only
was in Love with three Dead men, which were Dead long before my
time, the one was Caesar, for his Valour, the second Ovid, for his Wit,
and the third was our Countryman Shakespear, for his Comical and
Tragical Humour; but soon after we both Married two Worthy men,
and I will leave you to your own Husband, for you best know what he
is; As for my Husband, I know him to have the Valour of Caesar, the
Fancy, and Wit of Ovid, and the Tragical, especially Comical Art of
Shakespear. (*Sociable Letters,* letter 162)

Those modern readers who admire Cavendish for her daring and
courage in seeking print under her own name might be apt to
despair when they believe that find her playing the part of the
"woman behind the man" and subsuming her own ambitions into
the life of her husband. I am not sure that she is actually so self-
effacing.[21] Rather, she simply is able to move back and forth
between actual and potential roles for herself. She thought of
herself as a loyal wife but also as a woman at the head of an army
in the manner of Henrietta Maria.[22] Cavendish is both the inher-
itor of Amiot's Plutarch when she writes in the role of historian of
her husband's life and, at least in her own imagination, a potential subject for "historiography."

LIFE WRITING AS NARRATIVE

In the narrative section of *The Life of William,* the depiction of
military events functions in several ways. The recounting of
details of dates, places, and numbers of troops provides the factual background necessary to establish Cavendish as a historian
of a person. At the same time Cavendish is able to strengthen the
portrait of her husband as a likeable man. Early in Book I, Cavendish relates the following story:

In the meantime, there happened a great mutiny of the train-band
soldiers of the Bishopric at Durham, so that my Lord was forced to
remove thither in person, attended with some forces to appease
them; where at his arrival (I mention it by the way, and as a merry
passage) a jovial fellow used this expression, that he liked my Lord
very well, but not his company (meaning his soldiers). (*Life,* 11)

In the next paragraph, we learn that Newcastle "reduced [the mutinous soldiers] to their obedience and duty." Cavendish's anecdote of the jovial fellow is included, in part, to show that Newcastle was liked as a leader even by a mutineer. We may guess that "to mutiny" here meant something like "to fail to obey orders" rather than "to take up arms against one's leaders," so the man was by no means coward or a traitor. Trained bands were militias notorious for their lack of professional discipline, and Newcastle joked about them in his play *The Country Captain* (acted c. 1640, printed 1649).[23] At the same time, a mutiny was a serious threat. An astute reader would understand that Newcastle had coolly dealt with a potentially explosive situation.

The characterization of Newcastle as a likeable commander is interwoven with references to the necessity for military leaders to find money to prosecute wars. In the paragraph that follows the description of the mutiny, Cavendish continues,

> Some short time after, my Lord received from her Majesty the Queen, out of Holland, a small supply of money, viz. a little barrel of ducatoons, which amounted to about £500 sterling; which my Lord distributed amongst the officers of his new-raised army, to encourage them the better in their service. (*Life,* 12)

We may imagine that the officers of the new-raised army were delighted, but the point made by Cavendish is that the genial Newcastle did not in the end benefit personally from the Queen's gift. The story continues as the King finds occasion to review Newcastle's men: "but it seems his Majesty liked the troop so well, that he was pleased to command their stay to recruit [i.e., "add to"] his own army" (ibid., 12). Newcastle, easygoing as ever, does not complain about having to cede control of his freshly recruited men to the king, nor does Cavendish. Newcastle just gets on with the job, perhaps quietly putting aside any temporary anger or bitterness. The job, in Cavendish's telling, means returning to the matter of collecting money to prosecute the war:

> [I]n the later end of December 1642, [Newcastle] fell upon consultations how he might best proceed to serve his King and country; . . . well knowing, that no army can be governed without being constantly and regularly supported by provision and pay. Whereupon it was agreed, that the nobility and gentry of the several counties,

should select a certain number of themselves to raise money by a regular tax. (ibid., 15)

One might imagine that the nobles and gentry were not enthusiastic about being taxed twice, once by the Parliament and then again by the king in the person of Newcastle. On the other hand, the nobles and gentry were no doubt happy not to have a royalist army that was left "to free-quarter, and carve for themselves" (ibid., 15). Indeed, should any of the soldiers damage any privately owned property, the tax would be used "to repair those injuries" (ibid., 15).

It well may be that Newcastle was ordered to support Queen Henrietta Maria's landing at Burlington Key in February of 1642, but Cavendish casts the event in terms of Newcastle's gallantry, yet another important public quality of her likeable husband:

> My Lord, finding her Majesty in this condition [under attack from the Parliament by sea], drew his army near the place where she was, ready to attend and protect her Majesty's person. . . . About this time, her Majesty having some present occasion for money, my Lord presented her with £3000 sterling, which she graciously accepted of. (ibid., 19)

At the same time, the king was in need of ammunition, which Newcastle sent guarded by a party of 1,500, who were "well commanded." Unsurprisingly, "which party his Majesty was pleased to keep with him for his own service." Once again the genial Newcastle finds himself helping the king at his own inconvenience, nor do Newcastle's gallant attentions to Henrietta Maria abate:

> My Lord ordered the whole marching army to be in readiness to conduct her Majesty, which they did, he himself attending her Majesty in person. And after her Majesty had rested there some small time, she being desirous to proceed in her intended journey, no less than a formed army was able to secure her person; wherefore my Lord was resolved out of his fidelity and duty to supply her with an army of 7,000 horse and foot . . . rather than suffer her Majesty's person to be exposed to danger. (ibid., 23)

A final example of gallantry involves the wife of Sir Thomas Fairfax. She was captured by Newcastle and returned to her husband, but not returned unceremoniously. She was "within a few days sent to York in my Lord's own coach, and from thence very shortly after to Kingston-upon-Hull, where she desired to be attended by my Lord's coach and servants" (ibid., 26). Newcastle had no reason to keep control of Lady Fairfax, but neither was it necessary that he send her in his own coach attended by his own servants. Cavendish does not let such a gesture slip by unnoticed.

The second book of *The Life* begins with Newcastle, about to depart for the Continent, asking his steward "how much money he [Newcastle] had left; [and the steward] answered he had but £90" (43). Cavendish comes close to a direct response to Clarendon's remarks about "passion and despair" when she avers that Newcastle was "not at all startled at so small a sum, although his present design required much more, [but] was resolved to seek his fortune, even with that little" (43). An attentive reader might decide that Newcastle was, indeed, startled, but was careful not to show it. Cavendish also describes Newcastle's prudence. He, "being a wise man" knew that the loss at Marston Moor would be followed by a general collapse of the royalist cause "both in England, Scotland, and Ireland, [which] were lost and undone." Indeed, "there was no other way but either to quit the kingdom or submit to the enemy or die" (43). The story continues with Newcastle's marriage to Cavendish, the then Margaret Lucas, and it concludes with her journey to England in an attempt to compound for his estates.

MIXED GENRE

The second book then shifts genre away from narrative and becomes dominated by a group of spreadsheets that demonstrate lost rents, property by property, and that calculate lost interest on these rents at 6 percent compounded annually. Destruction of property is included as is the felling of forests. Cavendish does not forget to add in the losses incurred by Newcastle's brother Sir Charles, whose estates had been sequestered for eight years— only to be inherited in their diminished form by Newcastle in the early 1650s. The total loss sustained by Newcastle, £941,303, has been taken by some to be inflated, but Firth notes that the marquis of Worcester came up with a similar figure, £918,000, for his own losses (ibid., 79). For a modern reader, who expects the narrative thread from the first part of the second book to continue, the result is tedium and apparent irrelevance. For Cavendish's contemporaries, however, the effect would have been riveting and the relevance instantly would have been apparent. Here in black and white was to be found all of the details regarding the holdings a man who had been of one of the richest men in England and who still was a well-known public figure. Here, too, were all of the financial particulars that could be checked down to the last penny against comparable rents elsewhere. There was an obvious risk for Cavendish, of course, since it would have been easy enough for her figures to have been questioned in private in correspondence that survives today or even in public in lampoons. It already has been noted in this chapter that Cavendish was called a "whore" and an "atheist" in one such lampoon, but her figures presented in *The Life of William* were not challenged during her lifetime and were never seriously questioned thereafter.

A modern biography might print the spreadsheets found in the second book of *The Life of William,* but only in an appendix. The spreadsheets, it would be argued, provide support for biography but are not themselves biography. They are, however, a kind of life writing and they are as powerful in their own way as are letters or diaries in that they situate their subject's life in good times (before the wars) and in bad (thereafter). They mark the end of narrative, but they do not mark the end of effective life writing. Rather they signal the beginning of Cavendish's olio, her mix of genres.

Many letters that have survived from the time of Cavendish were first saved because they provided legal evidence of financial obligations undertaken or discharged. Often these letters also describe personal joys and sorrows, since money matters were not kept strictly separate from other aspects of life. This mixing of the personal and the financial is found in several places in the section dominated by spreadsheets. For example, one of Newcastle's favorite haunts, Clipston Park, had been a beauty spot be-

fore the war, but its forest was leveled by those who had bought
the property from the government during the Interregnum:

> [A]lthough his patience and wisdom is such, that I never perceived
> him sad or discontented for his own losses and misfortunes, yet when
> he beheld the ruins of that park, I observed him troubled, though he
> did little express it, only saying, he had been in hopes it would not
> have been so much defaced as he found it, there being not one timber-
> tree in it left for shelter [for the wildlife]. However, he patiently bore
> what could not be helped. (*Life,* 71)

Newcastle comes as close in this passage as he ever gets to Clarendon's "passion and despair." The impression given the reader,
however, is not of a man broken by having been defeated in battle
but rather of someone who sees wanton destruction directed
against nature and is in consequence saddened. Who, Cavendish
no doubt hoped, wouldn't feel sympathy for, and even like, a man
who was able to be touched in such a situation? In this passage,
Cavendish also provides a paradigm for emotional shift: public
sadness is transformed into equally public patient resignation.
Might not private anger and bitterness be transformed into public amiability and wit?

The spreadsheets are augmented by other financial and personal material. For example, Cavendish gives credit to Newcastle's family for helping him with "supplies of Moneys at several
times" (ibid., 69). That she should offer commendation to Newcastle's brother, Charles, is not surprising, since she and Charles
were good friends. That she should single out Lady Jane Cheyne,
Newcastle's oldest daughter, for praise is interesting in view of
the notion, commonly held these days, that Cavendish did not get
along well with her stepdaughters:

> The Lady Cheiny sold some few jewels which my Lord, her father,
> had left her, and some chamber-plate which she had from her grand-
> mother, and sent over the money to my Lord, besides £1000 of her
> portion. (ibid., 69)

Cavendish also notes the contributions of the youngest son,
Henry, who was earl of Ogle at the time of the publication of *The
Life of William:* "And now the Earl of Ogle did at several times

supply my Lord, his father, with such moneys as he had partly
obtained upon credit, and partly made by his marriage" (70). It
may be that Cavendish hoped that her judicious treatment in
print of her two surviving stepchildren would help reinforce her
credibility as a historian of a particular person, or, perhaps, she
sought to mend fences with them.[24] Whatever the case, the mixture of family anecdote and financial report works well as part of
an olio of life writing.

Cavendish looks not only at Newcastle's financial problems in
this portion of the second book but also at the sources of his
wealth in the first place. Newcastle's rise from being a young man
of modest means to a position from which he was able to fund his
own army came about largely through the good offices of three
women:

> Before the wars my Lord had as great an estate as any subject in the
> kingdom, descended upon him most by women, viz, by his grand-
> mother of his father's side, his own mother, and his first wife. What
> estate his grandfather left to his father Sir Charles Cavendish, I
> know not. (72)

Cavendish is vague about the contribution of the grandmother on
the father's side, though she is correct in noting that this woman,
Elizabeth Countess of Shrewsbury and often known as Bess of
Hardwick, "was very rich" (72). Cavendish is far more clear about
what came from the first wife:

> My Lord's first wife, who was daughter and heir of William Basset, of
> Blore, Esq.; widow to Henry Howard, younger son to Thomas, Earl of
> Suffolk, brought my Lord £2400 a year inheritance, between six and
> seven thousand pounds in money, and a jointure for her life of £800 a
> year. (72)

There tucked away in the section devoted to spreadsheets is a
fascinating piece of information and one that, in an indirect way,
fits with the notion of a woman being Caesar. While women
might not often lead armies, it was women who provided Newcastle with the wealth that he was to spend on troops employed to
defend his king.

Cavendish's third book is not so easily justified as part of an
olio of life writing. Much of it probably does belong in an appendix

in which there would be subdivisions such as one actually headed by Cavendish "A Particular of the Principal Garrisons and Governors of them, constituted by my Lord" (86). There follows the heading a simple three-page list of Newcastle's garrisons and the names of their commanders. This sort of life writing probably was not so very interesting to most of Cavendish's readers, excepting of course those like John Rushworth who were Civil War historians or those who might have looked for the names of kin among the commanders. In section three of Book III, "Of his Loyalty and Sufferings," Cavendish becomes repetitive and hence tedious.[25] At points like these, Cavendish is also in danger of overstating her case. Newcastle suffered, but, as Firth points out, the king did in fact restore much of what he lost, especially such property as had fallen into the hands of regicides (69, note 1). There is some relief from the litany of loss, as when Cavendish tells the story of a man who was on his way to see Newcastle and "was set upon by picaroons." These banditti turn out to be former soldiers of Newcastle, who free the man in honor of their one-time leader (85). For the most part, however, the third book wears on a reader's patience.

The fourth and final book, containing as it does a collection of Newcastle's and Cavendish's observations about life and their maxims, makes for a more pleasant read. In it, observation and maxim become kinds of life writing. The bulk of Book IV is organized as a listing of what follows after the phrase "I have heard my Lord say,"

> v / That great princes should not suffer their chief cities to be stronger than themselves. (121). . . . / vii / That the prince is richest, who is master of the purse; and he strongest that is master of the arms; and he wisest that can tell how to save the one, and use the others. (122)

It is easy to skip around from entry to entry, and the impression of Newcastle that a reader, now or in the seventeenth century, is liable to garner is quite positive. Newcastle's ideas are down to earth and the man who emerges is thoroughly amiable. Cavendish, in Book IV, is back on track in offering an interesting form of life writing. The reader might surmise that Newcastle has been able to put past disappointments behind him. If he still has feelings of anger and bitterness, they are diminished to a point approaching nil. Cavendish's own observations and maxims, which conclude *The Life of William,* are sometimes cynical, at least by contrast, with those of her husband. They, ironically, hint at her own anger and bitterness:

> xi / I observe, that spleen and malice, especially in this age, is grown to that height, that none will endure the praise of anybody besides themselves; nay, they'll rather praise the wicked than the good; the coward rather than the valiant. (145)

The cynicism of Cavendish, however, only serves to make her depiction of her husband's amiability come more to the fore.

So ends *The Life of William Cavendish, Duke of Newcastle.* But what of its place among other major instances of life writing in seventeenth-century England? A look at the circumstances surrounding the completion of John Aubrey's *Brief Lives* (first published 1813) reveals that Aubrey, while cognizant of the importance of his work, recoiled from the task of making it orderly and hoped that someone else would organize his notes in one way or another:

> I have tumultuously stitcht up what I have many years since collected: I hope, hereafter it may be an Incitement to some Ingeniose and publick-spirited young Man to polish and complete what I have delivered rough hewn, for I have not leisure to heighten my Stile.[26]

Anthony à Wood was, perhaps, not exactly the "young man" that Aubrey had in mind, but Wood did borrow heavily from Aubrey's work. Cavendish, who is sometimes faulted for laziness, at least finished the job of writing *The Life of William* herself and saw to it that the book was published. It is also true that Cavendish, while given to colorful anecdote, never includes anything quite like Aubrey's account of the death of Sir Philip Sidney, which, writes Aubrey, would not have happened when it did had Sidney followed doctor's orders and abstained from sex while ill. Aubrey is, of course, legendary for including curious pieces of information of dubious veracity in his lives. What then of Izaac Walton, whose *Lives* (1670) on the topic of Donne, Wotton, Hooker, and Herbert is generally taken more seriously than Aubrey's efforts? Walton's form of life writing is mostly narrative, but he interrupts its progress in a number of ways. He intersperses in the narrative the full text of three letters and a good deal of Donne's poetry as well as Donne's will. Walton ends his life of Donne with a list of characteristics of his subject that reads a little like the entries that are found in Cavendish's third book:

> He [Donne] was of Stature moderately tall, of a strait and equally-proportioned body, to which all of his words and actions gave an unexpressible addition of Comeliness. The melancholy and pleasant humor, were in him so contempered, that each gave advantage to the other, and made his Company one of the delights of Mankind.[27]

There are a total of eight entries on this list. Walton also includes an appendix, though it is not so labeled and is only indicated by a line running across the page. The appendix contains elegies by Dr. Corbet, Bishop of Oxford, Henry King, Bishop of Chichester, and Walton, himself. Walton, like Cavendish, casts himself as an unabashed appreciator of his subject, though Walton is not trying to create an olio by including all of this material. He does demonstrate, however, that narrative might be augmented with other forms of life writing.

More than twenty-five years ago Rosalie Colie—jokingly, I think—apologized for delivering lectures on the importance of genre at a time when "forms seem[ed] generally restrictions—the fetters from which we are dutybound to escape, or brands of an unimaginative establishmentarianism, or (at their worst) self-made prisons."[28] Some ten years later, Alastair Fowler unashamedly lamented, "If we are to have genres [today], they must be arrived at *de novo* rather than *ab ovo*."[29] Cavendish, living in seventeenth-century England, had a strong sense of genre, and she knew that she was writing in a mixture of forms. That mixture, that olio, was in her view both entertaining and fashionable. While it is probably true that some parts of *The Life of William* are stronger than others as examples of mixed genre even by seventeenth-century standards, *The Life of William* counted as a success then and, for those willing to consider it in the context of other books by Cavendish, counts as a success even now.[30]

NOTES

1. While Cavendish's autobiography, "A True Relation, " printed in *Nature's Pictures* (London, 1656), has received considerable attention in the last ten

years or so, *The Life of William Cavendish, Duke of Newcastle* is now rarely more than mentioned in passing. Elaine Hobby wrote that *The Life* was Cavendish's best-known book, and such may have been the case at and before the time of the publication of Hobby's book. Cavendish, in part thanks to Hobby, thereafter became better known for other writing. In any event, Hobby has little to say about *The Life* itself. Cf. Elaine Hobby, *Virtue of Necessity; English Women's Writing 1649–1688* (London: Virago, 1988), 81–83. Sara Mendelson sees *The Life* as part of a last, unsuccessful attempt by Cavendish and her husband to gain court favor and to rise in social standing. She points out that the book's publication coincided with the couple's 1667 trip to London, during which time Cavendish paid her famous visit to the Royal Society. Cf. Sara Mendelson, *The Mental World of Stuart Women: Three Studies* (London: Harvester, 1987), 50. Douglas Grant, in his now-classic study, took an approach more characteristic of the earlier part of the twentieth century: "[*The Life*] was also a memorial to Margaret's love and gratitude. She had found in [Newcastle's] company a happiness which it is highly unlikely she would have found in that of any other man. Not only did he complement her own weaknesses and tolerate her idiosyncrasies but he actively encouraged her writing, which to her was dearer than all else." See Douglas Grant, *Margaret the First* (London: Rupert Hart-Davis, 1957), 188.

2. Hunter writes of the continuing tendency among scholars to disregard shifts and developments in genre. Cf. Paul Hunter, *Before Novels: The Cultural Contexts of Eighteenth Century English Fiction* (New York: W. W. Norton, 1995), 5.

3. Reed Whittemore characterizes Plutarch as a moralist but not a prude. "Plutarch was committed to reporting and judging his nobles' flaws only when they surfaced in public. Luckily he was not a prude, and the process did not keep him from impressive thoroughness with many of his subjects." Cf. Reed Whittemore, *Pure Lives: The Early Biographers* (Baltimore: Johns Hopkins University Press, 1988), 6, 7.

4. Margaret Cavendish, *Natures Picture drawn by Fancies Pencil* (London, 1656), sig. C5.

5. Quoted from the *OED,* which in turn cites *Eikon Basilike,* xv (London, 1648).

6. The *OED* gives as one set of definitions: "A collection of various artistic or literary pieces, as engravings, verses, etc.; a miscellany; a musical medley." As an example it cites "Entertain them with a fashionable Oglio" (1691).

7. Nevertheless, Donald Stauffer, in a major study of early biography, has a difficult time getting beyond what he sees as crucial problems with the form of *The Life:* "The biography is individual and follows no pattern. Its particular merit lies in its *naïveté,* for its exuberance and verbosity cannot be interpreted as power or completeness in portrayal. After her fanfare of prefaces, wherein mountains travail, the ensuing life of the Duke of Newcastle seems somewhat unworthy of its heralds." Cf. Donald A. Stauffer, *English Biography Before 1700* (Cambridge: Harvard University Press, 1930), 153.

8. Edward Hyde, Earl of Clarendon, *Selections from The History of the Rebellion,* ed. G. Huehns (Oxford: Oxford University Press, 1978), 259. Claren-

don elsewhere in the section expands on his views regarding Newcastle's mental state after the battle, yet in the same paragraph, however, he praises his character more generally (ibid., 255, 256).

9. Margaret Cavendish, *The Life of William Cavendish, Duke of Newcastle,* ed. C. H. Firth (2nd ed., revised, London: Routledge, n. d.), 50, 51. Subsequent references are to this edition, given simply as *Life.*

10. "Biographical truth sharpens the focus on the larger question of relationship between fiction and fact in the Tudor-Stuart period. Biography—or life-writing, as with greater historical accuracy we should call it—itself occupies a middle ground between history and art, chronicle and drama, objective truth and creative invention—Holinshed and Shakespeare, so to speak." Judith H. Anderson, *Biographical Truth: The Representation of Historical Persons in Tudor-Stuart Writing* (New Haven: Yale University Press, 1984), 2.

11. Had Newcastle fathered such children, he most likely would have acknowledged them in the way that Charles II acknowledged the duke of Monmouth. Clarendon would have made mention of them, and they would have found their way into Restoration lampoons.

12. For instance, he was accused of "fornicating with the *Nine Muses,* or the Dean of *York's* daughters." British Library, Thomason Tracts E279 (6), 26 April, 1645, London.

13. Newcastle remarks about receiving the £2000 can be dated to 1661, when his former daughter-in-law and the widow to his first son died. At the time of her death, she was Elizabeth Stuart, Countess of Richmond, and her jointure reverted to Newcastle.

14. Horace Walpole, *Catalogue of the Royal and Noble Authors of England,* 2 vols. (London, 1759), 2: 13.

15. Margaret Cavendish, *Sociable Letters* (London, 1664), letter 30.

16. "As I was writing this life this story came in my mind, and methought I should have dealt hardly if I should have left it unwritten." Cf. Plutarch, *The Lives of the Noble Grecians and Romans Compared Together,* trans. Thomas North, modern edition by Roland Baughman (New York: Heritage Press, 1941), 362.

17. The wit is identified as Joseph Stansby by Grant: "Shame of her sex, Welbeck's illustrious whore, / The true man's hate and grief, plague of the poor, / The great atheistical philosophraster, / That owns no God, no devil, lord nor master" (Grant, *Margaret the First,* 199).

18. "He loved monarchy, as if it was the foundation and support of his own greatness; and the church, as it was well constituted for the splendour and security of the crown. . . . He had a particular reverence for the person of the king, and the more extraordinary devotion for that of the prince, as he had had the honour to be trusted with his education as governor" (Clarendon, *Selections,* 256).

19. Margaret Cavendish, *The World's Olio* (London, 1655), 133.

20. Elsewhere Cavendish questions the motives for Lucretia's suicide and concludes: "the Cause of Lucretia's Killing her self, was as much through Prudence & Wisdom as through Virtue" (*Sociable Letters,* letter 54).

21. Anne Shaver explains the rather baffling situation thus: "What to a con-

temporary reader may seem to be vacillation about women's worth comes not just from a modesty topos but also from a sincere effort to claim for her sex access to the virtues of men without having to give up the special virtues of women. This effort, though it can lead to apparent incoherence also produces a powerful challenge to clichés about gender." Cf. Shaver, Introduction to *The Convent of Pleasure and Other Plays* (Baltimore: Johns Hopkins University Press, 1999), 7.

22. Alexandra Bennett's edition of *Bell in Campo* and *The Sociable Companions* contains an appendix including documents relating to Henrietta Maria and other women as military commanders. Cf. Margaret Cavendish, *Bell in Campo* and *The Sociable Companions* (Peterborough, Ontario: Broadview Press, 2001), 213–19.

23. "*Vnd.* I am made a Captaine of the traindband Thomas, & this is my Commission, this very paper hath made me a Captaine. / *Tho.* Are you a paper-Captain; Sir, I had thought more had gon to the making up of a Captaine. / *Vnd.* They are fooles that thinke so: provided, he have the favour of the Lord Lieutenant of the County" (*The Country Captain* [London, 1649], 3). Newcastle continues the joke by implicating himself, for he was Lord Lieutenant of Nottinghamshire.

24. Two other stepchildren who might have been mentioned and who are not had died within the last ten years.

25. For instance: "He never minded his own interest more than his loyalty and duty, and upon that account never desired nor received anything from the Crown to enrich himself, but spent great sums in his Majesty's service. I have observed his ruined estate was like an earthquake, and his debts like thunderbolts, by which he was in danger of being utterly undone, had not patience and prudence, together with Heaven's blessings, saved him from that threatening ruin" (93).

26. John Aubrey, *Aubrey's Brief Lives,* ed. Oliver Lawson Dick (London: Secker and Warburg, 1949), xxi.

27. Izaak Walton, *The Lives of John Donne, Sir Henry Wotton, Richard Hooker, George Herbert, & Robert Sanderson,* ed. George Saintsbury (London, New York, Toronto: Humphrey Milford for Oxford University Press, n. d.), 83.

28. Rosalie Colie, *The Resources of Kind: Genre-Theory in the Renaissance* (Berkeley and Los Angeles: University of California Press, 1973), 1.

29. Alastair Fowler, *Kinds of Literature: An Introduction to the Theory of Genres and Modes* (Cambridge: Harvard University Press, 1982), v.

30. *The Life of William* went into a second edition shortly after the deaths of Cavendish and her husband, presumably because it was respected by those who read history and hence something that a publisher would be able to print without subsidy. It appears that the book also had a popular audience, for Samuel Pepys' wife liked it well enough to recommend it to her husband. The volume, one might say, was in circulation, for Mrs. Pepys had it on loan from a friend named Betty Turner. Cf Samuel Pepys, *The Diary of Samuel Pepys,* ed. Robert Latham and William Matthews, 11 vols. (Berkeley and Los Angeles: University of California Press, 1970–1983), 9:123.

The "Native Tongue" of the "Authoress": The Mythical Structure of Margaret Cavendish's Autobiographical Narrative

LINE COTTEGNIES

Cavendish's short autobiographical narrative, "A True Relation of my Birth, Breeding and Life," is an extraordinary text, although in the bulk of Cavendish's writings it has drawn relatively little critical attention until very recently, probably on account of its brevity.[1] Published in 1656 as the closing book of *Natures Pictures,* a collection of tales and fictional *varia,* it has been hailed as one of the first narrative, nonreligious and nonhistorical autobiographies to be published as such in England.[2] Indeed, in contrast with many autobiographical texts of the period, it did fulfill the "contractual effect" Philippe Lejeune (among others) described as central to the genre of "autobiography" as it was to become canonical in the eighteenth century—and defined as "a retrospective prose narrative of his or her own life written by a real person, with a special concern for his or her individuality and in particular the history of his or her personality."[3]

Like Rousseau, Cavendish makes a claim for absolute singularity, but like Sartre, she also remarks that writing is something anyone can do.[4] Lejeune's definition of course excluded important non-narrative texts, such as Montaigne's *Essais,* Burton's *Anatomy of Melancholy* or Browne's *Religio Medici,* which probably played an important part in Cavendish's autobiographical impulse. But it highlights what makes Cavendish's text deeply original, just like the 1626 autobiography of Montaigne's famous niece, Marie de Gournay: the retrospective, narrative drive, and the presence of this "essential autobiographical quest" that Domna Stanton describes as "the constitution of the self as subject."[5]

103

Additionally, Cavendish's "A True Relation" seems to illumi-
nate a topos of feminist criticism of female autobiography, the
tension, in Stanton's words, between a "pre-defined" and a "de-
viant" self (or between any version of the public/private divide),[6]
which could be designated as "the syndrome of the blindfolded
eyes," as a reference to an episode of Lady Halkett's autobiography, contemporary of Cavendish's: in this wonderful episode, emblematic of this conflict, the young woman is forbidden by her
mother to see her suitor and as a consequence decides to meet
him wearing a blindfold, thus reconciling her allegiance to the
parental injunction and an assertion of her own desire.[7] "A True
Relation" has indeed recently been studied as an example of an
early modern female subject finding her voice through self-
inscription,[8] and there is much that can be said for this approach.
But inconsistencies found in the text have sometimes led critics
such as Mary Beth Rose to conclude with Cavendish's failure in
overcoming self-contradictions induced by an oppressive ideology
(op. cit., passim). Other critics, on the contrary, have seen the
inconsistencies in the text not as a failure, but as the expression
of a modern insight into the idea of the textual nature of the self,
coinciding with a skeptical attitude towards the notion of truth.[9]
This hypothesis, which I will follow up, points to intriguing similarities between Cavendish and our postmodern subject, from
either end of a three-century period that saw the acme and
decline of the triumphant self.[10] But as Robert Mayer recently
reminded us in his study of Lucy Hutchinson, modern critics
often forget that in the seventeenth century, autobiography was
a historical genre, alongside biography (both "lifewriting").[11]
When Cavendish claims to be writing a true story, she seems to
be writing from within the tradition of the family memoirs.[12] Yet,
from the very beginning, she deliberately offers a critique of the
notion of memory, thus giving a twist to her whole enterprise as
the inclusion of her "life" into a collection of fictional tales already
suggested. In doing so, she frees her text and the genre of autobiography from their dependence on history. My claim is that the
narrative shows an awareness of identity as a literary construct[13] that Cavendish, selecting a series of arguments for their
resonance, expresses through a series of personal "myths," from
that of the loyal cavalier's submissive wife to that of the "authoress." Far from being a "failure," it is the celebration of herself

by an author consciously and artfully transmuting her life into writing, while offering a powerful critique of conventional writing modes. The text thus reveals a far-reaching skepticism concerning the very possibility of truth; as a consequence, it offers an overt reconsideration of rhetoric as the art of truth and contributes to freeing the genre of "autobiography" from its subservience to history.

The introductory epistle shrewdly starts with an attack on the rhetorical notion of *memoria,* firmly positioning Cavendish both as an early defendant of the Moderns against the Ancients and as a resolutely antihistorical writer. Like Marie de Gournay, who was attacked in similar terms,[14] she presents her "life" as a polemical defense against accusations of madness and plagiarism, and immediately places herself among a prestigious lineage. Her first concern is indeed to answer those who question her authorship of her texts on the ground that she does not seem to remember by heart what she has written: the best orators, she answers, Cicero himself, could not do it either, and, she adds, "the same is in writers" (151). Cavendish thus explicitly inserts herself into a prestigious series that includes the great ancient writers of fiction and philosophy: Homer, Virgil, Ovid, Euclid, Aristotle—all enlisted to defend freshness and creativity against the sterilization of invention by the dead weight of memory. None of these could have mustered sufficient memory to recite from their own works either, she claims, even though they are now invoked by modern scholars as constituting the Western heritage; again like Marie de Gournay, she concludes with a neat inversion of the initial proposition:

> But certainly they that remember their own wit least, have the most of it; for there is an old saying, and surely true, that the best wits have the worst memory . . . [G]reat memories are standing ponds that are made with rain; so that memory is nothing but the showers of other men's wits; and those brains are muddy that have not running springs of their own, that issue out still fresh and new.[15]

What is at stake here is her legitimacy as a writer, in the context of a humanistic training that focuses primarily on the teaching of topoi drawn from authorities and on rhetoric—which teaches that memory is primarily a practical faculty of eloquence, the memorization of the elements of speech in preparation for delivery.[16] Hobbes, who, incidentally, was highly critical of rhetoric, also attributes a psychological dimension to memory when he defines the latter and imagination as one and the same thing,[17] and as absolutely necessary to thinking. As he writes in his *Answer* to Davenant:

> Time and education begets experience; Experience begets memory; Memory begets Judgements, and Fancy; Judgment begets the strength and structure; and Fancy begets the ornaments of a Poeme. The Ancients therefore fabled not absurdly in making memory the mother of the Muses.[18]

Against this emphasis in Renaissance education on memory, which had led to the setting-up of the art of memory into a discipline,[19] Cavendish presents it as an obstacle to creation: "it's against nature for natural wits to remember; for it is impossible that the brain should retain and create; and we see in nature, death makes way for life; for if there were no death there would be no new life or lives" (152). She advocates a process of creation inspired by natural cycles, whereby only the mind not steeped into past authors and authorities is able to create new, original works. This she illustrates with the frontispiece to *Philosophical and Physical Opinions* (1655), in which she is represented in an empty room, without any book in sight, with a caption emphasizing her independence from past authors:

> Her Library on which She look's [*sic*]
> It is her Head her Thoughts her Books.
> Scorninge dead Ashes without fire
> For her owne Flames doe her Inspire.

(frontispiece)

She also famously uses the metaphor of the silkworm spinning its yarn out of its own bowels to describe the workings of her own mind: "if the senses bring no work in, [my thoughts] will work of themselves, like silk-worms that spins [*sic*] out of their own bowels" (173).[20] Her conception of intellectual and literary creation is here first empirically linked with the role of the senses in the creative process; but secondly creation can also be an autonomous, self-sufficient procedure taking place within her mind, independently from her will. Ironically, in the Epistle, the authors she invokes as being allegedly devoid of memory themselves are those that are used at school as the authorities to be taught and pilfered for commonplaces or topoi; and yet she presents them as having been modern in their days. The idea of the tabula rasa she had already expanded in 1655, reclaiming as a strength her lack of a conventional education—although she had also deplored it elsewhere[21]: "I have heard that learning spoils wit and the fancies of others, drive the fancies out of our own braines, as enemies to the nature, or at least troublesome guests that fill up all the rooms of the house."[22]

Intriguingly, Michel de Montaigne had also emphatically rejected the notion of *memoria,* repeatedly presenting himself as having a bad memory (thus legitimating his practice of approximate citation). This, as Michel Beaujour has shown, allowed him to create his own textual *memoria,* intensely personal, using the ruins and fragments of a bookish past as raw materials in his endless rewriting and expanding of the *Essays.*[23] According to Beaujour, the amnesia paradoxically and repeatedly invoked by Montaigne could be interpreted as a way of liberating eloquence (*elocutio*) from the weight of *memoria.* Other critics have seen this phenomenon as becoming generalized from the 1650s in French critical discourse.[24] But more fundamentally, Beaujour interprets Montaigne's critique of memory as a means of staging in and through the text the invention of a textual, immanent memory which engenders the figure of the subject manipulating the code (ibid., 117). This analysis can in many respects be extended to Cavendish. With her as well as with Montaigne, the questioning of memory is used to undermine rhetorics, and also to offer the basis for a discourse of the self affranchized from historical categories—in particular from the imperative of truth. As seen above, Cavendish offers a critique of the common notions of artificial invention, setting herself deliberately on the side of nature (as one among the "natural wits"). The metaphor of memory as a still pond conversely suggests that of invention as a creative gush, which becomes explicit towards the end of the text when she describes her ways of creating as a spontaneous, uncontrollable surging which must come out some way or other (172). But she does not reject all kinds of *memoria.* One of the most striking features of her introductory Epistle is the recurrence of phrases such as "I have heard" (six occurrences in the first paragraph), which points to her reliance on a secondhand knowledge mostly acquired orally,[25] substituted for the conventional magazine of learned authorities. This kind of memory, not mediatized by the written word, attributes a central part to the individual, empirical experience of the speaker through direct oral or visual testimony, to his or her knowledge of the world, and, most importantly, to common sense: "it hath been a long and true observation, that every one had rather speak than listen to what another says" (152). Cicero, Ovid, or the Duke of Newcastle are thus ironically put on a par in the text as secondhand sources authorizing her discourse.[26] The attack on learned *memoria* then allows her to comment indirectly upon the various uses of rhetoric among the world:

> I perceive that as most men have particular understandings, capacities, or ingenuities, and not a general; so in their discourses some can speak eloquently, and not learnedly; others learnedly and not eloquently; some wittily, and neither learned nor eloquent; and some will speak neither learnedly, eloquently, wittily, or rationally. (153)

After establishing empirical experience as a valid form of knowledge, she continues to undermine rhetoric, by separating eloquence (as the faculty to produce a fluent speech) from reason or wit, thus taking up a common accusation against rhetoric. For her, eloquence is an innate faculty, a character trait having little to do with education or training ("some will speak well as it were by chance," 153). But, if the natural gift is unnaturally developed by a formal education, it can evolve into a sophistic faculty producing inflated, empty discourses.

Cavendish thus endorses a common critique, which had already been put forth by Bacon or Hobbes (among others), that of the uncertain connection between rhetoric and truth; but she phrases it as a means of defending her own status as a writer. No doubt she includes herself among those whom she describes as having: "great capacities, as may be perceived in their discourse: but yet their speech is like those that are lame, which limp and halt, although the ground whereon they go is even, smooth, and firm" (154). The suspicion in which she holds rhetoric indirectly allows her to justify her own practice, which ignores writing con-

ventions. If a smooth, beautiful discourse, following all the rules
of the art, is not necessarily true or rational, then a "misshapen"
one might well be so—this is meant to apply to her writings:

> I desire all my readers and acquaintance to believe, though my words
> run stumbling out of my mouth, and my pen draws roughly on my
> paper, yet my thoughts move regular in my brain; for the several
> tracks or paths that contemplation hath made on my brain . . . are
> much smoother than the tongue in my mouth. (154)

The skeptical undermining of rhetoric allows for a defense of her
own writing practice here and elsewhere, but the metaphor of
physical disgrace, recurrent throughout the text, points to something more fundamental perhaps: an awareness of language as
literally disfiguring the self, the insight into identity as pure
interiority having to come to terms with externalization through
language. For the beautiful, rational ideas Cavendish knows she
has within her mind can hardly be adequately mediated through
discourse—the "habit" of thought as it is often described in contemporary texts.[27] As a matter of fact, "A True Relation" can
perhaps be read as the history of Cavendish's difficult relationship to language, which represents the means of bridging the gap
between the core of the inner personality and the outside; significantly, this gap is emblematized both by her speech impediment
("my words run stumbling out of my mouth"), on which she dwells
at great length as a major element of character formation, and by
her awkward handwriting, which is so bad that it produces a
"ragged rout" of letters (172).[28] Describing her activity as a
writer, she thus sees herself as a female general, with the page as
a battlefield on which her thoughts ("sent out in words," 172) are
made to march: when she thinks, her stream of thoughts is so
powerful and dense, she says, that they could "smother the conception in the brain" (172). But when some are let out, it gives
"the rest more liberty to place themselves in a more methodical
order, marching more regularly with my pen on the ground of
white paper." The military metaphor implicitly establishes a correspondence between her writing and Newcastle's past military
activities, but it also allows her to expand a physiological theory
of creation, superimposing a medical onto the military image.
Here again, Cavendish is concerned with bridging the gap be-

tween a totally internal process of thought and its physical tran-
scription in writing, the "sen[ding] out in words" (172). Thoughts
move faster than the hand; and as a consequence,

> my letters seem rather as a ragged rout than a well-armed body, for
> the brain being quicker in creating than the hand in writing or the
> memory in retaining, many fancies are lost, by reason they ofttimes
> outrun the pen, where I, to keep speed in the race, write so fast as I
> stay not so long as to write my letters plain. (172)

Significantly, the inadequacy with language extends to the learning of foreign languages as well, as she finds herself incapable of
learning any on account of her failing memory: "I had a natural
stupidity towards the learning of any other language than my
native tongue, for I could sooner and with more facility understand the sense, than remember the words, and for want of such
memory makes me so unlearned in foreign languages" (174).

The idea of a "native tongue," I would like to suggest, could in
fact be applied to her own idiosyncratic use of English, which "A
True Relation" clearly presents as having its roots in her family
history, as is apparent through the first half of this carefully
constructed narrative. In fact, it is possible to identify a series of
personal myths through which Cavendish constructs and represents her identity. The text adopts indeed a loose chronological
structure, retracing the past history of the family up to the Civil
War before focusing on Cavendish's present exile in the Low
Countries. But the narrative is not strictly chronological; it espouses a quasi-mythical structure to suggest the perfection of
pre–Civil War England: family life before the fracture of the war
is nostalgically described in a series of edenic, prelapsarian tab-
leaux, the first twenty years of her life condensed into stilted,
unreal scenes of family harmony. The only temporal landmarks
are the father's early death, dealt with in the first paragraph,
and the symbolical entry into time and mortality that is a consequence of the breaking out of the Civil War. It is this traumatic
event that is responsible first for the voluntary exile self-inflicted
by Cavendish on herself—when she leaves the protective environment of the family cell to seek her fortune at the court of
Henrietta Maria in Oxford—and then for the various deaths in
the family (two brothers, a sister, and finally her mother). Be-

tween these two tragic series of events, she describes the education and pastimes of the Lucas children on a mode suggesting
eternity, a perpetual life of leisure led under the governance of a
benevolent mother. The members of this microsociety of perfect
ladies and gentlemen are hardly individualized and appear as
almost interchangeable: "eight children, three sons and five
daughters . . . not any one crooked, or any ways deformed, . . .
but every ways proportionable; likewise well-featured, clear com-
plexions, brown hairs (but some lighter than others), sound
teeth, sweet breaths, plain speeches, tunable voices" (164). Margaret includes herself into this iconic, collective portrait, and
she emerges only later as an individual, when she leaves the
community. Meanwhile, the family is a perfect unit of twinlike
equals, a self-sufficient, self-contained society: "they did seldom
make visits, nor never went abroad with strangers in their company, but only themselves in a flock together, agreeing so well
that there seemed but one mind amongst them" (160). Later, the
family utopia is destroyed by the civil wars; but even before the
troubles, Margaret's desire to leave is interpreted as a fall from
grace, an original sin that soon appears irredeemable, as there
seems to be no turning back: "my mother said it would be a
disgrace for me to return out of the Court so soon after I was
placed" (162). Her mother, described at great lengths as a perfect,
heroic figure—an adjective also used in connection with her
father—becomes the embodiment of a rigid sense of honour
which Margaret is taught at her own expense.

The family myth has deep implications on her life as a writer.
Realizing too late what paradise she has lost, Cavendish describes how the homogeneous, profoundly equalitarian family
group constituted a warm, protective cell united by common
ethics and a common language, which she also loses as soon as
she leaves: "when I was gone from them, I was like one that had
no foundation to stand, or guide to direct me, which made me
afraid, lest I should wander with ignorance out of the ways of
honor, so that I knew not how to behave myself" (161). The sib-
lings also constituted her privileged public, under whose eyes she
was bred and thrived, "seldom out of their sight" (161), and for
whom she wrote her first texts.[29] But the consciousness of her
exile comes together with the traumatic discovery of a behavioral
disorder that is central in the history of her personality, that of

her "bashfulness"—and here Cavendish's autobiographical quest
shows intriguing similarities with Rousseau's *Confessions,* also
built around similar personal crises.[30] Confronted with unkind,
judgmental gazes, she withdraws into herself and is perceived as
a fool: "I durst neither look up with my eyes, nor speak, not be any
way sociable, insomuch as I was thought a natural fool" (162).
Characteristically for a person who defines herself through her
loyalty to the Royalist cause, she describes her troubles at court
as deriving from her faithfulness and loyalty to her family and
their values, and invents the myth of the stable self: "I was so
afraid to dishonour my friends and family by my indiscreet actions that I rather chose to be accounted a fool than to be thought
rude or wanton" (161–62). The shift from "I was *thought* a natural fool" to "I rather *chose to be accounted* a fool" (my emphasis) is
remarkable: it seems to show the voluntary reclaiming of a negative image as the basis for her public persona. Even though her
only option is to resort to marriage to flee from a court she abhors
("I was married from thence," 162), she writes the initial trauma
into a voluntary assertion of a new sense of her identity.[31] In this
founding moment, she radically chooses marginality and difference as a way of resisting the oppressive force of the others' gazes.
This is also apparent in her eccentricity in clothes, well documented by fascinated contemporaries, which proceeds from the
same choice of an exacerbated singularity:[32] "I always took
delight in a singularity, even in accoutrements of habits" (175).
The romanticizing of her inner difference at court can in many
respects be read as a founding gesture: "A True Relation" tells the
story of the self-willed, literary construction of the personality in
a hostile world, a self based on resistance to change. It tells us
about the deliberate invention of a private world and a singular
language in the face of adversity. In contrast with the subject of
the conversion narrative, a form of autobiography which Cavendish would have known,[33] she uses various strategies to emphasize the unshakeable stability of the self in a world marked by
mutability and change.

The celebration of the myth of the stable self naturally takes on
a political dimension. Throughout the narrative, Cavendish insists on the heroic nature of loyalty and constancy in a society
that values change: from her father's upholding of honor even in
the face of royal discontent (155–56), to the open-ended exile of

the Newcastles still hoping for better days, her emphasis is on merit as the stoical faculty to remain the same in the face of trouble. Significantly, her family is compared to "Job's children," helplessly falling under the blows of God's wrath: "this unnatural war came like a whirlwind, which felled down their houses, where some in the wars were crushed to death" (160).[34] Job embodies the constancy and fidelity to a cruel God in which the Newcastles can perceive echoes of their predicament. But the biblical reference makes clear that they are still hoping for divine retribution at the end of the day. Cavendish describes herself and the duke as perfectly loyal Cavaliers who could have outjobbed Job himself, not uttering one spiteful word against fortune: "we do submit, and are both content with what is, cannot be mended . . . we are both content, spending our time harmlessly" (171). Yet Cavendish's confused narration of her dealings with the Parliament slightly contradicts this vision of steely resolve; it highlights the difficulty of reconciling the image of adamancy to a reality demanding some measure of opportunism and flexibility. As Mary Beth Rose has pointed out,[35] the convoluted syntax (double negations, complex restrictive clauses, etc.) vividly renders her contradictory position as an unflaggingly loyal Cavalier entering into negotiations with Parliamentary committees to retrieve some of her husband's properties:

> I did not stand as a beggar at the Parliament door, for I never was at the Parliament House, nor stood I ever at the door, as I do know, or can remember, I am sure, not as a petitioner. Neither did I haunt the committees, for I never was at any, as a petitioner, but one in my life, which was called Goldsmiths' Hall, but I received neither gold nor silver from them, only an absolute refusal, I should have no share of my Lord's estate. (167)

The political myth of absolute resistance and loyalty takes a beating in this relation of a rather inglorious episode: the tension the text reveals derives from the clash between the celebration of the heroic, stable self and a world that obeys other rules.

As this passage reveals, Margaret Cavendish seems to be obsessed with setting false rumors about herself right; the autobiography as a whole can be read as a defensive device, aiming at producing her own truth (as the title itself intimates), for the benefit of her contemporaries and for after ages:

> [W]hatsoever I was addicted to, either in fashion of clothes, con-
> templation of thoughts, actions of life, they were lawful, honest,
> honourable, and modest, of which I can avouch to the world with a
> great confidence, because it is a pure truth. (175)

Like Rousseau and his use of a dual "I"—alternatively or con-
jointly himself as a child and himself as an adult reminiscing
about his past—Cavendish here adopts a twofold perspective:
the "I" of the author presently writing the narrative guarantees
the honesty of the "I" considered posthumously (as no longer in
existence), as is shown by the use of the preterite in this passage
("I was"). But contrary to Rousseau, whose split-up perception is
naturally justified by the temporal distance between the narrated events and the moment of the narration, Cavendish almost
schizophrenically adopts two different perspectives on herself at
once, immortalizing a posthumous figure of herself but above all
celebrating herself as the author manipulating the text ("I can
avouch . . .").

For the last myth she constructs for herself, at the end of the
narrative, is that of the self-acclaimed "authoress"—incidentally
coining a word.[36] She provocatively ends the "Relation" by claiming to be writing her life only to suit herself: "'tis to no purpose to
the readers, but it is to the authoress, because I write it for my
own sake, not theirs" (178). The shift from the third to the first
person draws attention to the textual nature of the figure of the
"authoress."[37] Cavendish is ostentatiously writing herself into a
female author. In spite of her apparent humbleness in the very
last lines, when she seems to confess her hopes to be remembered, what the text does is celebrate the power of the written
word that allows her to escape the common lot of women—
oblivion after death:

> Neither did I intend this piece for to delight, . . . but to tell the truth,
> lest after-ages should mistake, in not knowing I was daughter to one
> Master Lucas of St. Johns, near Colchester, in Essex, second wife to
> the Lord Marquis of Newcastle; for my Lord having had two wives, I
> might easily have been mistaken, especially if I should die and my
> Lord marry again. (178)

Against the predicament of women, whose social status was commonly defined in relation to men, she evokes her own dissolution

on a conditional mode, and the oblivion that she might have fallen into is no more than a posthumous, hypothetical proposition, denied by the existence of the very text whose concluding sentence it is.

With this variation on the topos of the *exegi monumentum,* the last page shrewdly echoes the critique of memory and the references to the art of writing in the prefatory Epistle, which gives the narrative a sense of closure as well as a circular structure. Cavendish had set forth with the intent to "write the true relation of [her] birth, breeding, and to this part of [her] life" (154). The paradox involved in the specularity of the initial formulation has been given full vent: writing the true story of her life, she has consciously created her own legend, and there is no truth outside the one the text sets forth. In a way not dissimilar to the role played by her eccentric clothes, the text is itself the space where she can will herself singular and "recreate" herself.[38] Cavendish thus sets herself the task of offering to the world her own truth, through a text that will be her own "monument of truth" (166), or "Fame's Tower" (177), for her and those she loved to be remembered in after ages. To this end, she playfully inscribes her own epitaph in the final lines, as if to indicate this is the kind of *memoria* she was eventually striving for. But it is above all the figure of the authoress writing her life, shaping and manipulating her image and the narrative that is immortalized by the text, in a manner irresistibly evoking Montaigne's *Essays.* Setting life-writing deliberately away from family memoirs and onto the side of fiction, this text stages a radical insight into the textuality of the self and of truth itself. It defines the notion of identity through a series of profoundly original personal myths, and finally inscribes in its center the figure of the writing authoress tinkering with the unfinished text of her life. Perhaps because it was too radical for her public, Cavendish omitted it from her second edition of *Natures Pictures* in 1671.[39]

NOTES

1. "A True Relation . . .", only twenty-seven folio pages, appeared as Book 11 of *Natures Pictures Drawn by Fancies Pencil to the Life* (London, 1656), 363–90. All quotations henceforth from *The Life of William Cavendish, Duke of Newcastle, to which is added the True Relation of my Birth, Breeding and Life by*

Margaret, Duchess of Newcastle, ed. C. H. Firth (London: Routledge and Sons, n.d.). Since the end of the nineteenth century, both texts have regularly been associated, although Cavendish had never intended them to be published together. The narrative is now regularly taught in universities, thanks in particular to Sylvia Bowerbank and Sara Mendelson's edition of it in *Paper Bodies: A Margaret Cavendish Reader* (Peterbourgh, Ontario: Broadview Press, 2000).

2. See Effie Botonaki, "Marching on the Catwalk and Marketing the Self: M. Cavendish's Autobiography", *a/b: Auto/Biography Studies* 13:2 (1998): 159–81, 159; Nancy S. Weitz, "Contextual Material for *A True Relation of my Birth, Breeding and Life*" (Brown Women Writers Project, www.wwp.brown.edu); L. Cottegnies, "Margaret Cavendish et l'autobiographie au XVIIe siècle: topographie d'un discours paradoxal," in *L'Autobiographie littéraire en Angleterre (XVIIe–XXe siècles): Géographies du moi,* ed. Frédéric Regard (Saint-Etienne: Université de Saint-Etienne, 2000): 35–55, 35.

3. Philippe Lejeune, *Le Pacte autobiographique* (Paris: Editions du Seuil, 1975), 14. See John Sturrock's definition of this pact as proceeding from "the determination with which every one of these writers marks him or herself off from other people, as an individual who has come to distinction in life by his or her own efforts and by the exercise of an essentially natural endowment" (289). See Sturrock, *The Language of Autobiography: Studies in the First Person Singular* (Cambridge: Cambridge University Press, 1993).

4. Cf. Jean-Jacques Rousseau, *Les Confessions* (Paris: Gallimard, Folio Classiques, 1973), 33; Jean-Paul Sartre, *Les Mots* (Paris: Gallimard, Folio Classiques, 1964), 213. Paul Delaney himself traces a line of autobiographical texts from Cavendish down to Rousseau. Cf. Paul Delaney, *British Autobiography in the Seventeenth Century* (New York: Columbia University Press, 1969), 160. See also Sidonie Smith, "'The Ragged Rout of Self': Margaret Cavendish's *True Relation* and the Heroics of Self-Disclosure," in *A Poetics of Women's Autobiography: Marginality and the Fiction of Self-Representation* (Bloomington and Indianapolis: Indiana University Press, 1987): 84–101; 85. As a defense for writing in *The Blazing World,* Cavendish writes that "it is in every one's power to do the like" (124).

5. Domna Stanton, "Autogynography: The Case of Marie de Gournay's *Apologie pour celle qui écrit,*" *Autobiography in French Literature, French Literature Series* XV (1985): 18–31, 19. It is unlikely that Cavendish ever read Marie de Gournay's self-defense, as it was never translated. Similarly to Lejeune, Georges Güsdorf defined autobiography as the "theodicy of the individual being," "a vision of the self," "a mythic tale" (cited in Robert Mayer, *History and the Early English Novel: Matters of Fact from Bacon to Defoe* [Cambridge: Cambridge University Press, 1997], 85.

6. Stanton, "Autogynography," 19.

7. A text not published until the nineteenth century. Cf. Anne, Lady Halkett, *The Autobiography,* ed. John Gough Nichols (London: Camden Society, New Series, 13, 1875), 12–13. See also Sandra Findley and Elaine Hobby, "Seventeenth-Century Women's Autobiography," in *1642: Literature and Power in the Seventeenth Century,* ed. Francis Barker et al. ([Colchester]: University of Essex, 1981), 17. Mary Beth Rose also bases her analysis of seventeenth-century

autobiography on the perception of the "felt conflict between self-effacement and self-assertion, between private and public life, and between individual personality and social role that gives shape to [women's] autobiography and which they seek to resolve through the art of autobiography" (247). See Mary Beth Rose, "Gender, Genre, and History: Seventeenth-Century Women and the Art of Autobiography," in *Women in the Middle Ages and the Renaissance. Literary and Historical Perspectives,* ed. Mary Beth Rose (Syracuse, NY: Syracuse University Press, 1986): 245–78, 247.

8. See Bella Brodzki and Celeste Schenk, eds., *Life/Lines: Theorizing Women's Autobiography* (Ithaca and London: Cornell University Press, 1988), 8–9; Mary Beth Rose, "Gender, Genre and History," 249–55; Cynthia Pomerleau, "The Emergence of Women's Autobiography in England," in *Women's Autobiography. Essays in Criticism,* ed. Estelle C. Jelinek (Bloomington and London: Indiana University Press, 1980), 22–23; Estelle C. Jelinek, "The Seventeenth Century: Psychological Beginnings," in *The Tradition of Women's Autobiography,* ed. Jelinek (Boston: Twayne Publishers, 1986), 28–29. For an approach that reconciles both ideas, see Smith, "The Ragged Rout of Self." While noting a concern in the text for the "self *qua* self," Smith concludes that she can be seen "struggling uncomfortably with an androcentric genre" (101).

9. For instance, Brodzki and Schenk, *Life/Lines,* 9, or Sandra Sherman, "Trembling Texts: Margaret Cavendish and the Dialectic of Authorship," *ELR* 24.1 (1994): 184–210, 209.

10. This is something which Brodzki also comments on (see *Life/Lines,* 9), seeing in Cavendish's position an adumbration of Roland Barthes' intuition: "The subject is merely an effect of language" (quoted in Brodzki and Schenk, *Life/Lines,* 5, 9).

11. Mayer, *History and the Early English Novel,* 85–86. Cavendish moves away from the tradition of the family memoirs, as Natalie Zemon Davis shows (154–57, 163–65). See Zemon Davis, "Gender and Genre: Women as Historical Writers, 1400–1820," in *Beyond their Sex: Learned Women of the European Past,* ed. Patricia H. Labalme (New York: New York University Press, 1980): 153–82.

12. These texts, like Cavendish's, usually started with a genealogy.

13. Botonaki, for instance, calls the text a "metatext, fixing her meaning upon her life" ("Marching on the Catwalk," 173).

14. Cf. "Apologie pour celle qui écrit," in *Fragments d'un discours féminin,* ed. Elyane Dezon-Jones (Paris: José Corti, 1988): 147–83.

15. "A True Relation" (152). Marie de Gournay had reached a similar conclusion already in 1626: "La mémoire est plus souvent faible que forte, comme on sait, entre les gens de jugement relevé" ("Memory is more often weak rather than strong, as it well known, among people of refined judgement," my translation). Cf. *L'Ombre de la Demoiselle de Gournay* (Paris, 1626), 9.

16. Cf. for instance Thomas Wilson, *The Arte of Rhetorique,* n. p., sig. f.3v. Quoted in Quentin Skinner, *Reason and Rhetoric in the Philosophy of Hobbes* (Cambridge: Cambridge University Press, 1996), 52.

17. Thomas Hobbes, *Leviathan,* ed. C. B. Macpherson (Harmondsworth: Penguin, 1968), 89.

18. Quoted in Skinner, *Reason and Rhetoric,* 370.

19. Cf. Robert Copland, *The Art of Memory* (London, 1548). See Skinner for an overlook of the curriculum in the seventeenth and eighteenth centuries, *Reason and Rhetoric,* esp. 19–211. On the art of memory, see Frances Yates, *The Art of Memory* (London: Routledge and Kegan Paul, 1966).

20. Elsewhere, Cavendish also uses the metaphor of the spider to describe how she creates. Cf. Sylvia Bowerbank, "The Spider's Delight: Margaret Cavendish and the 'Female Imagination'," *English Literary Renaissance* 14 (1984): 392–408.

21. *The Philosophical and Physical Opinions* (London, 1655), sig. A4.

22. Ibid., sig. [B4v].

23. Michel Beaujour, *Miroirs d'encre* (Paris: Editions du Seuil, 1980), 112, and also 113–31.

24. Cf. Bernard Beugnot, *La Mémoire du texte: essais de poétique classique* (Paris: Champion, 1994), 20.

25. Although it is a statement to be taken with some caution, she did claim to have read very little: "I have no acquaintance with old Authors, nor no familiarity with the moderns, I have received no instructions [sic] by learning" (*The Philosophical and Physical Opinions,* sig. A4).

26. Cf. 151.With some covert irony, Cavendish points out to her readers that although the Duke of Newcastle's failing memory marks him off as one of the "moderns," he nevertheless never forgets the good and harm done to him (151). This could be particularly ironical in the light of the Cavendishes' status as powerful patrons, which according to many accounted for the relative indulgence of the learned towards the eccentricities of Margaret.

27. See for instance Cowley and the "Wardrobe of rich Eloquence" ("To Mr. Hobs," v. 63–69). Cf. *The English Writings of Abraham Cowley,* ed. Alexander R. Waller (Cambridge: Cambridge University Press, 1905) 189. Cf. my *L'Eclipse du regard: la poésie anglaise du baroque au classicisme (1625–1660)* (Genève: Droz, 1997), 337–39.

28. To this, we could add her idiosyncratic syntax and spelling, which are erratic even by seventeenth-century standards, and cannot be totally accounted for by the lack of a formal education.

29. It is this family utopia that Cavendish seems to be trying to recreate in the frontispiece of *Natures Pictures,* in which she is presiding over a table of friends and family.

30. Rousseau's life is romanticized as a series of epiphanic moments of crisis, centered around the confession of a fault, a sin, even a perversion. Cf. Jean Starobinski, *La Transparence et l'obstacle* (Paris: Gallimard, 1971), 149–215.

31. Oddly, one is reminded here of the analysis Sartre made of Jean Genet's existential heroism, when Genet voluntarily chose to become the thug he was accused of being. Cf. Jean-Paul Sartre, *Saint Genet, comédien et martyr* (Paris: Gallimard, 1952), 23–63.

32. Cf. Samuel Pepys, *The Diary of Samuel Pepys,* eds. Robert Latham and William Matthews (London: G. Bell and Sons, 1983), 8:163–64, 186–87, 209, 243; and John Evelyn, *The Diary of John Evelyn,* ed. E. S. de Beer (Oxford: Clarendon Press, 1955), 3: 478.

33. Cf. Joan Webber for a still helpful analysis of the conversion narrative in the seventeenth century, *The Eloquent I: Style and Self in Seventeenth-Century Prose* (Madison, Milwaukee, London: University of Wisconsin Press, 1968).

34. The reference is to *Job,* 1:13–19.

35. Rose, "Gender, Genre, and History," 253. For a complementary study of Cavendish's rhetoric, see also Louise Stewart and Helen Wilcox, "'Why hath this Lady writ her own life?': Studying Early Female Autobiography," in *Teaching Women: Feminism and English Studies,* ed. Ann Thompson and Helen Wilcox (Manchester: Manchester University Press, 1989), 65–67.

36. The *OED* gives the first occurrence of "authoress" as designating a female author as Caxton, but it applies to the production of a spoken utterance. The second occurrence is an extract of Swift.

37. Cavendish also calls herself "Margaret the first" in the preface to *The Blazing World.* Cf. *The Blazing World and Other Writings,* ed. Kate Lilley (Harmondsworth: Penguin, 1992), 124.

38. It is tempting to exploit the pun "recreate"/"re-create" (172). For Cavendish, writing is a very serious "pastime."

39. See James Fitzmaurice for details about changes between the 1656 and 1671 edition of *Natures Pictures,* "Front Matter and the Physical Make-up of *Natures Pictures,*" *Women's Writing* 4.3 (1997): 353–67. It might be the case that Cavendish, disappointed with the Restoration, thought this text was no longer up-to-date.

Part II
Imaginative Writings

"Flattering Division": Margaret Cavendish's Poetics of Variety

HERO CHALMERS

Aɴʏoɴᴇ ᴇᴍᴇʀɢɪɴɢ ꜰʀᴏᴍ ᴛʜᴇ ᴠᴇʀᴛɪɢɪɴᴏᴜs ᴇxᴘᴇʀɪᴇɴᴄᴇ ᴏꜰ reading Cavendish's *Poems and Fancies* (1653) might be forgiven for accepting wholeheartedly the author's concluding confession that "my shallow wit could not tell how to order it to the best advantage."[1] While it would be disingenuous to deny that Cavendish is restricted by the limitations of her poetic technique, this essay will argue that *Poems and Fancies* emerges out of the conscious espousal of a poetics of "variety" which transcends mere muddleheadedness and finds analogues in existing works of rhetorical and literary theory as well as verse. Cavendish's poetic principles and practice reflect her cherished natural philosophy and carry with them ideological resonances which touch on her historical predicament.

Poems and Fancies is pervaded at all levels by her sense that:

> *Nature* most *Pleasure* doth to *Poets* give;
> If *Pleasures* in *Variety* do live.
> There every *Sense* by *Fancy* new is fed,
> Which *Fancy* in a *Torrent Braine* is bred.
>
> <div align="right">("Poets <i>have most</i> Pleasure," 152)</div>

The privileging of diversity in *Poems and Fancies* is echoed in a prefatory epistle from Cavendish's maid, Elizabeth Toppe, whose comments fortuitously anticipate the striking generic range of Cavendish's oeuvre:

> [N]*either can there be anything writ, that your* Honour *have not imployed your Pen in: As there is* Poeticall Fictions, Morall instructions, Philosophicall Opinions, Dialogues, Discourses, Poeticall Romances. (A5v)

The structure of *Poems and Fancies* is designed to favor a reading practice that thrives on eclecticism as Cavendish makes clear in her preface "*To Naturall* Philosophers":

> I desire all that are not quick in apprehending, or will not trouble themselves with such small things as *Atomes,* to skip this part of my *Book,* and view the *other,* for feare these may seem *tedious:* yet the *Subject* is *light,* and the *Chapters* short. Perchance the *other* may please better; if not the second, the third; if not the third, the fourth; if not the fourth, the fifth: and if they cannot please, for lack of *Wit,* they may please in *Variety,* for most *Palates* are greedy after *Change.* (A6v)

The text is divided into contrasting sections interspersed with prose epistles to the readers and bridging poems (or short collections of poems), subheaded "THE CLASPE," a label that seems to hint at the sections as beads on a necklace (47, 110, 155, [186] mispaginated 162). Whilst not all parts of the volume are rigidly thematically coherent, every section has its dominant mode or subject matter, be it atomistic natural philosophy, dialogues, so-called moral discourses, fairy poems, or mourning verses.

Although the end result may at first glance strike the modern reader merely as a baggy compendium, recognizable Renaissance precedents exist for Cavendish's method of gathering together diverse matter under varied subheadings. In particular, she appears to be influenced by contemporary rhetorical textbooks in seeking to demonstrate both thematic and formal variety. Her *Orations of Divers Sorts* (1662) confirms that she possessed some awareness of the structures of rhetorical handbooks, reflecting their division into topics and indeed the kinds of topics considered.[2]

Her propensity for dividing her material into sections and (within these) into poems on different aspects of a topic favors the Renaissance fondness for the text as anatomy. Such a structural principle necessarily embodies the "variety" on which she places a premium. Her earliest composition, *The Worlds Olio,* a prose work printed after *Poems and Fancies* in 1655, also adopts the method of anatomizing its material under subheadings.[3] As in *Poems and Fancies,* Cavendish conceives of this approach as offering something for all "*Palates*" as indicated by the titular metaphor of the "olio" or spicy stew. Her husband underlines this in a dedicatory poem which invites readers:

> Thus feast your Souls, the Bodies look you too.
> An *Olio* of Confections not refrain;
> For here's a sumptuous Banquet for your Brain:
> And this Imaginary Feast pray try,
> Censure your worst, so you the Book will buy.
> ("*To the Lady of* Newcastle," A6v)

Sections of *The Worlds Olio* entitled "*Short Essayes*" or presented as a series of numbered "Allegories" remind us that division and variation may be achieved by formal as well as thematic means (109–21, 95–107).

Hence, *Poems and Fancies,* offers the reader, for example, a masque, elegies under the heading "A REGISTER OF MOURN-FULL VERSES" and orations in "THE ANIMALL PARLIA-MENT" (155–60, [217–24] mispaginated 191–98, [225–37] mispaginated 199–211). Cavendish also experiments with differ-ent rhetorical figures in particular sections. Simile dominates throughout *Poems and Fancies* but is brought to the fore in a series of conceited poems, "*Comparing the* Tongue *to a* Wheele," "*Similizing the* Clouds *to* Horses," "*Similizing* Birds *to a* Ship" and so on (136, 142–43). Meanwhile, an "Epistle to Souldiers" heralds a collection of verses which adopt the exercise of applying metaphors of warfare to a range of subjects ([191–216], mispagi-nated 167–92). Although the poems, "*The* Hunting *of the* Hare" and "*The* Hunting *of the* Stag" may appear, at first to have no special connection with the two other poems, "*Of an* Island" and "*The* Ruine *of the* Island" which join them in an unlabeled sec-tion, closer inspection reveals the device of prosopopoeia as the rhetorical link (110–20). Elsewhere, a section of "DIALOGUES" (53–91) emulates the rhetoricians' emphasis on arguing from both sides of a question, a practice whose importance Cavendish recognizes when describing her own book of *Orations* as "Decla-mations, wherein I speak *Pro* and *Con.*"4

For Cavendish, the dialogue form provides an apt encapsula-tion of the multifaceted nature of thought or imagination, the "fancy" which she regards as essential nourishment for the plea-sures of variety offered by poetry.5 The embodiment of the diversity of thought and fancy in the form of the dialogue is apparent in Cavendish's "Dialogue *between* Melancholy, *and* Mirth." The poem evidently owes a debt to Milton's handling of this classic opposition in "L'Allegro" and "Il Penseroso," first printed in his *Poems* (1645). Yet, where Milton's poems are built around the poet's controlled and discrete invocations of the goddesses of Mirth and Melancholy in turn, Cavendish depicts a debate between the two in their own voices within one poem as the product of the irresistible, involuntary processes of her thoughts. "As I sate *Musing,* by my selfe alone," she begins, "My *Thoughts* on several things did work upon" (76). There follows a heady list of the multifarious topics covered by her thoughts, some of which seem to echo the meditations on different poetic modes implicit in Milton's two poems: *"Stately Towers," "Orchards, Gardens,* and fine *Bowers," "Nymphes, Shepheards,* and *Shepheardesses," "Court-ship"* and the *"Heroick"* (76).[6] Melancholy and Mirth simply emerge as two further *"Thoughts"* that surface from the melee, which leads the speaker to reflect, *"Thoughts* severall bee, in severall places dwell" (76). This conception of thought and of its primacy in ensuring the variety which Cavendish sees as underpinning poetry is also evident in her "Dialogue *betwixt* Wit, *and* Beauty." Here, Wit has the final word, asserting that "The *Mind,* as *Senses* all, delights in *Change"* and that:

> I can create *Ideas* in the *Braine,*
> Which to the *Mind* seem reall, though but fain'd.
> The *Mind* like to a *Shop* of *Toies* I fill,
> With fine *Conceits,* all sorts of *Humours* fell.
> I can the work of *Nature* imitate;
> And change my selfe into each severall *Shape*

> (82)

Wit's insistence that it can imitate "the work of *Nature"* serves as a reminder that Cavendish's formal and thematic commitment to variety in *Poems and Fancies* is inextricably connected to the natural philosophy that constitutes a central preoccupation in the text. The opening section of the volume outlines a notion of matter made up of differently shaped, self-moving atoms combining and recombining into diverse forms.[7] These theories provide the basis for her overall contention that "Great *Nature* by *Variations* lives" and connect with her vision of thought processes: "But

Motion to one *Forme* can nere constant be, / For *Life,* which *Motion* is, joyes in varietie" (*"Natures* Exercise, *and* Pastime," 139; *"The* Motion *of* Thoughts," 41).

The link between such tenets and the stylistic or structural makeup of *Poems and Fancies* is especially clear in the section entitled "FANCIES," which begins with a series of poems grouped around the loose conceit of Nature as a lady presiding over the running of a great house with her *"Bunch* of *Keyes"* hanging at her side (*"The severall* Keyes *of* Nature," 126). This leads to the diversity of Nature being figured in the itemizing variety suggestive of the recipe or recipe book, drawing in one instance on her favored metaphor of diversity, the "olio" ("Meat *drest for* Natures Dinner; *an* Ollio *for* Nature," 129). With macabre wit, Cavendish figures Death as "the *Cook* of *Nature"* who dresses meat in "severall waies to please her *Mind"*:

> Some Meates shee rosts with Feavers, burning hot,
> And some shee boiles with Dropsies in a Pot.
> Some for Gelly consuming by degrees,
> And some with Ulcers, Gravie out to squeese.
>
> ("Natures Cook," 127)

As the section proceeds, the recipe form becomes intertwined with another more conventionally poetic mode of separation into various component parts: the blazon. Hence *"A* Bisk *for* Natures Table" figures Nature taking:

> A *Fore-head* high, broad, smooth, and very sleek,
> A *large great Eye,* black, and very quick.
> A *Brow* that's *Arch'd,* or like a *Bow* that's bent,
> A *Rosie Cheek,* and in the midst a dent.
>
> These mixing all with *Pleasure,* and *Delight,*
> And strew upon them *Eyes* that's quick of *Sight;*
> Putting them in a *Dish* of *Admiration,*
> And serves them up with *Praises* of a *Nation.*[8]
>
> (129–30)

Cavendish's emphasis on the miscellaneous quality of Nature is further apparent in her device of deploying extended similes broken down into their constitutive elements to create the impression of a panoply of images passing rapidly before the reader's eye. In lines, "*Similizing the* Head *of* Man *to the* World":

> THE *Head* of *Man* is like the *World* made round,
> Where all the *Elements* in it are found.
> The *Braine,* as *Earth,* from whence all *Plants* do spring,
> And from the *Womb* it doth all *Creatures* bring.
> The *Fore-head, Nose,* like *Hills,* that do rise high,
> Which over-top the *Dales* that levell lye.
> The *Haire,* as *Trees,* which long in length do grow,
> And like its *Leaves* with *Wind* waves to, and fro.[9]
>
> (148)

Her method here recalls the technique of Phineas Fletcher's *The Purple Island; or, the Isle of Man* (1633) in which the poet ponders the spiritual fate of humanity by means of the sustained metaphor of man as an island created by God.[10]

Throughout *Poems and Fancies,* Cavendish favors rhetorical structures that create a list-like effect imitative of her vision of the flickering diversity of Nature that must animate poetry. Her opening poem in the first section, detailing Nature's role in the creation of the world, sets a precedent with its swift accumulations of personified participants in the task, as Nature abjures

> [. . .] strong *Destiny* to take some paines,
> Least she growe idle, let her Linke some Chaines:
> *Inconstancy,* and *Fortune,* turne a Wheele,
> Both are so wanton, cannot stand, but reele.
> And *Moisture* let her poure out *Water* forth,
> And *Heat* let her suck out, and raise up growth,
> And let sharp *Cold* stay things that run about,
> And *Drought* stop holes, to keepe the water out.
>
> ("*Nature calls a Councell,*" 1)

The sense of an almost breathless account of the multiplicity of Nature is heightened in the last few lines of this extract by its use of polysyndeton and conduplicatio ("And . . . let her . . ./And . . . let her"). Elsewhere, she brings the similarly dizzying multiplications of her belief that there are other imperceptible worlds within the visible world paradoxically within the reader's apprehension using the multifaceted rhetorical effect of asyndeton: "So in this *World* another *World* may bee, / That we do neither *touch, tast, smell, heare, see*" ("*It is hard to beleive* [sic], *that there are other* Worlds," 43). Her propensity for modes of itemization stressing variety is also apparent in the anaphoric structure of her list of competing thoughts that opens the "Dialogue *between* Melancholy, *and* Mirth":

> *Some* did large *Houses* build, and *Stately Towers,*
> Making *Orchards, Gardens,* and fine *Bowers:*
> And *some* in *Arts,* and *Sciences* delight,
> *Some* wars in Contradiction, *Reasons* fight.
> And some, as *Kings,* do governe, rule a *State;*
> *Some privie Counsellors,* and *Judges* are.
> *Some Priests,* which do preach *Peace,* and *Godly life,*
> Others *Tumultuous* are, and full of *strife.*
>
> (76)

Cavendish's preference for poetry imitative of the diversity of Nature entails the notion that such a poetics bespeaks elevated social status:

> GIVE *Mee* the *Free,* and *Noble Stile,*
> Which seems *uncurb'd,* though it be *wild:*
> Though *It* runs wild about, *It* cares not where;
> *It* shewes more *Courage,* then *It* doth of *Feare.*
> Give me a *Stile* that *Nature* frames, not *Art:*
> For *Art* doth seem to take the *Pedants* part.
> And that seemes *Noble,* which is *Easie, Free,*
> Not to be bound with ore-nice *Pedantry.*
>
> ("THE CLASPE," 110)

The impetus to stress these associations is enhanced by her desire to reinforce a sense of her own and her husband's aristocratic standing threatened by Parliament's sequestration of their property and their exile as royalists. The volume's connection with their political plight filters through in numerous ways both in its expressions of royalist sentiments and in Cavendish's allusions to the circumstances of its composition during her trip to London between November 1651 and March 1653 to petition Parliament for a portion of her husband's estates.[11] In commending the "*Variety*" of *Poems and Fancies* to the reader in the metaphor of a generous feast, Cavendish implies that her volume, with its "*Free,* and *Noble Stile*" and composition, aspires to become a no-

tional substitute for the aristocratic rites of hospitality that political circumstances have denied the Newcastles: "I wish heartily
my *Braine* had been *Richer,* to make you a fine *Entertainment:*
truly I should have spar'd no *Cost*" ("*To Naturall* Philosophers,"
A6v). A similar conceit appears in *The Worlds Olio,* where the
central idea of the text as "Sumptuous Banquet" finds an echo in
her request to *"those that do not like my Book, which is my House,
I pray them to pass by, for I have not any entertainment fit for
their Palats"* (A3v). The sense that *Poems and Fancies* somehow
stands in for the sequestered Newcastle estates and the lifestyle
connected with them also emerges in Cavendish's recurrent use
of images of building or rebuilding the great house. In the opening poem, *"Nature calls a Councell,"* this metaphor serves to
unify the activities of the multifarious participants in Nature's
creation of the universe (2). Elsewhere too, the transformative
powers of Cavendish's poetics of free fancy give rise to poems
such as "A Dialogue *between a* Bountifull Knight, *and a* Castle
ruin'd in War," or the allegories *"Natures House"* and "The *Fort,
or Castle* of *Hope,"* which continue to provide textual embodi-
ments of reconstruction or resistance to siege (89, 133, [193] mispaginated 169).

In portraying the creation of *Poems and Fancies* as a sublima-
tion of the energies that she would otherwise use in managing
her husband's household, Cavendish's wish to identify herself
with aristocratic magnanimity feeds into a predilection for a poetics of similar largesse or richness:

> [M]y Lords Estate being taken away, [I] had nothing for Huswifery, or
> thrifty Industry to imploy my selfe in; having no Stock to work on. For
> Housewifery is a discreet Management, and ordering all in Private,
> and Household Affaires, seeing nothing spoil'd, or Profusely spent,
> that every thing has its proper Place . . . But Thriftiness is something
> stricter; for good Housewifery may be used in great Expenses; but
> Thriftiness signifies a Saving, or a getting; as to increase their Stock,
> or Estate. For Thrift weighs, and measures out all Expence. It is just
> as in Poetry: for good Husbandry in Poetry, is, when there is great
> store of Fancy well order'd, not only in fine Language, but proper
> Phrases, and significant Words. And Thrift in Poetry, is, when there
> is but little Fancy, which is not onely spun to the last Thread, but the
> Thread is drawne so small, as it is scarce perceived. (A7r)

Although Cavendish is relatively cautious here in her rejection of "Thrift" in favor of a more expansive policy of household management and poetic composition, her poem, *"Of* Poets, *and their* Theft,"* leaves the reader in no doubt that thrifty poets are no better than botched-up court interlopers. Of the best poets, she writes:

> Their *Notes* great *Nature* set, not *Art* so taught:
> So *Fancies,* in the *Braine* that *Nature* wrought,
> Are *best;* what *Imitation* makes, are naught.
>
> . . . .
>
> There's *None* should *Places* have in *Fames high Court,*
> But those that first do win *Inventions Fort:*
> Not *Messengers,* that onely make *Report.*
>
> To *Messengers* Rewards of *Thanks* are due,
> For their great *Paines,* telling their *Message* true.
> But not the *Honour* to *Invention new.*
>
> Many there are, that *Sutes* will make to weare,
> Of severall *Patches* stole, both here and there;
> That to the *World* they *Gallants* may appeare.
>
> And the *Poore Vulgar,* which but little know,
> Do *Reverence all,* that makes a *Glistring Shew;*
> Examines not, the *same* how they came to.
>
> Then do they call their *Friends,* and all their *Kin,*
> They *Factions* make, the *Ignorant* to bring:
> And with their help, into *Fames Court* get in.

(123–24)

Asserting that *"Fancy* is the *Eye,* gives *Life* to all," Cavendish here propounds her conviction that "Invention" must be the root of her cherished poetry of imaginative freshness and diversity (125). In "A Dialogue *betwixt* Wit, *and* Beauty" too, the endless novelty and changeability of Wit is associated with invention:

> For *Wit* is *fresh,* and *new,* doth sport, and play,
> And runs about the *Humour* every way.
>
> . . . .

Wit's ingenious, doth new *Inventions* find,
To ease the *Body,* recreate the *Mind.*[12]

(81)

Cavendish's clear preference for invention over imitation that fuels her poetics of fancy and variety cannot simply be reduced to the feminine rejection of rule and method with which Sylvia Bowerbank credits her. Bowerbank's claim that Cavendish finds herself at odds with "prevailing literary attitudes" is based on a notion of the seventeenth-century literary climate as dominated by Horatian notions of the imitation of previous authors as the touchstone of good composition.[13] Yet, Cavendish's approach represents an internally consistent poetics that echoes a clearly discernible sense of the importance of invention in both classical and Renaissance thought. Traditional rhetorical theory places "invention" (in the sense of choosing fit subject matter) as the first of its five parts above those concerned with style and presentation, and some Renaissance apologists for poetry clearly deploy the term in a way that privileges imaginative creativity in the manner favored by Cavendish.[14]

While Cavendish does claim in *Poems and Fancies* that a feminine sensibility is ideally suited to poetry that feeds on fancy and the rejection of *"Rule & Method,"* the fact that her conception of poetry keys into a tradition of valuing literary invention warns us against reading this simply as a gesture of self-marginalizing female incapacity ("TO ALL NOBLE, AND WORTHY LADIES," A3r). In this prefatory epistle, her preference for invention is played out through an extended metaphor of female dressing, crafts, and needlework:

> Besides, *Poetry,* which is built upon *Fancy, Women* may claime, as a *worke* belonging most properly to themselves: for I have observ'd, that their *Braines* work usually in a *Fantasticall motion;* as in their *severall,* and *various dresses,* in their many and singular choices of *Cloaths,* and *Ribbons,* and the like; in their *curious shadowing,* and *mixing of Colours,* in their *Wrought workes,* and divers sorts of *Stitches* they imploy their *Needle,* and many *Curious* things they make, as *Flowers, Boxes, Baskets* with *Beads, Shells, Silke, Strawe,* or any thing else . . . and thus their *Thoughts* are imployed perpetually with *Fancies.* For *Fancy* goeth not so much by *Rule & Method,* as by *Choice:* and if I have chosen my *Silke* with *fresh col-*

ours, and *matcht* them in *good shadows,* although the *stitches* be not very true, yet it will please the *Eye.* (A3r)

Her remarks are somewhat reminiscent of George Puttenham's comparison between the need for "Poesie" to "shew it self either gallant or gorgious" and the "silkes" or "tyssewes & costly embroderies" proper to the dress of "great Madames of honour" in their "courtly habillements."[15] However, where Cavendish valorizes fine or curious feminine adornment, she does so with the purpose of celebrating imaginative creativity and not poetic ornamentation per se, elsewhere opposing "Fancy" to the *"Silver Lace"* and *"glistering Shews"* of decorative language ([238] mispaginated 212).

In embodying her poetics of variety in metaphors of female self-adornment, she finds a further means of suggesting that the rich diversity of *Poems and Fancies* provides a surrogate for her threatened aristocratic status, implied here by the fine and decorative dressing associated with a courtly feminine aesthetic. Her husband's opening dedicatory poem prefigures this motif in the volume with its alliance between *"Your* New-borne, sublime Fancies" and *"the* Richer Dressings *of each Line"* ("TO THE LADY NEWCASTLE," A1r). The multifariousness of Nature, so crucial to Cavendish's conception of a poetics of particolored fancy, is similarly figured in terms of dazzlingly adorned female costume in her poem, *"Natures* Dresse" (127).[16]

A comparison with Robert Herrick's volume *Hesperides* (1648) (from which Cavendish appears to have got the idea for her fairy poems) shows how she draws on a use of female adornment to embody a poetics of spontaneity and diversity that identifies itself specifically with a royalist sensibility.[17] Herrick's poem, *"Delight in Disorder"* anticipates Cavendish's rejection of the pedantry of *"Art"* in favour of the *"Free,* and *Noble Stile, /* Which seems *uncurb'd,* though it be *wild"* ("THE CLASPE," 110), using the semiotics of feminine decorative dress favored in *Poems and Fancies:*

> A Sweet disorder in the dresse
> Kindles in cloathes a wantonnesse:
> A Lawne about the shoulders thrown
> Into a fine distraction:
> An erring Lace, which here and there

> Enthralls the Crimson Stomacher:
> A Cuffe neglectfull, and thereby
> Ribbands to flow confusedly:
> A winning wave (deserving Note)
> In the tempestuous petticote:
> A carelesse shooe-string, in whose tye
> I see a wilde civility:
> Doth more bewitch me, then when Art
> Is too precise in every part.[18]

Read in the context of *Hesperides* as a whole, Herrick's lines can be seen to bear out the ethos of "cleanly-*Wantonnesse*" set out in *"The Argument of his Book"* and implicitly designed to challenge a notion of Puritan repressiveness.[19] His encapsulation of this ideologically weighted spirit of mirth in the figure of his *"Mad maiden"* muse as in the delightful negligence of feminine adornment shares common ground with Cavendish's identifications of a feminine aesthetic in the exuberantly multivalent fancy for which she begs license as the lifeblood of poetry.[20]

The juxtaposition between Herrick and Cavendish helps to reinforce our sense that the variousness of *Poems and Fancies* should not be read simply as a sign of chaotic muddle. For both poets engage a familiar paradox in which variety is regarded not as the root of disintegration but as an essential basis of order. It is this concept which lies behind Herrick's structuring oxymorons: "cleanly-*Wantonnesse*," "sweet disorder," and "wilde civility."

The account of the creation of the world that opens *Poems and Fancies* highlights the need both for a variety of disparate components (*"Motion," "Life," "Forme," "Matter," "Moisture," "Heat," "Cold"* and so on) and for their ultimate cooperation: "First *Nature* spake, my *Friends* if we agree, / We can, and may do a fine *Worke,* said she" (*"Nature calls a Councell,"* 1). In Cavendish's atomistic view of matter, the independent oscillation of separate particles provides the foundation for coherent forms:

> Small *Atomes* of themselves a *World* may make,
> As being subtle, and of every shape:
> And as they dance about, fit places finde,
> Such *Formes* as best agree, make every kinde.
>
> ("*A World made by* Atomes," 5)

In "*The* Motion *of* Thoughts," she depicts the vision of "a glorious *Light*" in perpetual motion:

> This *Motion* working, running severall waies,
> Did seeme a *Contradiction* for to raise;
> . . . .
> Yet at the last, all severall *Motions* run
> Into the first *Prime Motion* which begun.
> In various *Formes* and *Shapes* did *Life* run through,
> *Life* from *Eternity,* but *Shapes* still new.
>
> (40)

Cavendish's vision culminates in an uncharacteristically religious recognition that, for all its Diversity, the "*Light*" is

> . . . a *Union, Knowledge, Power* and *Might;*
> *Wisdome, Justice, Truth, Providence,* all one,
> No *Attribute* is with it selfe alone.
>
> (41)

Music provides a recurrent metaphor for the concept of pleasing order achieved through variety. In her poem, "Similizing the *Heart* to a *Harp,* the *Head* to an *Organ,* the *Tongue* to a *Lute,* to make a *Consort* of *Musick,*" Cavendish claims:

> Witty light *Aires* are pleasant to the *Eare,*
> *Straines* of *Description* all *Delights* to heare.
> In *Quavers* of *Similizing* lies great *Art,*
> *Flourishes* of *Eloquence* a sweet part.
> Stops of *Reproofe,* wherein there must be skill,
> *Flattering Division* delights the *Mind* still.
>
> (137)

To the conceit of the harmony arrived at by means of a diversity of instruments, Cavendish adds the notion of "*Flattering Division*" meaning the pleasure to be derived when longer notes are divided up into a variety of shorter, quicker ones to embellish a melody.[21] Musical metaphors are accompanied by those of dancing, with Nature showing her best face when the diverse energies of the dance move towards a coherent whole. In her poem "*Similizing the* Windes *to* Musick":

All that this *Musick* meets, it moves to dance,
If *Bodies* yeilding [*sic*] be with a *Compliance*.
The *Clouds* do dance in circle, hand in hand,
Wherein the mids [*sic*] the *Worldly Ball* doth stand.

(138)

In a universe where "Motion *is the* Life *of all things*" (19), the disparate atoms are pictured as united in the dance: "*ATOMES* will dance, and measures keep just time; / And one by one will hold round circle line," ("Motion *directs, while* Atomes *dance*," 17).

A number of analogues exist for Cavendish's images of a universe of pattern or order emerging out of diversity and change. Sir John Davies's *Orchestra* (1596) is rooted in the metaphor of the dance of Creation that resurfaces in *Poems and Fancies*. In *Orchestra,* Antinous tells Penelope:

Dauncing bright lady, then began to be,
When the first seedes whereof the world did spring
The Fire, Ayre, Earth, and water did agree,
By Loves perswasion, Natures mighty King,
To leave their first disordred [*sic*] combating;
    And in a daunce such measure to observe
    As all the world their motion should preserve.[22]

The notion, used by Davies here, of the various and conflicting elements combining and recombining in coherent forms frequently reappears, not least in Du Bartas's account of the world's creation, much reprinted in Joshua Sylvester's translation as *The Divine Weeks and Works*.[23] Du Bartas's partly scientific approach must have interested Cavendish, who was clearly aware of this translation, which she mentions in her *Philosophical and Physical Opinions* (1655) (a2r). Du Bartas shares Cavendish's sense that the creation of the world emerges out of an agreement between potentially dissonant, separate components coming together in endlessly varied combination. Of the four elements he writes:

And sith but changing their degree and place;
They frame the various Formes, wherewith the face
Of this faire World is so imbellished:
As six sweet Notes, curiously varied,

In skilfull Musike make a hundred kindes
Of Heavenly sounds, that ravish hardest minds,
And with Division of a choise device,
The Hearers soules out at their eares intice:
Or, as of twice twelve *Letters,* thus transposed,
This World of Words is variously composed;
And of these Words, in divers order sowne,
This sacred *Volume* that you read, is growne
(Through gracious succour of th'*Eternall Deitie*)
Rich in discourse, with infinite Varietie.[24]

(I.1.2.261–74)

Like Cavendish, he repeatedly returns to the idea of variety as a defining marvel of Nature and, in this extract, even begins to link this, as Cavendish does, with the poetics of the written text.[25] As in *Poems and Fancies,* musical "Division" also serves to encapsulate his conception of the coherent patterns that emerge out of a principle of diversity.[26]

First printed closer to the time of *Poems and Fancies,* Sir John Denham's poem *Cooper's Hill* provides a model of Nature particularly sympathetic to Cavendish's own. The sense that she knew *Cooper's Hill* is reinforced by the fact that the final stages of her poem, "*The* hunting *of the* Stag" (116) echo Denham's use of the stag hunt as a metaphor for the betrayal and destruction of Charles I.[27] Describing the ideal location of his poem, Denham asserts:

Here Nature, whether more intent to please
Us or her selfe with strange varieties
. . . .
Wisely she knew the harmony of things
As well, as that of sounds from discord springs,
Such was the discord, which did first disperse
Forme, order, beauty through the universe;
While driness, moysture; coldnesse heat resists;
All that we have, and that we are subsists;
While the steepe horrid roughnesse of the wood
Strives with the gentle calmnesse of the flood.
Such huge extreames, when Nature doth unite
Wonder from thence results, from thence delight.

(12–13)

Denham's poem, originally printed in 1642, the year of the out-
break of the Revolution, reminds us of the potential attractiveness for royalists of the notion that division and difference ultimately generate harmony and order (a notion embodied in the
heroic couplet form favored by both Denham and Cavendish).
Such ideological resonances surface in Cavendish's depiction of
the cohesion of disparate components in creating the world as a
resistance to the disintegrating force of death portrayed as a
political usurper:

> Saies *Nature,* I am of another minde,
> If we let *Death* alone, we soon shall finde,
> He wars will make, and raise a mighty power,
> If we divert him not, may us devoure.
> He is ambitious, will in triumph sit,
> Envies my workes, and seekes my State to get.
>
> ("*Nature calls a Councell,*" 2)

The comparison between *Poems and Fancies* and the model of
order through variety apparent in Denham and others helps to
support the idea that variety represents a conscious and coherent
principle in Cavendish's volume. Despite its notable peculiarities
her first printed text emerges as a work clearly influenced by the
cross-currents of contemporary poetry. While we cannot prove
conclusively that Cavendish read all the texts in relation to
which I have situated *Poems and Fancies,* the evidence for their
impact appears strong. After all, although she is eager to suggest
that she has "*read but little*" that might diminish the originality
of her natural philosophy, extensive discussions of literary texts
and authors in *Sociable Letters* indicate that she was a voracious
and critically alert reader of a range of works, including Homer in
English translation, Shakespeare, contemporary verse, satires,
and romance.[28] Yet, having established this, a final caveat is
called for. *Poems and Fancies* exhibits a degree of fascination
with variety and change that exceeds the balance and fixity upon
which the analogues I have explored ultimately place such a
premium. Where Davies, Du Bartas, and Denham insist that
nothing emerges "by chance" in an ultimately orderly Creation,
for example, Cavendish allows for the idea that Nature may
throw up troubling irregularities:

> TIS severall *Figur'd Atomes* that make *Change,*
> When severall *Bodies* meet as they do range.
> For if they sympathise, and do agree,
> They joyne together, as one *Body* bee.
> But if they joyne like to a *Rabble-rout,*
> Without all order running in and out;
> Then *disproportionable* things they make,
> Because they did not their right places take.[29]
> ("*What* Atomes *make* Change," 9)

Cavendish's particular vision of matter as composed of endlessly self-moving atoms cannot fail to leave readers with the image of a universe in flux:

> But *Motion* she perswades new *Formes* to make,
> For *Motion* doth in *Change* great pleasure take.
> And makes all *Atomes* run from place to place;
> That *Figures young* he might have to imbrace.
> For some short time, she will make much of *one,*
> But afterwards away from *them* will run.
> And thus are most things in the World undone,
> And by her *Change,* do *young ones* take *old's* roome.
> ("Motion *makes* Atomes *a* Bawd
> *for* Figure," [18] mispaginated 20)

Given the way in which she roots her poetics of variety in this model of a multifarious, atomistic Nature, such a vision can, at times, trigger a sense of the instability not only of the universe of matter but of the poetic text itself. In a preface "*To Naturall* Philosophers" she portrays her work as constantly making and unmaking itself subject to the reader's interpretation, drawing out the analogy between self-moving atoms and the inherent instability and variousness she attributes to poetry:

> I cannot say, I have not heard of *Atomes,* and *Figures,* and *Motion,* and *Matter;* but not thoroughly *reason'd* on: but if I do erre, it is no great matter; for my *Discourse* of them is not to be accounted *Authentick:* so if there be any thing worthy of noting, it is a good Chance; if not, there is no harm done, nor time lost . . . And the Reason why I write it in *Verse,* is, because I thought *Errours* might better passe there, then in *Prose;* since *Poets* write most *Fiction,* and *Fiction* is not given for *Truth,* but *Pastime;* and I feare my *Atomes* will be as small

Pastime, as themselves: for nothing can be lesse then an *Atome.* But my desire that they should please the *Readers,* is as big as the *World* they make; and my *Feares* are of the same *bulk;* yet my *Hopes* fall to a single *Atome* agen: and so shall I remaine an unsettled *Atome,* or a confus'd *heape,* till I heare my *Censure.* If I be prais'd, it fixes them; but if I am condemned, I shall be *Annihilated* to nothing. (A6r)

Cavendish's image of perpetually mobile atoms then, can feed a curiously metamorphic conception of her volume that serves to forestall the fixed meanings that might invite literary, scientific, or political criticism. Likening her "Verses" to "Chast Penelope's Work," she implicitly invites the reader to conceive of a text that weaves and unweaves itself in tune with the tireless dance of her atoms ("TO POETS," 122).

NOTES

1. Margaret Cavendish, *Poems and Fancies* (1653; facsimile reprint, Menston: Scolar Press, 1972), [238] (mispaginated 212). Subsequent references to *Poems and Fancies* are to this edition and given in brackets in the text. Numbers denote page references as there is no line numbering.

2. Her orations concerned with the management of the state, for example, share subjects such as "Peace and Warre," "levying of mony," and "the severall kinds of Governments," listed under "Deliberative" orations by R[obert] F[age] in setting out the categories of "Demonstrative," "Judiciall," and "Deliberative" oration in his *A Compendium of the Art of Logick and Rhetorick* (London, 1651). See Margaret Cavendish, *Orations of Divers Sorts* (London, 1662), 1–77, 251–56, 281–87; Fage, 141, 143, 157. Fage's "Judiciall" orations are suggested by Cavendish's section of speeches set "In Several Courts of Judicature" (78–99). See also Thomas Wilson's explanations under the subheadings "Of an Oration Judicial," "Oration Judicial: What It Is," and subsequent sections in Wilson, *The Art of Rhetoric* (1560), ed. Peter E. Medine (University Park: Pennsylvania State University Press, 1994), lines 120–32. Both Cavendish's legal and political orations find counterparts in Richard Rainolde's "Oracion Civill or Judiciall" and his "Oracion . . . prefferyng a Monarchie, conteinying all other states of the common wealthe" in Rainolde, *A Booke Called the Foundacion of Rhetorike* (London, 1563), sig. a4r. His outline of contents in the dedicatory epistle to Robert Dudley also adumbrates other topics covered by Cavendish: "The duetie of a subjecte, the worthie state of nobilitie, the preheminent dignitie and Majestie of a Prince, the office of counsailours. . . . the office of a Judge or Magestrate" (a2v). His oration "concerning the goodly state of Mariage" (D2v–P3r) finds a counterpart in Cavendish's series of "Marriage Orations" (198–203).

3. The period of composition of *The Worlds Olio* is indicated in "An Epistle to the Reader" which comments that, "This Book, most of it was written five year since," see Margaret Cavendish, *The Worlds Olio* (London, 1655), A3v. Subsequent references are to this edition and given in brackets in the text.

4. Margaret Cavendish, *CCXI Sociable Letters* (London, 1664), c2r.

5. See, for example, "THE CLASPE," "Similizing the Braine to a Garden," "Similizing Thoughts" and "Of Thoughts" (*Poems and Fancies*, 47, 136–37, 145–[46], mispaginated 156).

6. See Milton, "L'Allegro," especially lines 67–72, 77, 119–24, 87; "Il Penseroso," lines 27–29, 50, 86, 104, 116–20 in John Milton, *Complete Shorter Poems*, ed. John Carey (London: Longman, 1971). Cavendish's identification of Melancholy with "Ravens hoarse," "The Tolling Bell," "a thick dark Grove," "hollow Caves . . . or lowly Cell" (77, 78) also strongly recall Milton, "L'Allegro," lines 3, 5, 7; "Il Penseroso," lines 83, 133, 169.

7. See in particular, "A Worlde made by foure Atomes" and the prose note that follows it (31).

8. See also, for example, "A Hodge-Podge for Natures Table" (130–31); "A Tart" (131–32).

9. For other instances of the same technique, see "Similizing the Mind" (143); "Similizing Navigation," ([146], mispaginated 156); "Similizing the Sea to Meadowes, and Pastures, the Mariners to Shepheards, the Mast to a May-pole, Fishes to Beasts," ([146]-147 mispaginated 156–47).

10. See Phineas Fletcher, *The Purple Island; or, the Isle of Man* (London, 1633). Cavendish may also have had Fletcher's poem in her mind when writing the two poems "Of an Island" (116–18) and "The Ruine of the Island" (118–120) that echo its allegorical use of the corruption of a once-paradisal island. However, Cavendish's allegory is more suggestive of a commentary on the disruption of England by civil war than of the universal spiritual corruption of mankind. Cavendish's "Of two Hearts" (140–41) is also redolent of Fletcher's copious expansion on the metaphor of man as landscape. Francis Quarles's commendatory poem to Fletcher, printed in *The Purple Island* ([A]4r-v), also utilizes the device of the subdivided extended simile, starting in this case from the premise that "Mans Bodies like a house." Cavendish's "Natures House" (133) works along related lines although it concentrates more on the house as a metaphor for human moral virtues.

11. For descriptions of this visit, see Margaret Cavendish, *Natures Picture Drawn by Fancies Pencil to the Life* (London, 1656), 379–82; *The Life of the Thrice Noble, High and Puissant Prince William Cavendishe* (London, 1667), 70–74. Douglas Grant, *Margaret the First: a Biography of Margaret Cavendish, Duchess of Newcastle 1623–1673* (London: Rupert Hart-Davis, 1957), 108–32, establishes the dates of the visit. In an epistle "TO THE READER" (A7r) Cavendish notes that she began writing *Poems and Fancies* "since I came into England, being eight Yeares out, and nine Months in," and in her next work, *Philosophical Fancies* (London, 1653), admits that she is in a hurry to get her work printed owing to her "desire (to have those Works Printed in England, which I wrote in England, before I leave England)" (B6r–B6v). The opening dedicatory epistle of *Poems and Fancies* addresses Charles Cavendish, "MY

Noble Brother-in-Law," thanking him for accompanying her on her petitioning trip and making pointed reference to the harshness of the times (A2v). For a fuller exploration of these kinds of sentiments as part of a deliberate strategy of royalist resistance in the face of exile on the part of Cavendish and her husband, see Hero Chalmers, "Dismantling the Myth of 'Mad Madge': the Cultural Context of Margaret Cavendish's Authorial Self-Presentation," *Women's Writing* 4 (1997): 323–39.

12. For examples of other favorable comments on invention in *Poems and Fancies,* see "The Purchase of Poets, or a Dialogue betwixt the Poets, and Fame, and Homers Marriage" (57); "Similizing the Braine to a Garden" (137); "Of Thoughts" ([146] mispaginated 156); "Of small Creatures, such as we call Fairies" ([186] mispaginated 162). Cavendish's emphasis on invention also appears to be reflected in the Elizabeth Toppe's prefatory epistle to *Poems and Fancies* where she describes her mistress as "not onely the first English Poet of your Sex, but the first that ever wrote this way: therefore whosoever that writes afterwards, must own you for their Pattern, from whence they take their Sample; and a line by which they measure their Conceits and Fancies" (A5v). See also "Of invention" in *The Worlds Olio* (26).

13. Sylvia Bowerbank, "The Spider's Delight: Margaret Cavendish and the "Female" Imagination," *English Literary Renaissance* 14 (1984): 392–408 (394, 395).

14. See Richard A. Lanham, *A Handlist of Rhetorical Terms,* 2nd ed. (Berkeley: University of California Press, 1991), 91–92, 165–66; Wilson, *Art of Rhetoric,* 9, 49. George Gascoigne, "Certayne Notes of Instruction Concerning the Making of Verse or Ryme in English," in G. Gregory Smith, ed., *Elizabethan Critical Essays,* 2 vols., 1:47–48, links poetic skill in invention with the avoidance of clichés. Sir Philip Sidney, *A Defence of Poetry,* ed. Jan Van Dorsten (Oxford: Oxford University Press, 1966), 23, praises the poet for being "lifted up with the vigour of his own invention," see also 41, 53. Sidney, in *Astrophil and Stella,* in *A Critical Edition of the Major Works,* ed. Katherine Duncan-Jones (Oxford: Oxford University Press, 1992), famously plays on the term "invention" (taken to mean both poetic decoration and substantial, freshly conceived subject matter) in the first sonnet in order to fuel a critical debate between Horatian imitation and the more Aristotelian notion of the need for poets to emulate nature or life in finding their material. There is a link here with Cavendish's conception of the true poetry of invention emerging out of the imitation of Nature in *Poems and Fancies,* see above, 126–29.

15. George Puttenham, *The Arte of English Poesie,* in G. Gregory Smith, *Elizabethan Critical Essays,* 2:3–193 (142).

16. See also "Natures Cabinet" (126) and the descriptions of "A Lady drest by Love" and "A Lady drest by Youth" in "Fantasmes Masque" (157, 158).

17. Robert Herrick, *Hesperides; or, the Works Both Humane and Divine of Robert Herrick Esq.* (1648; facsimile reprint, Menston: Scolar Press, 1969). For fairy poems in *Hesperides,* see "The Fairie Temple: or, Oberons Chappell" (101–5), "Oberons Feast" (136–37), "Oberon's Palace" (191–94). For equivalents in *Poems and Fancies,* see "The Fairy Queen" ([172–75] mispaginated 148–51), "The Pastime, and Recreation of the Queen of Fairies in Fairy-land, the Center

of the Earth" ([175–77] mispaginated 151–53), "The Pastime of the Queen of Fairies, when she comes upon the Earth out of the Center" ([177–79] mispaginated 153–55), "Her descending downe" ([179] mispaginated 155), "Of small Creatures, such as we call Fairies" ([186] mispaginated 162), "The City of the Fairies" ([187] mispaginated 163), "The Fairies in the Braine, may be the causes of many thoughts" ([187–88] mispaginated 163–164), "A Battle between King Oberon, and the Pygmees" ([203–10] mispaginated 179–86).

18. Herrick, *Hesperides,* 29. Lois Potter, *Secret Rites and Secret Writing: Royalist Literature, 1641–1660* (Cambridge: Cambridge University Press, 1989), 143, uses Herrick's poem to illustrate her contention that "the female counterpart of the 'wild' cavalier is the careless, even eccentric, lady."

19. Herrick, *Hesperides,* 1. For suggestive readings of Hesperides as a royalist text, see, for example, Thomas N. Corns, *Uncloistered Virtue: English Political Literature, 1640–1660* (Oxford: Clarendon Press, 1992), 91–128; Leah Marcus, *The Politics of Mirth: Jonson, Herrick, Milton, Marvell, and the Defence of Old Holiday Pastimes* (Chicago: University of Chicago Press, 1986), 140–68; Nigel Smith, *Literature and Revolution in England, 1640–1660* (New Haven: Yale University Press, 1994), 250, 260, 262.

20. Herrick, "To his Muse," in *Hesperides,* 1. For a further instance of Herrick's linking the energy necessary to good poetry with virtuous, yet "wanton" femininity, see "A request to the Graces" (343).

21. For this explanation of the Renaissance meaning of "division" in music, see *The Divine Weeks and Works of Guillaume de Saluste Sieur Du Bartas,* translated by Johsua Sylvester, ed. Susan Snyder, 2 vols. (Oxford: Clarendon Press, 1979), 2:774. For other examples of musical order in variety in *Poems and Fancies,* see "According as the Notes in Musicke agree with the Motions of the Heart, or Braine, such Passions are produced thereby" (40), "The Fairy Queen" (148).

22. John Davies, *Orchestra; or, a Poeme of Dauncing,* in *The Poems of Sir John Davies,* ed. Clare Howard (New York: Columbia University Press, 1941), 70.

23. There were nine sixteenth- and seventeenth-century editions of Sylvester's translation, beginning in 1592 and ending in 1641. The translation was based on Du Bartas's *La Semaine ou Creation du monde* (1578) and *La Seconde Semaine* (1584), see *The Divine Weeks and Works,* 1: 5.

24. Anne Bradstreet, whose *The Tenth Muse Lately Sprung Up in America* (1650) was printed in London shortly before Cavendish's petitioning visit, is also avowedly influenced by Du Bartas's handling of the elements, see "To her most Honoured Father Thomas Dudley Esq.; these humbly presented" lines 29–35 and "The Four Elements," lines 1–24, in *The Poems of Anne Bradstreet,* ed. Robert Hutchinson (New York: Dover Publications, 1969). Fletcher, *Purple Island,* 11, also recognizes the necessity for the "peacefull fight, and fighting peace" of the four elements in the creation of the world.

25. For other examples of Du Bartas's focus on variety in Nature, see *The Divine Weeks and Works,* I.1.3.837–40, 859–64; I.1.5.63–70.

26. He also uses the metaphor of a harmonious dance in *The Divine Weeks and Works,* I.1.3.3–4.

27. John Denham, *Coopers Hill. A Poeme. The Second Edition with Additions* (London, 1650), 14–15.

28. *Grounds of Natural Philosophy* (London, 1668), A2v. See also, for example, *Poems and Fancies,* A6r; *Philosophical and Physical Opinions* (1655), B2r, B3v–B4v; *Sociable Letters,* 259, 244–48, 338, 151, 152, 160. See also *Sociable Letters,* 7, 62, 257, 300–305.

29. See Davies, *Orchestra,* 71; Denham, *Coopers Hill,* 4; Bartas, *The Divine Weeks and Works,* I.1.1. The language that Cavendish uses to describe the behavior of atoms in this quotation (as, for example in "Of the sound of Waters, Aire, Flame, more then Earth, or Aire without Flame," 28) shows how her theory of self-moving atoms might carry with it a disturbing sense that they provided a natural model for political insurrection. Indeed, atoms begin to disappear from Cavendish's natural philosophy as early as her second printed work, *Philosophical Fancies* (London, 1653), and in the second edition of her *Philosophical and Physical Opinions* (London, 1663) she explains this specifically in language that acknowledges the implicit threat posed by her earlier theories to conceptions of the preeminence of absolute monarchy as a form of human government (c2r–c2v).

Romantic Fiction, Moral Anxiety, and Social Capital in Cavendish's "Assaulted and Pursued Chastity"

NANCY WEITZ

WHILE CAVENDISH'S IMAGINATIVE FICTION CLEARLY BELONGS TO the broad collective genre of narrative prose, many of her stories resonate with elements of other genres, particularly those that had traditionally participated in a moral project, such as the conduct book, the masque, and the allegory. We don't tend to think of Cavendish as a moralist, since her work is so varied, contradictory, often self-aggrandizing, and decidedly nonreligious, but she was not exempt from social and historical pressures to promote virtue and castigate vice in her writings—even when the object or aim of a given piece is clearly something other. These pressures lead to—and in hindsight help to explain—conflicts in the prose narrative "Assaulted and Pursued Chastity." There is no question that Cavendish's work in toto displays a high degree of multivalence and multivocality. Anna Battigelli asserts that after 1655, Cavendish focused "on the conflicts that arose from multiple and conflicting sensibilities. Repeatedly, she turned to narrative frames that contained multiple and competing perspectives, no one of which can be identified unproblematically with Cavendish's own perspective."[1] One such narrative frame is the use of Boccaccian storytellers in *Natures Pictures,* the volume that contains "Assaulted and Pursued Chastity."

However, the conflicts contained within "Assaulted and Pursued Chastity" alone are not the result of fractured narrative voices, but Cavendish's need to serve more than one master: the divergent aims of the narrative lead to inconsistencies in the resulting meaning of the text. The forces at work are Cavendish's own authorial goals, her understanding of reader expectations, her adherence to generic and modal conventions, and finally her own reputation. The key element in this group of conflicting aims is chastity, the principal female virtue, which not only bears titular importance in the plot and moral message of the story but also impinges crucially on Cavendish's authorial ethos and her choice of genre for this message.

The idea that early modern women writers were in constant struggle with their reputation for virtue has been well documented and explored.[2] Writing about chastity allowed women to defy the link between silence and chastity ostensibly in the service of usefulness and virtue, yet they did not always obediently reproduce the chastity topos that male writers employed, nor, on the other hand, did they simply resist the wholesale exaltation of the virtue. Women writers negotiated with the representations and ideological encodings that they had received from male writers in order to reclaim chastity as a potent quality that is neither canceled out by female speech nor always already decayed by the seductive lure of women's chaste beauty. In general, women writers present an altered picture of chastity, one that gives men back responsibility for their own desirous response to female beauty. They also question the ways exemplars have been and can be used to illustrate women's virtue and abilities.

Cavendish was overt in her anxiety that her writings might impinge upon her own reputation, as many of the prefaces to her imaginative writings—her prose fiction, drama, and poetry—testify.[3] Hero Chalmers argues persuasively that Cavendish uses wifely obedience and her Royalist links to support her publication and create "a climate amenable to the notion of chaste feminine display."[4] By the mid-seventeenth century, even conduct books such as Richard Brathwait's *English Gentlewoman* gave permission to virtuous women to appear in public as an example for others to emulate:

> Yet far be it from me, to be so regularly strict, or Laconically severe, as to exclude Women from all publick societies. Meetings may they have, and improve them, to their benefit . . . A modest and well Behaved Woman may by her frequent or resort to publike places, conferre no lesse benefit to such as observe her behavior, than occasion of profit to her private family, where shee is Overseer. . . . These

are such mirrors of modesty, patternes of piety, as they would not for a world transgresse the bounds of Civility. These are Matrons in their houses, Models in publike places.[5]

Although the climate was slowly changing for women to be seen abroad and assert themselves in writing, they had to adhere closely to social and moral codes, particularly in the content and form of their writings.

In addition to her awareness of the perceived impropriety of publication, Cavendish was highly conscious of gendered divisions in her potential audience. It is nearly impossible to discuss the author's work without taking into account the prefatory material in her books. Not surprisingly, her appeals to male readers (notably her brother-in-law, Sir Charles Cavendish, and assorted "Natural Philosophers") dwell upon her lack of formal education; her appeals to women, however, are mostly concerned with defending her writings against "dishonesty." This presupposes both that chastity was the first and foremost concern for all women (and, consequently, women would be quick to notice its lack in other women) and that she was aware that writing had long been a suspect activity for women. Her defensive strategy is to encourage other women to follow her lead, claiming that writing is a wholesome way to spend time that actually deflects desire *away* from unchaste activities. She pleads to "All Noble, and Worthy Ladies,"

> Condemne me not as a dishonour of your Sex, for setting forth this Work; for it is harmlesse and free from all dishonesty. . . . Wives, Sisters, & Daughters, may imploy their time no worse than in honest, Innocent, and harmless Fancies; which, if they do, Men shall have no cause to feare, that when they go abroad in their absence, they shall receive Injury by their loose Carriages. Neither will women be desirous to Gossip abroad, when their Thoughts are well imployed at home.[6]

This attempt to gain the approval of women readers for her books by suggesting they themselves try writing is a ploy to instill what Kenneth Burke termed *consubstantiality*: the author's concerns for her own reputation for moral virtue are intimately tied to her apparent care for her readers' moral well-being.

This anxiety was never more apparent than when she approached the gray area of romance, which popular genre was tainted by a long-standing reputation for immorality, especially in regard to women readers. Suzanne Hull has shown that women had been a significant audience for fiction during the early development of the prose narrative,[7] and romantic fiction remained popular throughout the sixteenth and seventeenth centuries despite moralists' condemnation. According to the Humanist educator Juan Vives,

> It can not lightly be a chaste mind that is occupied with thinking on armour and tourney and man's valiance. What places among these be for chastity unarmed and weak? . . . Moreover, whereto readst thou other men's love and glozing words and by little and little drinkest the enticements of the poison unknowing and many times ware and wittingly. . . . I marvel that wise fathers will suffer their daughters or that husbands will suffer their wives or that manners and customs of people will dissemble and overlook that women shall use to read wantonness.[8]

One hundred and fifty years later, Restoration conduct books would exhibit the same level of suspicion about the moral content of the romantic fiction:

> [Women] do read how this Virgin leaves her Countrey, and her Parents, to run after that Stranger; another is in love in a moment, when she reads that she hath received Letters from such and such a Gallant, and how they have appointed private places where to meet together. These are but cunning lessons, to learn young Maids to sin more wittily.[9]

Whether it be the male-dominated tales of Vives' day or the adventures of a Restoration heroine, romance posed a threat to the female reader's ability to differentiate positive from negative examples and severely tested her strength of will to resist her natural inclination toward sensuality.[10] Even male readers were at risk: a sixteenth-century commentator on Ariosto's *Orlando Furioso* warned that the reader of such a romance was safe only because an allegorical truth was concealed within its siren's song.[11] Responsible moral writers were obliged to consider the impact their words would have upon their female reader in order to lead her toward virtue, away from vice, and to hide the contradictions hidden within the "truly chaste" ideal.[12] In the preface to *Natures Pictures,* Cavendish worries that her book will smack of romance:

> Though some of these Stories be Romancical, I would not be thought
> to delight in Romances, having never read a whole one in my life. . . .
> I hope, that this Work will rather quench Passion, than enflame it;
> will beget chast Thoughts, nourish the love of Virtue . . . and instruct
> Life: will damn Vices, kill Follies, prevent Errors, forwarn Youth, and
> arm the Mind against Misfortunes; and in a word, will admonish,
> direct, and perswade to that which is best in all kinds.[13]

This avowal exhibits full recognition of the widespread belief in romance's immorality even while Cavendish clearly delights in the possibilities the genre offers for spinning a tale. James Fitzmaurice sees Cavendish's reliance on the stylistic tenets of French romance (whether consciously or otherwise) as closely allied to her ideals of writing under the power of "fancy."[14]

Leaving aside the problems inherent with romance, chastity posed a difficulty for discussion because its very position as the pinnacle of virtue and anathema to lust makes it the inescapable partner of lust: every mention of chastity carries with it that absent presence. In Foucauldian terms, even the discursive prohibition of sexual desires reinscribes those desires whether largely within the limits of the literary work or by directly addressing the desires of the reader.[15] Jeremy Taylor acknowledges this problem when he worries that his readers may find fuel for their lust even in his pious admonitions against sin. In the preface to his chapter on chastity, Taylor cautions:

> Reader stay, and read not the advices of the following Section, unless
> thou hast a chast spirit, or desirest to be chast, or at least art apt to
> consider whether you ought or no. For there are some spirits so Athe-
> istical, and some so wholly possessed with a spirit of uncleanness,
> that they turn the most prudent and chast discourses into dirt and
> filthy apprehensions; like cholerick stomachs, changing their very
> Cordials and medicines into bitterness; and in a literal sense turning
> the grace of God into wantonness. They study cases of conscience in
> the matter of carnal sins, not to avoid, but to learn ways how to offend
> God and pollute their own spirits; and search their houses with a
> Sunbeam, that they may be instructed in all the corners nastiness.[16]

Taylor makes much of the idea that the reader's intention and attitude toward the material is crucial to the eventual good effects of his text, but he does not absolve himself, as author, from responsibility for attempting to make a wrong reading impossible:

> I have used all the care I could, in the following periods, that I might neither be wanting to assist those that need it, nor yet minister any occasion of fancy or vainer thoughts to those that need them not. If any man will snatch the pure taper from my hand, and hold it to the Devil, he will only burn his own fingers, but shall not rob me of the reward of my care and good intention, since I have taken heed how to express the following duties, and given him caution how to read them.[17]

Cavendish appears especially aware of the male literary tradition's overt concern for producing a chaste response in the reader and the most typical methods for approaching that response. While "Assaulted and Pursued Chastity" does not use allegory per se to recuperate her romance, Cavendish is no stranger to emblematic figures, which pepper her works, especially her dramas. The text resonates with allegorical figures and ideas reminiscent of Milton's *Mask Presented at Ludlow Castle* [*Comus*]. In both texts, the retention of the heroine's chastity— the heroine as the manifestation of chastity, in fact—is the focus for the narrative. However, unlike Milton's *Mask,* which celebrates the spiritual powers of the Lady and bestows heavenly rewards on her as possessor of true virtue, Cavendish's construction of chastity somewhat indirectly allows the heroine to reach a position of great social and political power, despite (possibly due to) the author's obliteration of the religious mystery with which generations of writers before her imbued the virtue: the brief appearances of the spiritual realm in the tale proves heaven to be pretty feeble, or at least largely uninterested in human virtue. And whereas Milton makes sharp distinctions between good and evil, right and wrong,[18] Cavendish's tale contains an ideological rift that allows its messages to float along, slipping ambiguously in and out of moral categories, and in many ways prefigures Richardson's *Pamela.* In her essay on the story, Marina Leslie argues compellingly that through her figurations of empire Cavendish's vision of potent chastity emblematizes the tension between disordered times and the absolute monarchy of the Caroline court.[19] While one can trace the political disjunctions radiating from the narrative and view chastity as a metaphor of events on the "world's stage," the text also responds to an examination of the moral contradictions deeply rooted within Cavendish's construction of the virtue, which exists not only as a political metaphor but as a synecdoche for social relations. The relationship between chaste female beauty and male desire—more specifically, the *impetus* for male desire—is the locus for Cavendish's ideological conflict. Her support of women's innocence clashes with her reproduction of the traditionally male Petrarchan rhetoric one expects to find in a romantic narrative that inherently blames women for seducing men into desiring them.

Milton's attention to such issues as chastity, rape, and individual responsibility is less concerned with the worldly implications of human interaction than with the spiritual consequences of that interaction. Rape, for Milton, remains liminal, off-side: it is an example of sin or a temptation to sin, usually committed or threatened allegorically. Milton, however, is by no means oblivious to propriety in social conduct, but the social remains subordinate to the spiritual; human interaction provides a sort of evidence of spiritual status. How does chastity protect a woman from sexual assault, and what happens to a woman's spiritual status when she is victimized by rape? His *Mask* presents a sexual struggle as a particular example of the general claim that faith protects the goodly believer from "each thing of sin and guilt."[20] Catherine Belsey says in her study of Milton, "*Comus* is about rape."[21] I would shift the emphasis slightly to suggest that the masque is mainly concerned with celebrating the power of chastity to repel sexual violence, but this theme is not without its inconsistencies. Milton may not steadfastly support the categorical insistence upon the unchastity of a rape victim found in Vives' *Instruction of a Christian Woman:* "It is an evil keeper that cannot keep one thing well committed to her keeping . . . which no man will take from her against her will, nor touch it, except she be willing herself."[22] However, the conflicting ideologies that allow women to be blamed for the effect they have upon men are not completely absent in Milton's work. Milton supports the Augustinian notion that sexuality of any kind beyond the bounds of marriage necessarily falls within the category of concupiscence for both parties, consenting or otherwise, as sin infects all it touches.

Cavendish's philosophy of rape differs quite radically from Milton's: heaven only sometimes favors the chaste with protection from ravishment, and then usually through human aid and not heaven-sent agents like Thyrsis and Sabrina. Her attitude is far more pragmatic, and the contradictions in her representation of chastity under assault are most apparent in a discrepancy between the purpose she claims for her tale and the narrative itself. This discrepancy indicates a conflict between the woman writer's method of self-authorization—the way she justifies what she writes—and the story she really wants to tell. While Milton asks of the Lady only her steadfast refusal to give in to Comus's temptations, thus allowing Comus to bear the brunt of culpability as long as she doesn't fall victim to him, Cavendish allows her heroine to be in some degree responsible for her seducer's attraction. The seducer is in fact only very faintly demonized for persecuting his prey, an attitude that undercuts the virtue's importance as anything more than a maneuver for catching a husband, even while Cavendish shows the worldly power that chastity can bring. The explanation Cavendish gives for writing her tale is rich with resonances of earlier discussions of rape and the relationship between chastity and beauty, and she reproduces the conflicts that those discussions contain. The author's evident aim is to "shew young Women the danger of Travelling without Parents, Husbands, or particular Friends, to guard them."[23] It is important to quote this passage at length:

> Though Virtue is a good Guard, yet it doth not always protect their Persons, without other Assistance: for though Virtue guards, yet Youth and Beauty betrays; and the Treachery of the one, is more than the Safety of the other; for Young, Beautiful, and Virtuous Women, if they wander alone, find but very often rude entertainment from the Masculine Sex, witness Jacob's Daughter Dinah, which Schechem forced: and others, whose Forcement is mentioned in holy Scripture, and in Histories of less Authority (sans nombre): which shews that Heaven doth not always protect the Persons of Virtuous Souls from rude Violences; neither doth it always leave Virtue destitute, but sometimes sends a Human Help; yet so, as never but where Necessity was the Cause of their Dangers, and not Ignorance, Indiscretion, or Curiosity: for, Heaven never helps, but those that could not avoid the Danger. . . . But to conclude, I say, Those are in particular favoured

by Heaven, that are protected from Violence and Scandal, in a
wandring-life, or a Travelling-condition. (394–95)

The mercurial and unpredictable divinity that Cavendish describes is much more allied to the pagan and natural powers that
she most often calls upon in her works, particularly Fortune and
the Fates. And there is nothing especially elect or divine in her
chastity that would allow it to reliably bring divine rewards. Like
Dorothy Leigh in *A Mothers Blessing,* Cavendish suggests that
chastity alone does not have the power to fend off those who are
determined to transgress, but unlike Leigh, Cavendish does not
invest the virtue with an alternative mysterious religious significance.[24] To Cavendish, chastity functions as a social virtue, such
as courtesy, which keeps the (polite) world running in a smooth
and orderly fashion but can be upset at any time by someone who
does not recognize its place and its worth.

Thus women alone and abroad are likely to fall prey to the
mercy of men, which puts them in great danger indeed, like
Dinah, whose travels led to her rape. It is important that Cavendish makes a distinction between women who are left alone
by the ravages of war or other necessity and those who stray
off through ignorance, indiscretion, or curiosity, which are all
vices. Here Cavendish alters the idea that Brathwait explicates
in *The English Gentlewoman,* when he writes, "Had Dinah never
roaved, shee had prov'd a Diana, and had never been ravished";
and, "Dinah may be a proper Embleme for the eye; shee seldome
strayes abroad, but shee is in danger of ravishing."[25] Brathwait
implies that Dinah's violation was first and foremost caused by
her own actions—it was her traveling abroad (necessary or otherwise) that is to be condemned for creating the opportunity for
her to be seen and desired by her ravisher. Cavendish, however,
acknowledges that Dinah's travels provided the opportunity for
her to be raped, but she shifts the responsibility for the crime
onto the shoulders of the "Masculine Sex" and its "rude entertainment" of women—as long as those travels were not undertaken
for vicious or trivial reasons. Cavendish is not willing to exempt
women utterly from responsibility for being victimized, but she is
willing to take into consideration which actions may have contributed to the assault. Men, on the other hand, are never to be

trusted on first acquaintance—it is a woman's duty to expect treachery from them before she should blithely trust them.

Yet this pro-woman stance is belied by Cavendish's personifications of Virtue, Youth, and Beauty (resonant with Shakespeare's in *Rape of Lucrece*), which reproduce the Petrarchan tradition of emblematic literature and undercut her attempt to assign blame for rape to the "Masculine sex." Shakespeare's battleground is Lucrece's face, wherein the colors of Virtue and Beauty strive for preeminence.[26] Cavendish pits Virtue against Youth and Beauty as a figure for the struggle between the virtuous woman and the ravisher. This metaphorical relationship, however, does not perfectly correspond: the conflict moves from two separate human adversaries to battling qualities all contained within only one of the human figures. If the assaulted woman's own Youth and Beauty betray her Virtue, regardless of the reason she is placed in such a position, then the ravisher is merely a neutral force that needs the willingness of at least some part of the woman in order to perform his rape. Thus Cavendish's own deployment of the male rhetoric of chastity serves to betray her theory that rape is a crime of assault against a wholly innocent victim.

The story itself, like its preface, slips elusively in and out of agreement with these two conflicting positions—woman as innocent victim/woman as culpable victim. It also dramatizes the personified struggle between Youth/Beauty and Virtue (with the ravisher looming in the background) as a different triangulation that maintains the displaced female/female struggle: heroine and bawd (with ravisher in the background).[27] "Assaulted and Pursued Chastity" contains an argument reminiscent of the "Beauty is nature's coin" speech delivered by Comus in Milton's *Mask,* but—significantly—in Cavendish's reworking of the struggle, the sophistic side is presented by a woman, the female bawd employed by the married Prince to persuade the heroine to accept his seductions willingly:

> Her Mistress began to read her Lectures of Nature, telling her, She should use her Beauty while she had it, and not to waste her Youth idly, but to make the best profit of both, to purchase Pleasure and Delight: besides, said she, Nature hath made nothing in vain, but to some useful End. . . . Wherefore it is a sin against Nature to be reserved and coy. (397–98)

This economic argument summarizes much of Comus's more pro-
tracted points of logic. But the similarity between the bawd's
words and those of Comus is evident:

> List Lady, be not coy, and be not cozen'd
> With that same vaunted name Virginity;
> Beauty is nature's coin, must not be hoarded,
> But must be current, and the good thereof
> Consists in mutual and partak'n bliss.[28]

Put into the mouth of a woman agent for an absent "buyer,"
however, the clear-cut one-on-one, male/female struggle between
good and evil becomes a more insidiously mediated and bartered
exchange between the market forces that are used metaphoric-
ally in the speech. The bawd's dispassionate persuasions only
indirectly serve her own ends, which are literally monetary, and
she is free from the ravisher's charged emotions and sexual passion toward the object of persuasion. Though the heroine is apparently as savvy to the fallaciousness of this argument as the
Lady in the masque, her only recourse is deception: "The young
Lady, being of a quick apprehension, began to suspect some
Design and Treachery against her . . . and dissembling her
discovery as well as she could for the present, gave her thanks for
her Counsel" (399).

The dispassionate nature of the mediated situation is one reason for the heroine's rejection of overt argumentation as a strategy for retaining her virtue, but she has another reason as well
for turning to active deception to gain her release:

> Her confidence of the Gods protection of Virtue gave her Courage. . . .
> But when [her Mistress] was gone, considering in what a dangerous
> condition she stood, and that the Gods would not hear her if she lazily
> called for help, and watch'd for Miracles, neglecting Natural Means:
> whereupon she thought the best way was, secretly to convey her self
> out of that place, and trust her self again to Chance. (399)

In direct opposition to the Lady's stalwart and passive faith in
divine protection, the pragmatic heroine of "Assaulted and Pursued Chastity" decides that the gods will only watch over her
safety if she acts quickly and wisely in her own defense. Chastity is not enough on its own: it must be complemented by heroic

action. In fact, the action the heroine takes is surprisingly outward-directed: she manages to get a pistol and hide it in her chamber, and, in a nod to Lucrece, she announces, "I am in no ways to be found by wicked Persons, but in Death: for whilst I live, I will live in Honour" (403). Cavendish revises this moment of sacrificial suicide, however, by having the heroine suddenly turn the pistol on her seducer, shoot and injure him: "Stay, stay, said she: I will first build me a Temple of Fame upon your Grave, where all young Virgins shall come and offer at my Shrine; and in the midst of these words, shot him" (404). In addition to the heroine's proactive stance, the language with which she discusses chastity diverges from that of most women writers. In the body of the text, the "heaven" of the preface becomes "the gods" of classical literature, which departure serves to further reduce the mysterious quality of the virtue's Christian resonance and introduce the arbitrariness of chance and whim.

So, why is chastity so crucial for a woman that she must encounter a multitude of dangers in her effort to protect it? Cavendish appears to undercut the threat to the heroine's chastity thoroughly with the comic ending, effectively trivializing Travellia's self-defense into a plot device for catching a husband.[29] But in Cavendish's conception, the social importance of the virtue cannot be overestimated. Certainly conduct books since the Reformation agree either explicitly or tacitly that attracting a good husband is one of the major goals for a woman, but the possibility that this worldly goal could openly displace attention to a woman's spiritual salvation emerges in the seventeenth century. Advice books began to acknowledge that a chaste appearance can be "put on" like a new gown to please a prospective mate—that, in fact, chastity can be bartered like social capital: Brathwait insists, "Let modesty suit you, that a discreeter mate may chuse you."[30] That chastity (or its appearance) is an essential quality for a prospective bride gives the unmarried woman with a reputation for chastity a certain amount of power over her social condition, and even though the property of chastity was most often bartered between men (the father and the husband-to-be), it allows Cavendish the space to imagine the power that a chaste orphan could wield over her future. In fact, Cavendish takes this exchange of capital to its extreme in her narrative: the heroine of the tale exchanges the ownership of her chastity for an empire, which could only have come into the possession of both the heroine and her pursuer via the adventures they encounter, the armies they lead, and the lands they conquer while the prince chases her all over the world: chastity doesn't merely buy the heroine her prince, it buys the prince and wins them both an empire.

Cavendish's overtly pragmatic view of chastity as a powerful social tool is radical for women writers of her time, who generally adopt a more spiritual approach to the virtue, whether through sincere piety or as a mean of constructing a pious ethos. Despite her prefaces, she fits her own description, which Sylvia Brown uses to describe a character one of her plays: "Here is no teacher who 'will admonish, direct and perswade to that which is best in all kinds,' but rather a manipulator of kinds of moral categories."[31] Mihoko Suzuki sees Cavendish as a satirist, who deploys satire's ironic doubleness and its disjunctive form in negotiating the gaps and fissures of seemingly authoritative patriarchal structures."[32] Indeed, Cavendish's manipulations are not only a self-serving evasion of condemnation; her moral twists and turns are also her attempts to negotiate between a number of conflicting ideologies: the misogynistic, the Petrarchan and Neoplatonist, and what Kenneth Burke would call a developing "scientistic" ideology emerging with the works of Descartes, Locke, Boyle, and Hobbes. Her forays into natural philosophy along with her elevation of the social power of chastity over a mystical, religious model suggest her affiliation with a more secularized society. Yet, the fact remains that chastity, however defined, is still the fundamental and crucial facet of female virtue designed to protect the ethos of the female author.

NOTES

1. Anna Battigelli, *Margaret Cavendish and the Exiles of the Mind* (Lexington: University Press of Kentucky, 1998), 73. Emma Rees takes a different position, claiming that "Cavendish herself is the only clearly defined character in the first book of *Natures Pictures*." See Rees, "*Heavens Library* and *Natures Pictures*: Platonic paradigms and trial by genre," *Women's Writing* 4.3 (1997): 369–81; in particular 375.

2. There are too many excellent studies of women's writing and authorial strategies in the period to list them all here. Those which have been most informative for me include: Patricia Crawford, "Women's Published Writings

1600–1700," in *Women in English Society,* ed. Mary Prior (London and New York: Methuen, 1985): 211–82; Gary F. Waller, "Struggling into Discourse: The Emergence of Renaissance Women's Writing," in *Silent but for the Word,* ed. Margaret P. Hannay (Kent, Ohio: Kent State University Press, 1985): 238–91; Elaine Hobby, *Virtue of Necessity: English Women's Writing 1649–88* (Ann Arbor: University of Michigan Press, 1989); Wendy Wall, *The Imprint of Gender: Authorship and Publication in the English Renaissance* (Ithaca: Cornell University Press, 1993); and Ann Rosalind Jones, *The Currency of Eros: Women's Love Lyric in Europe, 1540–1620* (Bloomington and Indianapolis: Indiana University Press, 1990). This connection between silence and chastity has been widely remarked: see for example Wendy Wall, *The Imprint of Gender,* chapter 5; and Peter Stallybrass, who notes that in the early modern period, "Silence, the closed mouth, is made the sign of chastity," in "Patriarchal Territories: the Body Enclosed," in *Rewriting the Renaissance: The Discourses of Sexual Difference in Early Modern Europe,* eds. Maureen Quilligan, et al. (Chicago and London: University of Chicago Press, 1986), 127.

3. Sylvia Brown explores Cavendish's anxiety about appearing "wanton" in "Margaret Cavendish: Strategies Rhetorical and Philosophical Against the Charges of Wantonness, Or Her excuses for Writing So Much," in *Critical Matrix* 6 (1991): 20–45. See also Jacqueline Pearson who examines the link between silent and speaking women in Cavendish's drama in "'Women may discourse . . . as well as men': Speaking and Silent Women in the Plays of Margaret Cavendish, Duchess of Newcastle," *Tulsa Studies in Women's Literature* 4 (1985): 33–45.

4. Hero Chalmers, "Dismantling the Myth of 'Mad Madge': the cultural context of Margaret Cavendish's authorial self-presentation," *Women's Writing* 4.3 (1997): 323–39. Sophie Tomlinson makes a case for Cavendish having seen other aristocratic women perform in masques, which provided a precedent for her own public display in "'My Brain the Stage': Margaret Cavendish and the Fantasy of Female Performance," in *Women Texts and Histories 1575–1760,* eds. Clare Brant and Diane Purkiss (London: Routledge, 1992): 134–63. They both remark that Cavendish's notion of "decorous" female heroism was drawn from Caroline drama and court masques.

5. Richard Brathwait, *The English Gentlewoman* (London, 1631), 50, 52.

6. Cavendish, *Poems and Fancies* (London, 1653), unnumbered prefatory material.

7. Hull writes, "The emergence of women as a reading public, recognized by authors and booksellers, coincides with the fiction explosion in the last quarter of the sixteenth century and raises interesting questions on the possible influence of women on the development of literature in the late Elizabethan period." See *Chaste, Silent, and Obedient* (San Marino, Calif.: Huntington Library, 1983), 75.

8. Vives, *Instruction of a Christen Woman,* trans. Richard Hyrde (London, 1529?), sigs. E3ᵛ–E4.

9. Robert Codrington, *Decency in Conversation Amongst Women* (London, 1664), 168.

10. There have been many studies of medieval and Renaissance misogyny

and beliefs in women's predilection for sensuality. See, for example, Pamela Benson, *The Invention of the Renaissance Woman* (University Park: Pennsylvania State University Press, 1992); R. Howard Bloch, *Medieval Misogyny and the Invention of Western Romantic Love* (Chicago and London: University of Chicago Press), 1991; Peter Brown, *The Body and Society: Men, Women, and Sexual Renunciation in Early Christianity* (New York: Columbia University Press, 1988); John Bugge, *Virginitas: An Essay in the History of a Medieval Ideal. International Archives of the History of Ideas* 17 (The Hague: Martinus Nijhoff, 1975); Vern Bullough, et. al., *The Subordinated Sex: A History of Attitudes Towards Women* (Athens: University of Georgia Press, 1988); Kathryn Gravdal, *Ravishing Maidens: Writing Rape in Medieval French Literature and Law* (Philadelphia: University of Pennsylvania Press, 1991); Katherine Usher Henderson, and Barbara F. McManus, ed., *Half Humankind: Contexts and Texts of the Controversy about Women, 1540–1640* (Urbana and Chicago: University of Illinois Press, 1985); Thomas Laqueur, *Making Sex: Body and Gender from the Greeks to Freud* (Cambridge: Harvard University Press, 1990); Gerda Lerner, *The Creation of Patriarchy* (New York and Oxford: Oxford University Press, 1986); Ian MacLean, *The Renaissance Notion of Woman* (Cambridge: Cambridge University Press, 1980); Glenda McLeod, *Virtue and Venom: Catalogs of Women from Antiquity to the Renaissance* (Ann Arbor: University of Michigan Press, 1991); Linda Woodbridge, *Women and the English Renaissance: Literature and the Nature of Womankind, 1540-1620* (Urbana and Chicago: University of Illinois Press, 1984).

11. Gordon Teskey paraphrases Simone Fornari. See the entry on "Allegory" in the *Spenser Encyclopedia,* ed. A. C. Hamilton (Toronto and London: University of Toronto and Routledge Presses, 1990), 20–21.

12. I've written about these contradictions elsewhere; in brief: a tradition of using abstract and figurative language to represent chastity builds contradictions into that ideal even while it obscures those contradictions. In literature, chastity ostensibly shields women from sexual attention, yet the physical beauty of the chaste woman frequently invites it. See my "Metaphor and the Mystification of Chastity in Juan Luis Vives' *Instruction of a Christen Woman,*" in *Menacing Virgins: Representations of Virginity in the Middle Ages and Renaissance,* ed. Kathleen Kelly and Marina Leslie (Newark: University of Delaware Press, 1999), 132–45.

13. Cavendish, *Natures Picture* (London, 1671), sig. C1.

14. James Fitzmaurice, "Fancy and the Family: Self-Characterizations of Margaret Cavendish," *Huntington Library Quarterly* 53 (1990): 200.

15. Michel Foucault, *The History of Sexuality. Volume 1: An Introduction* (New York: Vintage Books, 1990), *passim.*

16. Jeremy Taylor, *The Rule and Exercises of Holy Living,* 10th ed. (London, 1674), 65.

17. Taylor, *Rule,* 65.

18. I qualify this point vigorously in my essay on Milton's masque, "Chastity, Rape, and Ideology in the Castlehaven Testimonies and Milton's Ludlow *Mask,*" *Milton Studies* 32 (1995): 153–68.

19. See Marina Leslie, "Evading Rape and Embracing Empire in Margaret Cavendish's Assaulted and Pursued Chastity," in *Menacing Virgins,* 179–97.

20. John Milton, *Complete Poems and Major Prose,* ed. Merritt Y. Hughes (New York, 1957), 457. My quotations from *A Mask* and *Paradise Lost* are from this edition, and all line numbers are cited in the text.

21. Catherine Belsey, *John Milton: Language, Gender, Power* (Oxford: Basil Blackwell, 1988), 46.

22. Vives, *Instruction,* sig. G4.

23. Cavendish, *Natures Picture,* 394. All subsequent quotations are from this edition and are cited in the text.

24. Leigh shapes the mystery of chastity to serve women only and exclude men utterly: "Here is this great and wofull shame taken from women by God, working in a woman: man can claime no part in it." Dorothy Leigh, *The Mother's Blessing: or, Godly Counsel of a Gentlewoman not long deceased, left behind for her children* (London, 1616), 35.

25. Richard Brathwait, *The English Gentlewoman,* 50, 86.

26. See Nancy Vickers, "'This Heraldry in Lucrece' Face,'" in *The Female Body in Western Culture: Contemporary Perspectives,* ed. Susan Rubin Suleiman (Cambridge: Harvard University Press, 1986), 209–22.

27. The topos of the evil woman who, for monetary or other reasons, imprisons young women and works as an agent for their seduction (while the seducer only makes occasional appearances) becomes a commonplace in eighteenth-century novels. See, for example, Samuel Richardson's *Clarissa* and even Mary Wollstonecraft's *The Wrongs of Women: Or, Maria.*

28. John Milton, *Comus,* in *Complete Poems and Major Prose,* ed. Merritt Y. Hughes (New York, 1957), lines 737–41.

29. This is a conventional device. See Suzanne Gossett's "'Best Men are Molded out of Faults': Marrying the Rapist in Jacobean Drama," *ELR* 14 (1984): 305-27.

30. Brathwait, *The English Gentlewoman,* 24.

31. Brown, "Margaret Cavendish: Strategies Rhetorical and Philosophical," 29.

32. Mihoko Suzuki, "Margaret Cavendish and the Female Satirist," *SEL* 37 (1997), 484.

Science and Satire: The Lucianic Voice of Margaret Cavendish's *Description of a New World Called the Blazing World*

SARAH HUTTON

THE VERY RANGE OF MARGARET CAVENDISH'S WRITINGS IS CHAL-lenging to her modern readers, since her subject matter includes both fact and fiction, philosophy and fantasy. Admirers and critics alike have tended to emphasize her singularity, and the obvious inconsistencies in her thinking. In her own day she was widely regarded as eccentric, if not crack-brained—"a mad, conceited and ridiculous woman," in Samuel Pepys's now notorious phrase.[1] Her reputation for eccentricity has meant that her claims to be taken seriously as a *femme savante* have, until recently, been ignored. She has been dismissed as an intellectual lightweight and her writings on natural philosophy treated as if they confirmed Pepys's opinion.[2] However, for all her fabled shyness in real life, she was, in her writing, a witty mistress of the art of self-presentation, who adopted, as occasion demanded, the stance of a stridently outspoken critic of male attitudes, or the pose of self-deprecation, with the result that one is never quite sure how firmly her tongue is in her cheek. In this essay I want to examine the baffling blend of comic and serious elements in Cavendish's writing, by focusing on *Blazing World* as a satire on contemporary science. In particular I shall suggest that Cavendish's model is the Greek satirist Lucian of Samosata.

CAVENDISH AND NATURAL PHILOSOPHY

In her own day Margaret Cavendish received recognition of a sort as a lady of scientific learning: on 30 May 1667, she was invited to

161

visit the Royal Society, where various experiments were performed for her interest and entertainment.[3] This visit was an
exceptional one in the Royal Society's normal business. She never
won acceptance as a female virtuoso. In the year preceding her
visit to the Royal Society, Margaret Cavendish had published a
work that was highly critical of the experimentalism that was the
hallmark of the Royal Society's scientific method. This was her
Observations on Experimental Philosophy (London, 1666). A year
after her visit she published *The Grounds of Natural Philosophy*
(London, 1668).[4] Together, *Observations* and *Grounds* are Cavendish's most important books on natural philosophy. They could
also be described as Cavendish's most *systematic* pieces of writing on that subject. This is especially true of *Grounds of Natural
Philosophy,* which is the most carefully ordered of all her writings
on natural philosophy (or science). Starting with a definition of
matter or body, *Grounds of Natural Philosophy* progresses from
general definitions to cover natural phenomena, human beings,
animals, and metals, clearly illustrating her a priori approach.
The Appendix discusses immaterial substance, God, and the possibility that other worlds exist. *Observations on Experimental
Philosophy* covers a wide range of topics. The first part, "An Argumental Discourse concerning some Principal Subjects in Natural Philosophy," summarizes her philosophical opinions in the
form of a debate with herself that covers such topics as sense
perception, experimentalism, "the production of fire by Flint and
Steel," "Pores," water, salt, heat and cold, atoms, the heavenly
bodies, microscopes, and telescopes.[5] The second part, "Further
Observations upon the Experimental Philosophy" discusses ancient learning, matter and motion, animal spirits, God, the soul,
various diseases and their remedies, and chemistry. There is no
clear order to the arrangement of the topics. But a number of
over-arching themes are clear enough, notably Cavendish's concept of nature as "a self-moving and consequently self-living and
self-knowing infinite body."[6] Her *Observations on Experimental
Philosophy* is more polemical than her *Grounds of Natural Philosophy,* since it undertakes a critique of experimental science.
Written, as I have noted, before her visit to the Royal Society in
1667, the book takes as its starting position the view that knowledge derived via the senses is unreliable. Observation is not an
adequate basis for investigating the nature of things because it

"is more apt to be deluded than Reason."[7] Instead she proposes an a priori approach where

> Reason must direct first how sense ought to work, and so much as the Rational knowledg is more noble then the Sensitive, so much is the Speculative part of Philosophy more noble then the Mechanical.[8]

Since sense must defer to reason, the true method of investigation is not deductive via experiment but through reasonable discourse:

> Sense . . . cannot be the ground of Reason, no more then Art can be the ground of Nature. Wherefore discourse shall sooner find or trace Nature's corporeal figurative motions, then deluding Arts can inform the Senses.[9]

Cavendish repeatedly uses the same adjective, "deluding," to describe experiments and the high-tech investigatory equiment of her day (telescopes and microscopes).

> But our age being more for deluding Experiments then rational arguments, which some call a *tedious babble,* doth prefer Sense before Reason, and trusts more to deceiving sight of their eyes, and deluding glasses, then to the perception of clear and regular Reason; nay many will not admit of rational arguments, but the bare authority of an Experimental Philosophy is suffered then to decide all Controversies and to pronounce the Truth without any appeal to Reason, as if they onely had Infinite Truth of Nature, and impressed all knowledge to themselves. Thus Reason must stoop to Sense, and the Conceptor to the Artist, which will be the way to bring in Ignorance, instead of advance knowledg.[10]

In a thinly veiled attack on Robert Hooke's *Micrographia* (1665),[11] she reserves her strongest criticism for "the lately invented Art of Micrography," on practical and epistemological grounds:

> for I cannot perceive any great advantage this Art doth bring us. Also the Ecclipse [sic] of the Sun and Moon was not found out by Telescopes nor the motion of the Loadstone, nor the Art of the Card, nor Art of Guns and Gun-powder, nor the Art of Printing, and the like by Microscopes; if it be true that Telescopes make appear the spots in

the Sun and Moon, or discover some new Stars, what benefit is that to
us? Or if Microscopes do truly represent the external parts and su-
perficies of some minute Creatures, what advantages it our knowledge? For unless they could discover their interior, corporeal, figured
motions and the obscure actions of Nature, or the causes which make
such and such Creatures, I see no benefit or advantage they yield to
man.[12]

BLAZING WORLD

In the same volume as *Observations on Experimental Philosophy*
Cavendish published her utopian fiction, *A Description of a New
World Called the Blazing World,* a text that cross-references back
to her other writings. While the more metaphysical discussions
in *Observations* echo *Philosophical Letters,* many of the scientific
opinions expressed in *Observations on Experimental Philosophy*
are echoed in its companion text, *Blazing World.* The most obvious example is the discussion of micrography—the microscopic
examination of fleas, nettles, stings, and the eyes of flies are all
treated in *Observations.* Likewise, the opinions about the nature
of the sun rehearsed in *Observations* are re-echoed in *Blazing
World.* In the former Cavendish propounds a diversity of opinions, admitting to a measure of agonisticism as to the truth of the
matter, but giving reasons for the opinion she holds:

> There are divers opinions concerning the Matter or Substance of the
> Sun: Some imagine the Sun to be a solid Body set on fire: Others,
> That it is a fluid Body of Fire: and others again that it is only a body of
> Light, and not of fire, so that I know not which to adhere to: but yet I
> do rather believe the Sun to be a solid, than a fluid Body, by reason
> fluid Bodies are more inconstant in their motions than solid Bodies;
> witness Lightening, which is a fluid fire. . . . yet to our perception it
> appears not to be a fluid but a solid body, by reason it keeps con-
> stantly the same exterior figure, and never appears either ebbing or
> flowing, or flashing, as lightening is; nor does the whole of its Body
> dissolve and change into another time.[13]

Cavendish here conveys the impression of a bewildering variety
of opinions ("I know not which to adhere to"). In *Blazing World,*
the same range of opinions is advanced, with a similar sense of
the confusion arising from conflicting opinions:

The Sun, as much as they could observe, they related to be a firm or solid Stone of a vast bigness, of colour yellowish and of an extraordinary splendour . . . Some would have the sun hot in itself. . . . Others . . . thought it more probable that the Sun was not actually hot, but onely by the reflection of its light, so that its heat was an effect of its light; both being immaterial. But this opinion again was laughed at by others and rejected as ridiculous, who . . . believed both the light and heat of the sun proceeded from a swift Circular motion of the aethereal Globules. . . . Thus they argued concerning the heat and light of the Sun, but, which is remarkable, none did say that the sun was a globous fluid body and had a swift circular motion, but all agreed it was fixed and firm like a centre, and therefore they generally called it the Sun-stone.[14]

In this way, despite their disagreements between themselves, Cavendish's *virtuosi,* or scientific experts, endorse opinions she propounds in *Observations:* the last observation cited concurs with her own statement in *Observations,* "I do rather believe the Sun to be a solid than a fluid body." Furthermore, in *Observations,* Cavendish presents her ideas through dialogues with herself. So also, on *Blazing World,* the Empress comes to an understanding of the nature of things through dialogue, either with her virtuosi or with the Duchess. The Empress's conversations with her scientific experts are examples of the discursive method of investigation advocated in *Observations,* where she proposed "discourse" as a means of discovering "Nature's corporeal figurative motions."[16]

By virtue of the fact that it describes an ideal fictional society, *New Blazing World* invites comparison with Thomas More's *Utopia.* Like More, Cavendish gives some account of the state and government of the empire ruled by the heroine, as well as information about aspects of life in her empire—what the inhabitants look like, the recreations they take, what they eat, how peace is maintained. However, the social and political arrangements of the empire are given very little space in the narrative. The majority of the tale is occupied by conversations between the Empress and her virtuosi. The very term "virtuosi" alludes to the gentlemen of the Royal Society, so often referred to by this sobriquet. And indeed, the topics of discussion include the kind of topics then being investigated by the Royal Society—the worm-men, bear-men, ape-men, fish-men, and others—answer the Empress's enquiries about the make-up of the physical world, about the advantages of microscopes and telescopes as tools of investigation, and about the merits of new philosophical systems proposed by Descartes and Hobbes.[17] The Empress's investigations are not confined to natural philosophy, but also extend to metaphysical discussions about the nature of the soul,[18] and an encounter with some mathematicians (spider-men) and a group of orators and logicians (magpie-, parrot-, and jackdaw-men). These scientific and philosophical conversations take up the major part of the book. And it is these discussions that her modern readers are apt to find tedious. Beyond the fact that Cavendish indulges in a game of one-upmanship on the part of the leading lady of the story, their significance is largely lost on a twentieth-century audience. However, the subject matter and range of the Empress's discussions show that Margaret Cavendish had her finger on the pulse of the intellectual revolution of the seventeenth century. For want of an edition that identifies all the references to the now dead learning of Cavendish's time, it is difficult for her modern readers to appreciate the extensiveness and detail of her invocation of contemporary science and philosophy. Among the more obvious ones, Harvey and the circulation of the blood, J. B. van Helmont's concept of "blas," Hobbes's account of the formation of ice and of the phenomenon of thunder, Descartes' opinion of the motion of the sun, Henry More's theory of "plastic nature," not to mention Robert Hooke's researches in microscopy, the Royal Society's experiments in weighing air.[19] These are all highly topical for Cavendish's time. And sprinkled in amongst them are opinions culled from Cavendish's own philosophical writings. The intellectual debates in which these topics are discussed appear to be the equivalent of the factual descriptions of the works of Solomon's House in Bacon's *New Atlantis*. As a scientific utopia, therefore, *New Blazing World* sits more closely to Bacon's *New Atlantis* than to More's *Utopia*.[20]

Cavendish, like Bacon, proposes a new system of natural philosophy. In so doing she criticizes contemporary thought as much as, or even more than, received opinion. The publication of *Blazing World* in the same volume as *Observations on Experimental Philosophy*, suggests that it was intended as a fictional shopwindow for Cavendish's own philosophy of nature, rather as *New Atlantis* was for Bacon's program for the advancement of learning. Like Francis Bacon, Cavendish uses her narrative unashamedly as a vehicle for her own ideas. Not only does she have the heroine, the Empress, endorse a philosophy of nature remarkably similar to that set out in *Observations,* but Cavendish introduces into the tale a persona of herself, with her own name as adviser and chief confidante to the heroine. Described as "singular both in accoutrements, behaviour and discourse,"[21] the fictional Duchess has the unmistakable hallmarks of the authorial duchess's public persona. Furthermore, as we have seen, much of the subject matter of the Empress's conversations finds parallels in Cavendish's other books. As we have just seen, many of the conversations between the Empress and the virtuosi in *Blazing World* arrive at conclusions, that echo views Cavendish herself propounds in her nonfictional writings. *Blazing World* includes several instances where the virtuosi produce conclusions remarkably similar to Cavendish's own general philosophy of nature. For example, when quizzed by the Empress about the doctrine of forms, the worm-men tell her,

> that they did not understand what she meant by this expression. "For," said they, "there is no beginning in nature, no not of particulars, by reason Nature is Eternal and Infinite, and her particulars are subject to infinite changes and transformations by virtue of their own corporeal, figurative self-motions; so that there's nothing new in Nature, nor properly a beginning of anything."[22]

The juxtapositioning of *Observations on Natural Philosophy* and *Blazing World* within the same volume bears a striking resemblance to the volume in which Francis Bacon's *Sylva sylvarum* and *New Atlantis* were published. As a fictional realization of the scientific method propounded in the nonfictional companion text, *Blazing World* stands in the same relation to *Observations* as *New Atlantis* does to *Sylva sylvarum.* Furthermore, when claiming a serious purpose of her book Cavendish echoes Francis Bacon's view that fiction (or fable) has a role in promoting new ideas. Reason, she writes, "requires sometimes the help of fancy to recreate the mind and withdraw it from its more serious contemplations."[23] Cavendish's claim, already cited, that fiction has a role as a vehicle for philosophical and scientific ideas echoes Bacon's view.

One major difference from Bacon is that Cavendish uses satire as a means of criticizing contemporary natural philosophy. Satire also differentiates *Blazing World* from *Observations*. Although both texts offer critiques of contemporary scientific theories, they do so in very different ways. Even though *Observations* has no clear structural arrangement, Cavendish propounds her views rationally, adducing arguments in support of her case. By contrast, the Empress's debating society in *Blazing World* is the occasion of satire. To readers who are not conversant with the now-dead theories current in Cavendish's time the extent to which they are satirical is not immediately apparent. Apart from the fact that most of Cavendish's references to contemporary scientific and philosophical theories are anonymous, another reason for our difficulties in recognizing them is the fact that she distorts them, sometimes almost beyond recognition. Her technique is the simple one of abbreviation and out-of-context citation alongside a handful of alternative opinions. For example, on the question of the relative motion of the sun and the earth, Copernican, Tychonic, and Ptolomaic theories are cited, each on the heels, so to speak, of the previous one. Then, without further explanation we move on to rival opinions on the moon and stars:

> [S]ome said, they perceived that the Sun stood still and the Earth did move, about it; others were of the opinion that they both did move; and others said again that the Earth stood still and the Sun did move; some counted more stars than others; some discovered new stars never seen before; some fell into a great dispute with others concerning the bigness of the Stars, some said the Moon was another World like their Terrestrial Globe and the spots therein were Hills and Valleys; but others would have the spots to be the Terrestrial parts and the smooth and glossie parts the Sea.[24]

The resulting impression is of a jumble of conflicting opinions, most of which seem simply absurd.

In addition to representing contemporary scientific opinion as ridiculous and contradictory, *Blazing World* exposes what Cavendish sees as the futility of much philosophical speculation, and the sheer impracticality of much scientific investigation. For example, her Empress quizzes the experimental scientists (the bear-men) about the composition of the universe and various natural phenomena like wind, tides, snow, and thunder. The bear-men are unable to offer any cogent explanation, so the Empress makes the very practical suggestion that they use their telescopes to observe the sky.[25] But they cannot agree on what they see. Their telescopes having proved useless, she orders them to break them, whereupon the experimenters admit that all their endeavors were solely for the purpose of having arguments with one another and not for any practical purpose. They admit, in fact, that they are fools:

> The Bear-men, being exceedingly troubled at her Majesty's displeasure concerning their Telescopes, kneel'd down and in humblest manner petitioned that they might not be broken; "for", said they, "we take more delight in Artificial delusions than in natural truths. Besides, we shall want employments for our senses and subjects for arguments; for were there nothing but truth and no falsehood, there would be no occasion for to dispute, and by this means we should want the aim and pleasure of our endeavours in confuting and contradicting each other; neither would one man be thought wiser than another, but all would either be alike knowing and wise, or all would be fools, wherefore we most humbly beseech your imperial Majesty to spare our Glasses, which are our only delight, and as dear to us as our lives."[26]

Cavendish's satire on contemporary thought does not mean that the intellectual world did not interest her. Apart from the amount of space given over to hearing from the various "virtuosi," her debates with the worm-men, fish-men, bear-men, and others are an opportunity for the Empress to speak her own mind on a number of the topics discussed, not simply opportunities for skeptical comments on the irrelevance or contradictoriness of the doctrines propounded. And, indeed, although Cavendish satirizes contemporary philosophy and science for its muddled pointlessness, she does, in the end, show the experimentalists (bird-men, bear-men, fish-men, and worm-men) in a better light, applying their knowledge to practical ends during the war conducted to rescue the Duchess's native country. This group of virtuosi are the astronomers, natural scientists, and experimental scientists—that is, representatives of new thinking. The alchemists, scholastic logicians, Galenic physicians are conspicuous by their absence. Caricatures of contemporary scientific theory form a backdrop against which her own "singular" theories appear less

absurd—as we have already observed, on several occasions it is a
Cavendish theory that is put forward as the most "rational" explanation of the phenomenon under discussion. However, it is by
no means always the case that a "Cavendish opinion" wins the
debate—for example the fish-men's explanation of tides and cur-
rents in the sea is *not* the one propounded in *Observations*. Besides, there is an element of self-satire in Cavendish's presentation of her fictional persona. Unashamedly egocentric, the
fictional duchess is introduced to the heroine as "not one of the
most learned, eloquent, witty and ingenious" of women. When
asked "whether she could write," the Duchess's soul replies in the
affirmative, with the qualification, "but not so intelligibly that
any reader whatsoever may understand it," noting that the spirit
which recommended her to the Empress "is ignorant of my handwriting."[27]

Where *Observations on Experimental Philosophy* aims to provide a serious critique of contemporary natural philosophy, its
companion piece, *Blazing World,* contains much that defies us to
take it seriously. Cavendish presents it as a work of fiction, a
fantasy so light that you don't have to give it a second thought.
The prologue to the reader invites us to treat it as a mere whimsy,
"a Piece of Fancy." And, as she reminds her reader, "the end of
Fancy is Fiction," and fiction needs no basis in reality:

> Fictions are an issue of man's Fancy, framed in his own Mind accord-
> ing as he pleases, without regard, whether the thing he fancies be
> really existent without his mind or not.[28]

LUCIAN OF SAMOSATA

In spite of the fact that the scientific content of *Blazing World*
suggests an affinity with Bacon's *New Atlantis,* the satirical element in *Blazing World* sets it apart from *New Atlantis,* which is
devoted to a serious picture of Bacon's scientific program in action. In respect of its satirical element, Cavendish's text recalls
More's *Utopia.* However, as a satire on scientific ideas and practices, *Blazing World* has no precedent in More's fiction. And the
miscellany of animal-like inhabitants with which the Blazing
World is peopled has no parallel among either the citizens of
Utopia or of Bensalem. Rather, they anticipate the creatures

from *Gulliver's Travels.* For a generic precedent to Cavendish's story, we must look beyond Bacon and More, to a figure on whom More himself drew, Lucian of Samosata. It is Margaret Cavendish who gives us a clue as to the satirical pedigree for her story. At the beginining of her narrative she makes two pointed disclaimers. Her story, she says, "is a description of a New World, not such as Lucian's or the French-man's World in the Moon, but a world of my own Creating, which I call the Blazing-World."[29] The second of these, "the Frenchman's World in the moon," is a direct allusion to Cyrano de Bergerac's *Histoire comique contenant les États et Empires de la lune* (*Comical Story about the Empire of the Moon*) which was published in French in 1657. The first reference is to the classical satirist, Lucian of Samosata, whose extensive repertoire of tales includes two cast as imaginary voyages to other worlds, *Ikaromenippos, or the Sky Man* and *A True Relation* (or, in the Loeb translation, *A True Story;* Latin, *Vera historia*). Both Lucian and Cyrano specialized in fiction that pokes fun at contemporary philosophical and scientific ideas. The attraction of Lucian in the Renaissance and seventeenth century derived in large measure form his tantalizing mixture of nonsense and gravity (*joco-serium*).[30] For this reason Lucianic dialogues had tremendous appeal, not simply for their entertainment value but also as a vehicle for expressing novel, heterodox, and even dangerous ideas.[31] The Lucianic blend of seriousness and comedy underlies both Cyrano's *Histoire comique* and More's *Utopia:* and it is Lucian's special brand of intellectual satire-cum-science-fiction that matches *Blazing World* most exactly.

Cavendish's knowledge of Lucian must have included *A True Relation* and *Ikaromenippus.* Her knowledge of Lucian may well have extended beyond these two dialogues, for instance to *Philosophers for Sale* or *The Fisherman.* The title of *Blazing World* is itself an allusion to the "world of lights" encountered in *A True Relation* and referred to later in Cavendish's story. These direct pointers to Lucian alert her readers to the Lucianic mold of her story, evident also in her use of the fantastic journey and her ridicule of learned opinion. In particular, the way in which she sets about this recalls Lucian. Although his tales purport to have the serious intention of laying bare truth, Lucian's fantasy worlds, like Cavendish's, have a carnivalesque quality. Where the Empress encounters bear-men, fish-men, parrot-men, worm-men, and the like, so also Lucian's travellers also encounter fantastical creatures, such as the flea-archers of *A True Story*. She criticizes the microscopists and telescopists most effectively by lampooning them, so that in her account optical enhancement offered by their instruments becomes grotesque visual distortion: such an insignificant and despicable creature as a fly or a louse becomes "a strange and miraculous Creature," if not a monster, while the whale defies inspection ("alas the shape of the whale was so big that its circumference went beyond the magnifying quality of the Glass . . ."),[31] but when viewed in reverse, it appeared "no bigger than a sprat." The crowning absurdity is the bear-men's attempt to detect a vacuum with the help of their "glasses"—"they could by no means contrive such glasses by the help of which they could spy out a *Vacuum*."[33] A further dimension to this joke is that Cavendish herself denied the existence of a vacuum.

Cavendish's technique of selecting from a wide range of scientific and philosophical opinions may be compared to the method Lucian claims to follow in another dialogue, *The Dead Come to Life, or the Fisherman*. In this tale, the protagonist, named Frankness, defends himself against the charge that he has insulted the philosophers, by saying that he took his opinions from them, "Culling them like a bee, I make a show with them before men who applaud and recognise where and from whom and how I gathered each flower."[34] So also with Cavendish, part of the fun derives from recognizing the snippets of theory she has her Empress and the virtuosi expound. But, of course, in Cavendish's story, as in Lucian's, the game is not simply one of source-spotting, but of exploding the authorities cited. As Plato comments to Frankness, "you got your shafts from us as you admit, and then turned them against us."[35] Cavendish's method of poking fun at learned opinion by a combination of reduction and intermixture, which I have already described—what might be described as a "sound bite" method of distortion—corresponds exactly to Lucian's satirical method.

In *Blazing World*, Cavendish's heroine shares the curiosity of Lucian's narrator in *Ikaromenippus*, as well as his dissatisfaction with the explanations he is offered. Like the Empress, he has questions about the sun, stars, lightening, thunder, rain, snow,

and hail. Like the Empress, he finds that the experts "contradictory and inconsistent." He despairs of ever discovering the
truth because every view put forward can be countered by another. Furthermore, the experts assert dogmatically opinions
that are at best hypothetical. Zeus himself condemns the philosophers as "lazy, disputatious, vainglorious, quick-tempered, glut-
tonous, addle-pated," and charges them with teaching "insoluble
fallacies."

In his *True Relation,* Lucian takes the stance of a purveyor of
mere fictions, his subject matter being "things which I have neither seen nor had to do with nor learned from others—which in
fact do not exist at all," and he exhorts his reader not to believe
what he writes ("my readers should on no account believe in
them"). Honesty about lying is the central paradox of Lucian's
True Story ("I am not telling a word of the truth").[36] Margaret
Cavendish, as we have already observed, makes plain at the out-
set that *Blazing World* is just a "Piece of Fancy." The effect of this
is, immediately, to reduce to fictions the "scientific" theories of
respectable authorities with which her narrative is littered. By
this technique she immediately adds substance to her contention
in *Observations* and elsewhere that experiments are delusory,
and that "most of these Arts are Fallacies, rather than discoveries of Truth; for sense deludes more then it gives a true information."[37] Of course, this also reduces opinions that may be identified as Cavendish's own to a similar illusory nostrums. It is not
the case that Cavendish's own opinions stand out as sensible
against a farrago of nonsense. They are blended into the same
burlesque mix, so that, within the boundaries of the tale, it is
impossible to form a clear idea of where the author stands. This is
a Lucianic technique and it is compounded by yet another feature
of the Lucianic narrative, namely the elusiveness of the authorial
voice. For Lucian constructs one or more persona for the author
that makes it difficult to attribute to him the views expressed in
the narrative. So also with *Blazing World,* Cavendish supplies
two separate figures who may be identified with her real life self:
the Empress and the Duchess, the latter character named after
herself. And, as I have already noted some identifiably Cavendish views are put into the mouths of virtuosi. We should, moreover, be alive to the fact that Cavendish does not confine the

technique of adopting a mask of irony to her fiction, but that she employs it elsewhere—most obviously in her famous self-deprecating remarks:

> [I]f I err, I ask their pardon, and pray them to consider the Nature of our sex, which makes us, for the most part, obstinate and wilful in our opinions, and most commonly impertinently foolish.[38]

Since the marginalization of Lucian during the nineteenth-century redrawing of the classical canon, it is easy to forget that he was one of the most widely translated and imitated Greek authors from the Renaissance until the nineteenth century.[39] Margaret Cavendish may have been directed to Lucian through her reading of Ben Jonson.[40] She may have read the English translation by Thomas Hickes,[41] but she may also have encountered Lucian in French translation during her exile in Paris.[42] It was here in 1654 that Perrot d'Ablancourt published his translation that was to set the mould for Restoration England.[43] The Lucian of French taste was to influence Dryden's view into the next century. To Dryden, Lucian was "the Philosopher, and eminent Sophist," renowned for his wit, a moralist who set out "to expose the Mock Philosophers," and whose wit "was full of Urbanity, *Attic* salt which the French call fine Raillery; not obscene, not gross, not rude, but facetious, well-Mannered and well bred."[44] So also with Cavendish—in exploding contemporary scientific and philosophical theories, she is jocular, occasionally acerbic, but never harsh. Her caricatures of contemporary schools of thought may be grotesque but they are never gross. Hers is an urbane and elegant satire, that lampoons but does not excoriate—an example of what Perrot d'Ablancourt called "la bonne Raillerie," which mocks without wounding ("raille sans blesser") thereby demonstrating "une bonne naissance . . . nourrie dans les belles conversations."[45]

It has been suggested that Cavendish's natural philosophy should be understood in the context of seventeenth-century skepticism.[46] However, I would argue that *Blazing World* is not so much skeptical as Lucianic. This does of course entail a measure of skepticism about the authority and truth-value of philosophical and scientific opinion. But this is less an echo of Pyrrho or Sextus

Empiricus, so much as of the irreverent, elusive, but jocular voice of Lucian. Arguably, the final paradox of Cavendish's fantastical fiction is that it has made her a victim of her own success. So successful was she in exploding the serious pretensions of natural philosophers that she undermined her own claims for serious attention. Unless we recognize the Lucianic strategies deployed, we are in danger of taking it at Pepys's valuation of Margaret the first, namely "mad, conceited and ridiculous."[47]

NOTES

1. *The Diary of Samuel Pepys,* ed. R. Latham, 11 vols. (London: Bell, 1970–83), 9:123. The women among her contemporaries were no more charitable: Katherine Jones, Lady Ranelagh anticipates Pepys when she tells her brother, that Cavendish "scapes Bedlam onely by being to rich to be sent theather" (Katherine Ranelagh to Richard Boyle 13th April 1667, B. L. Althorp Papers B4). For the reaction of Mary Evelyn, see Francis Harris, "Living in the Neighbourhood of Science: Mary Evelyn, Margaret Cavendish and the Greshamites," in *Women, Science and Medicine,* ed. Lynette Hunter, and Sarah Hutton (Stroud: Alan Sutton, 1997): 198–217.

2. An extreme example is G. D. Meyer's chapter, "The Fantastic Duchess of Newcastle" in his *The Scientific Lady in England, 1650–1760* (Berkeley: University of California Press, 1955), where she is described as "too extravagant to be epitomised as the first scientific Lady" (2). For a contrasting view, see L. T. Sarasohn, "A Science Turned Upside Down: Feminism and the Natural Philosophy of Margaret Cavendish," *Huntington Library Quarterly* 47 (1984): 289–307, and my "Anne Conway, Margaret Cavendish and Seventeenth-Century Scientific Thought," *Women, Science and Medicine,* eds. Hunter and Hutton, 218–34; Anna Battigelli, *Margaret Cavendish and the Exiles of the Mind* (Lexington: University Press of Kentucky, 1998).

3. On Margaret Cavendish's visit to the Royal Society, see S. Mintz, "The Duchess of Newcastle's Visit to the Royal Society," *Journal of English and Germanic Philology* 51 (1952): 168–76.

4. Although presented as a second edition of her *Philosophical and Physical Opinions* (printed in 1655), *Observations* differs significantly from that work, both in presentation and in content. A modern edition by Eileen O'Neill was recently published (Cambridge: Cambridge University Press, 2001).

5. "The Table of all the Principle Subjects Contained and Discoursed in this Book," *Observations upon Experimental Philosophy* (London, 1666), no pagination.

6. Ibid., 135.

7. Ibid., 6.

8. Ibid., "Further Observations," 3–4. "Further Observations" is a separately paginated section of *Observations*.

9. Ibid., 6.

10. Ibid., "Further Observations," 4.

11. Robert Hooke, *Micrographia or Some Physiological Descriptions of Minute Bodies Made by Magnifying Glasses with Observations and Enquiries thereupon* (London, 1665).

12. *Observations*, sig. C2.

13. Ibid., 154.

14. *The Description of a New World Called the Blazing World* (London, 1666), 19–20. For a modern edition, see *An Anthology of Seventeenth-Century Fiction*, ed. Paul Salzman (Oxford: Oxford University Press, 1991).

15. *Observations*, 154.

16. Ibid., 6.

17. On Margaret Cavendish and Hobbes, see my "In Dialogue with Thomas Hobbes: Margaret Cavendish's Natural Philosophy," in *Women's Writing* 4 (1997): 421–32. On Cavendish's critique of contemporary philosophy, see Susan James, "The Innovations of Margaret Cavendish," *The British Journal for the History of Philosophy* 7 (1999): 219–44.

18. For further discussion, see my "Margaret Cavendish and Henry More," *A Princely Brave Woman*, ed. Stephen Clucas (forthcoming).

19. *Blazing World*, in *An Anthology of Seventeenth-Century Fiction*, respectively 273, 267, 266, 295, 269–71, 286.

20. Line Cottegnies points out some of the parallels with Bacon in the notes to her French translation of *Blazing World—Le Monde Glorieux*, trans. and postface by Line Cottegnies (Paris: José Corti, 1999).

21. *An Anthology of Seventeenth-Century Fiction*, 341.

22. *Blazing World* (1666), 45.

23. Ibid., sig. b*[2].

24. Ibid., 26. Controversy about the lunar landscape was sparked by Galileo's telescopic observations, recounted in his *Sidereus Nuncius* (1610) The reference to the moon as "another world" is probably to John Wilkins, *The Discovery of a New World in the Moon* (London, 1640) and Francis Godwin, *The Man in the Moone* (London, 1638). Also Cyrano de Bergerac *Histoire comique contenant les États et empires de la lune* (Paris, 1657), which draws on Godwin. Godwin, like William Gilbert (*De mundo nostro sublunari philosophia nova*, 1651) and Johannes Kepler (*Somnium sive astronomia lunaris*, published 1634, written before 1609) explains the the dark areas as land and bright areas as water. For an overview see M. H. Nicolson, *A World in the Moon. A Study of the Changing Attitude towards the Moon in the Seventeenth and Eighteenth Centuries* (Northampton, Mass.: Smith College Studies in Modern Languages, 1936); Nicolson, *Voyages to the Moon* (New York: Macmillan, 1960) and S. Dick, *Plurality of Worlds: The Extra-Terrestrial Life Debate from Democritus to Kant* (Cambridge: Cambridge University Press, 1982).

25. *Blazing World*, 26–27.

26. Ibid., 28. There is, incidentally, more than an element of tongue-in-cheek

here. Margaret's husband, William Cavendish, Duke of Newcastle, was an expert on optics and particularly interested in developing telescopes for military purposes. In fact, the next appearance of the bear-men and their telescopes is in the episode at the end of the story, where we find the bear-men putting their telescopes to practical use during the Empress's military campaign to rescue her home country.

27. Ibid., 89–90.

28. Ibid., sig. b*[2].

29. Ibid., .sig. b*[3].

30. Many of the adjectives used to describe Lucian fit Cavendish's *New Blazing World* almost exactly—Duncan, for example talks of Lucian's "intellectual play, teasing impersonality, a glittering and superficial virtuosity" which "resist analysis in formal neo-Aristotelian terms" (11 and 15). Donald Duncan, *Ben Jonson and the Lucianic Tradition* (Cambridge: Cambridge University Press, 1979).

31. See Letizia Panizza, "The Semantic Field of "paradox" in 16th and 17th Century Italy from Truth in Appearance False to Falsehood in Appearance True. A Preliminary Investigation," in *Il Vocabolario della République des Lettres,* ed. M. Fattori (Florence: Olschki, 1997), 197–220.

32. *Blazing World,* 32.

33. Ibid., 33

34. *The Dead Come to Life, or the Fisherman,* 6. All quotations from Lucian are taken from the Loeb Classical Library edition, *Lucian with an English translation,* ed. A.M. Harmon (London: Heineman; New York: Macmillan, 1913).

35. Ibid., 7.

36. *A True Story,* 1.4.

37. *Observations,* sig. d.

38. Ibid., 12

39. See Duncan, *Ben Jonson.* Also C. Robinson, *Lucian and his Influence* (London: Duckworth, 1979). For Lucian in the sixteenth and seventeenth centuries, see Letizia Panizza, "Lucian and the *volgare* Translations and Transformations," in *Lucianus vivus et redivivus,* eds. C. Ligota and L. Panizza (forthcoming).

40. Duncan, *Ben Jonson* and Robinson, *Lucian.* A voyage to the moon, for instance, is a motif in three of Jonson's masques, *News from the New World Discovered in the Moon, Icaromenippus,* and *Lovers Made Men.*

41. *Certaine select dialogues of Lucian, together with his true historie* (Oxford, 1634). Another translation, *Part of Lucian made English,* by Jasper Mayne, was printed in 1664.

42. *Lucien de la traduction de N. Perrot, Sr d'Ablancourt* (Paris, 1654).

43. Duncan, *Ben Jonson,* 183.

44. John Dryden, *The Life of Lucian,* published in *The Works of Lucian* (London, 1711), printed in *The Works of John Dryden,* general editor A. Roper (Berkeley, Los Angeles, and London: University of California Press, 1989), 20:209 and 220.

45. On Perrot d'Ablancourt, see E. Bury, "Un sophiste impérial à l'Academie. Lucien en France au XVIIe siècle," in *Lucianus vivus,* eds. Ligota and Panizza (forthcoming).

46. Lisa T. Sarasohn, "A Science Turned upside down." On the rise of skepticism in this period, see R.H. Popkin, *The History of Scepticism from Erasmus to Spinoza* (rev. ed., Berkeley: University of California Press, 1979).

47. *The Diary of Samuel Pepys,* ed. Robert Latham, and William Matthews, 11 vols. (London: G. Bell and Sons, 1974), 9:123.

NB: A version of this paper was given at the Margaret Cavendish Conference in Paris in 1999. I am grateful to Line Cottegnies for the opportunity to speak at the conference.

Fantastic Realism: Margaret Cavendish and the Possibilities of Drama

ALEXANDRA G. BENNETT

> Theater may also be understood as a symptomatic cultural site that ruthlessly maps out normative spectatorial positions by occluding its own means of production. And yet—any set of seemingly rigid positions is available for revision. Conservative and patriarchal, the theater is also, in a complex sense, the place of play.
>
> —Elin Diamond[1]

OVER THE PAST FIFTEEN YEARS, THE PLAYS OF MARGARET CAVENDISH have undergone a renaissance in reception, both within the scholarly community and in actual performance, though we know of no staged spectacles during Cavendish's own lifetime.[2] Yet while they have been celebrated for their imaginative freedom, they have also been criticized for being "structurally incoherent."[3] This harsh assessment posits an absence of narrative or character continuity as well as a failure to adhere to the dictates of neoclassical aesthetics (a value system set out most clearly in Horace's *Ars Poetica,* which Thomas Drant had translated into English in 1567), in which the unities of time, place, and action accompany the ideals of appropriateness and decorum.[4] Linda Payne, Sophie Tomlinson, Susan Wiseman, Gweno Williams, and others have argued persuasively that Cavendish is engaged in another kind of project in writing plays intended primarily for the theater of her own imagination, unbound by the cruel necessities of embodied action or stylistic convention as the expectations of previous generations of readers anticipated.[5] Yet some consideration of those stylistic conventions may provide a framework for exploring the uses to which Cavendish put her explicit decision to write *plays* in particular rather than, or in addition to, letters, poems, and other prose works.

Far from being a result of simple or mere technical ineptitude (as early-twentieth-century critics such as Henry Ten Eyck Perry and Douglas Grant posit), the lack of unity in the plot construc-tions of her dramas is a result of a deliberate, conscious choice.[6] Rather than working from older models or in traditional modes, Cavendish deliberately employs both the mimetic practice and the mutable promise of the dramatic form, elements that permit an episodic or scenic approach to contemporary life. Conse-quently, her depictions of gender, agency, and conduct in these plays demonstrate that she was not wholly concerned with the notions of either class or gender as necessarily definable mono-lithic categories that must and do maintain particular, consistent characteristics. Rather, what seems to interest her in her drama, as in her own public conduct, is the wide range and variety of behavior employable by unique, separable individuals set against certain societal expectations. An exploration of the aes-thetic claims she makes in the many "Prologue[s] to the Readers" that frame her plays, along with contextual readings of two of her diverse dramatic works (*Bell in Campo* [1662] and *The Sociable Companions* [1668]), will demonstrate some of the ways in which the potentially fragmentary nature of drama itself allowed the duchess to intertwine the legendary fantasy of her imagination with contemporary reality, providing a series of snapshots of seventeenth-century life and the possibilities of agency therein.

In the poem "A General Prologue to all my Playes" which pref-aces the plays in her first folio, Cavendish makes what looks like a conventional disclaimer of the quality of the works that follow, warning "[n]oble Readers, do not think my Playes, / Are such as have been writ in former daies; / As *Johnson, Shakespear, Beau-mont, Fletcher* writ."[7] Her mention of these Renaissance authors is neither simple self-effacement nor remembrance of a pre-Revolutionary golden age, for it draws particular attention to her use of an anthology publication format (large, elaborate, impres-sive, and expensive folio printing) previously used in drama only to immortalize the collected works of established and popular writers such as these men.[8] Moreover, this passage, along with the ten prefatory epistles to the readers of her plays, demons-trates her familiarity with the details of their works, particularly with those of Jonson. Her husband, the duke of Newcastle, had been a patron of Jonson's before the Civil War and had himself composed several plays in imitation of his "comedy of humors"; given her adoration of Newcastle and admiration for Jonson, it would not be surprising for her own works to emulate theirs.

Unlike her husband, however, Cavendish boldly claims all responsibility and credit for her writing in her prefatory material, making the extent of her own individual agency explicit. Later in the "General Prologue," she announces:

> All my Playes Plots, my own poor brain did make;
> From *Plutarchs* story I ne'r took a Plot,
> Nor from Romances, nor from *Don Quixot,*
> As others have, for to assist their Wit,
> But I upon my own Foundation writ.[9]

She deliberately disdains the practice of borrowing either subject material or literary style from previous writers in this passage. Moreover, she mentions Jonson by name precisely to indicate that she does not follow him, however much she may admire his works.[10] Though it is entirely possible that Jonson influenced her through his patronal and compositional connections with William Cavendish, the Duchess refused to become a slavish adherent to his dramatic principles, or to those of any other playwright. In the epistle to the readers that prefaces her second volume of dramatic works, she remarks: "When I call this new one, *Plays,* I do not believe to have given it a very proper Title: for it would be too great a fondness to my Works to think such Plays as these suitable to ancient Rules, in which I pretend no skill; or agreeable to the modern Humor, to which I dare acknowledg my aversion."[11]

She reinforces her resistance to the idea of following a set pattern elsewhere in her preliminary epistles. While she claims to be all in favor of the idea that "Playes are to present the general Follies, Vanities, Vices, Humours, Dispositions, Passions, Affections, Fashions, Customs, Manners, and practices of the whole World of Mankind,"[12] she is much more interested in the point that these aspects of human nature are to be expressed through "several" or "particular persons."[13] In repeating the reference to specific individuals no fewer than five times in the same sentence, she privileges the importance of distinctive characters over that of the traits they apparently represent, rewriting dramatic theory in order to suit her project.[14] Later in the same epistle, she anticipates precisely the kinds of objections that critics have since raised about her plays; in answer to the charge that they do not follow the unities of time, place, and action, she writes:

> [F]or though Ben Johnson as I have heard was of that opinion, that a Comedy cannot be good, nor is a natural or true Comedy, if it should present more than one dayes action, yet his Comedies that he hath published, could never be the actions of one day; for could any rational person think that the whole Play of the Fox could be the action of one day? or can any rational person think that the whole Play of the Alchymist could be the action of one day?[15]

Jonson may well have claimed that the classical rules of the unities should be maintained in order to produce "true" comedy, but his practices are far from his preaching, Cavendish argues. She, on the other hand, will not lay claim to ideals that her writing cannot or will not support. Subsequent objections to her plays on these neoclassical grounds, therefore, have misinterpreted the literary goals she has set out for herself and her readers—in fact, these are the very grounds *against* which she defines her work. Since these expectations are unrealistic, "neither Usual, Probable, nor Natural," and hardly conducive to presenting "natural dispositions and practices," the artificial constraints they impose are inimical to her ideas.[16] The mimetic possibilities afforded by drama as a genre, then, are what draw Cavendish to write plays, and what she intends to exploit in their composition.

Linda Payne has argued that Cavendish's rejection of the predetermined rules of theatrical composition implies a rejection of masculine boundaries and an embracing of "fancy" as a realm of female literary endeavor: "[t]he Duchess, not finding her dreams flesh, could at least give them substance on paper."[17] This interpretation celebrates Cavendish's endless inventiveness, though it also seems to suit the image of "Mad Madge" as a scribbler prone to imaginative excess; looking at the duchess's project as a mimetic presentation of ideas in accordance with the progression of actual events and the nature of the world around her allows us

to read her works in a slightly different way. What might appear
to be unrelated plotlines become richly indicative of the complex-
ities in which Cavendish is interested. Moreover, this generic
flexibility also gives Cavendish the room or potential to imagine
change in the world she depicts rather than limiting herself to
imitating what she sees. Elin Diamond, in arguing for a "feminist
mimesis," remarks that such a practice "would take the relation
to the real as productive, not referential, geared to change, not to
reproducing the same"; Cavendish's dramatic works engage in
precisely this process.[18] While the idea of universal traits, abilities, or ideals is deliberately countered in her intermingling of
diverse situations, each of which brings out different dimensions
in the others that make up a given play, she is also able to depict
forms of agency denied to individual women in her cultural environment. Consequently, her drama is a powerful intermixture
of reality and fantasy: her imaginative resolution of concrete situations departs from mirroring social mores exactly, while her
ultimate grounding in "the World" implies that "fancy" is not
quite sufficient as an all-encompassing literary category for what
she is trying to achieve. She may allege that all of her characters
and scenes are simply from her own mind and for her own amuse-
ment ("Sometime for want of work, I'm forced to play, / And idly to
cast my time away," she claims),[19] but this representation of her
efforts may also be a self-deprecating shield for the more radical
aspects of her work.

Though her dramatic writings are hugely diverse in their set-
tings, subject matter, and theatrical approaches, two examples
give us a glimpse into some of the ways in which Cavendish
employs dramatic genres for her own purposes. In *Bell in Campo*
(published in two parts in her 1662 folio collection), she sets out a
central plot in which the remarkable achievements of Lady Victoria (wife of a noble general) and her adherents are presented as
admirable configurations of female ability, nobility, and courage.
The women follow their husbands to war, create their own army,
and ultimately rescue the men from imminent peril. However,
readings of *Bell in Campo* as "a utopian fantasy"[20] may risk
overlooking the historical and political contexts of the play,
which show that the characters here are not entirely imaginary. I
have argued elsewhere that Cavendish was not short of live and
literary materials on which to base her characters and their ac-

tions, and the circumstances in which they find themselves, including the reality of losing husbands, brothers, and friends in battle, were probably drawn from actual events on both sides of the Channel.[21] The ultimate triumph of Lady Victoria's forces can certainly be read as the author's mimetic engagement with the military causes and environments that so affected her own life; however, there are also several subplots and tangents in *Bell in Campo* that add crucial dimensions to the course of the main plot. The rewards that the women of the "Amazonian Army"[22] ultimately attain are not necessarily universally applied, and women are subjected to far more trials than those the female soldiers undergo. Not all of the women in the play decide to accompany their spouses abroad: Madam Jantil (whose name suggests the aristocratic virtue of gentility) and Madam Passionate reluctantly stay behind and are ultimately widowed by the war. With their husbands newly dead, these women are left similarly wealthy, and importunate and indigent suitors subsequently besiege them as the latest and most valuable entries on the marriage market. The means each of them chooses to employ in handling this difficult situation provide contrasting contexts, both fantastic and realistic, for the military main plot.

Jantil manages to avoid falling victim to the rapacity of the men vying for her attention only by retiring utterly from the world. Possessed of an incredible fortune, she not only provides handsomely for all of her household servants upon her husband's demise, but gives detailed instructions for building a secluded cloister around her husband's tomb, a monument unbelievable in its lavish opulence:

> First I will have a marble piece raised from the ground about half a mans height or something more, and something longer than my Husbands dead body, and then my Husbands Image Carved out of Marble to be laid thereupon . . . also let there be two Statues, one for *Mercury,* and another for *Pallas,* these two Statues to stand at his head . . . on the right side of his figure, let there be a Statue for *Mars* . . . and on the left hand a Statue for *Hymen* . . . and at the feet of the figure let there be placed a Statue for *Fortune* also.[23]

Her page-and-a-half-long discourse enumerating precisely how many pillars, symbols, statues (including the stances in which they should be carved), and portraits are to appear in this fabulous mausoleum is fantastic in the extreme: no widow of the seventeenth-century English or Continental wars would have been able to afford either to build such a structure or to shut herself up in it until her own death as Jantil does. Intriguingly, Cavendish immediately proceeds to undercut this imaginary extravagance, for Jantil's servant inquires, "It shall be done, but why will not your Ladyship have my Lords figure cast in brass?" From out of the romanticized and wholly irrational portrayal of her idealized grief comes Jantil's answer: "Because the Wars ruin Tombs before Time doth, and metals being useful therein are often taken away by necessity, and we seldome see any ancient Monuments but what are made of Stone, for covetousness is apt to rob Monuments of metal, committing Sacrilege on the dead, for metals are soonest melted into profit."[24] Even a perfect display of mourning cannot remain untouched by the brutal realities of a country at war, though the idealized nature of her conduct appears far removed from actual practices.

Yet Jantil's self-confinement in her monastic quarters can also be seen not simply as the expression of her excessive devotion to her dead spouse, but as a means of evading the depredations of the living for one as young and potentially vulnerable as she is. By contrast, her fellow widow Madam Passionate does not take this path, and suffers as a consequence. In concordance with her name, she initially appears to outdo Jantil in venting her grief, fainting over and over again in between bouts of hysterics, yet eventually she recovers enough to take comfort in having her breakfast in bed and makes arrangements to sell her husband's goods at auction, realizing that "the World esteems and respects nothing so much as riches."[25] Not surprisingly, no fewer than three wooers accost her, each man interested only in her money as a means to ease and social advancement. Eventually, Passionate marries her youngest and most flattering suitor, who immediately dispossesses her of power, money, and belongings. She arrives onstage near the end of the play to bemoan her loss of control over herself, her servants, and her estate:

[A]ll my Servants slight and neglect me, following those that command the purse, for this idle young fellow which I have married first seized on all my goods, then let Leases for many lives out of my Lands, for which he had great fines, and now he cuts down all my Woods, and sells all my Lands of Inheritance, which I foolishly and fondly delivered by deed of gift, the first day I married, devesting myself of all power, which power had I kept in my own hands I might have been used better, whereas now when he comes home drunk, he swears and storms, and kicks me out of my warm Bed, and makes me sit shivering and shaking in the Cold, whilst my Maid takes my place.[26]

This is a remarkable contrast to the fates of those women who follow their husbands to battle and win such glory in the field, or who can afford to hide themselves entirely from the world. In handing over all of her property to her new husband, Passionate has left herself entirely subject to his will and protection or lack thereof. Her fate consequently sheds an interesting light on the list of decrees that ends *Bell in Campo*. As a reward for the achievements of the warrior women, "a blank for the Female Army to write their designs and demands" is issued, on which those women list eleven stipulations, beginning with "[t]hat all women shall hereafter in this Kingdome be Mistriss in their own Houses and Families" and ending with "[t]hat they shall be of their Husbands Counsel."[27]

S. Wiseman remarks that "they articulate demands for domestic autonomy which seem petty in comparison to the great triumphs of the Lady Victoria."[28] Cavendish's deliberate juxtaposition of the Jantil and Passionate subplots and intermingling of their fates with those of Lady Victoria and her army makes it clear that she uses these contrasts to examine the nature and effects of different forms of agency. Once Lady Victoria and her followers have given up their prerogatives to their husbands in the male army, after all, they too might find themselves in Passionate's position, with all the trappings of glory and position but no authority behind them. The case of an individual bereft of independence is, as Passionate shows, a miserable one, and the only way to prevent that particular case from becoming widespread is to insist publicly upon the conferral of power upon women in the spheres to which they will return once the tumultuous era of war is over. Some women, Cavendish shows us, get an opportunity to act in the theater of war, but those who do not must find other ways of asserting themselves or risk losing everything they may have. An unequivocal standard of female or noble conduct, a single vision of the category "woman" or "aristocrat," does not and indeed cannot exist, even within the world of a play; but a play-world can provide the opportunity for some women to take control over their own destinies in new ways.

The mutable environment created by the dramatic form provides an ideal setting for Cavendish's later comic satire, *The Sociable Companions, or The Female Wits* (1668). Like *Bell in Campo, The Sociable Companions* showcases the potential for female agency within a variety of contemporary circumstances, but it is also more overt in its deliberate thwarting of generic conventions. Set at the close of the Civil War, the male characters (Captain Valour, Will Fullwit, and Harry Sencible) learn that the royal army has been cashiered and, long bereft of their estates and family wealth, console themselves with each others' company and long drinking sessions in London's taverns. Frustrated by their poverty and relative powerlessness in the postwar marriage market, their sisters Peg, Jane, and Anne decide to take matters into their own hands and find their own wealthy husbands. Enlisting the aid of the older gossip Mistress Informer, they determine that the wealthiest men in town are Get-all, a usurer, Plead-all, a lawyer, and Cure-all, a physician, and devise creative plans to trick each of them into marriage. Their brothers agree to act out their parts in the intrigue, and also dupe the old Lady Riches into marrying their friend Dick Traveller. At the same time, young Mistress Prudence, the wealthy only child of Master Save-all, is inundated by waves of eager young suitors but refuses them all in favor of an old, wise, and wealthy man who woos her for love rather than money. By the play's end, the three sisters happily marry the men of their choosing, and Mistress Prudence joins them after making a public speech to her young suitors defending her selection of a spouse.

Even more than in *Bell in Campo,* the dramatic form here provides ample opportunity for Cavendish to indulge in pointed social commentary.[29] In the opening scene involving the cashiered soldiers, their Colonel bitterly undercuts the standard social values of law and honor (the very things most comedies strive ultimately to uphold in their conclusions) by remarking "there is no such thing as Law, nor no such thing as Honour, but what Man feigns or makes; but the truth is, that which men call Law and Honour, is Power and Force: for the Strongest give Law; and Power makes Honour as it pleases."[30] Immediately afterwards, the women note the hardships they face as a result of their brothers' lack of money, but Mistress Prudence snaps that "[i]f their brothers had been as wise as my Father, not to have been so vain to have show'd their Valour, they might have been so prudent as to have kept their Estates; and so you and they would not have lost your Portions by the folly of your Brothers."[31] The conditions of both plotlines are thereby inextricably entwined and similarly destabilized in the play's first moments: love, honor, and valor are all very well and good, but money makes this new world go around. The play turns audience expectations of comic setting and romantic values upside down to highlight and mirror the disruption of social order brought on by civil war.

However, the very upheaval and destruction of the status quo is precisely what permits the kind of license and inventiveness all of the women show in their various forays into the marriage market. Since the world as they know it has been turned on its head, Peg, Anne, and Jane all employ carnivalesque means to entrap the men who each have contributed to the decay of the landed classes in England. Jane dresses as a clerk to work her way into the affections of Plead-all, and Anne visits Cure-all alone, to be "surprised" there by her brother, who threatens to kill her for her perceived impropriety unless the doctor marries her to save her life and reputation. Most notably, however, Peg sues Get-all in Spiritual Court for the maintenance of a child she claims was begotten through a Platonic "Conjunction of Souls," wherein "the Idea of a Man, by the help of a strong imagination, may beget a Child."[32] Her technique is a striking blend of actuality and absurdity: while it was indeed possible to prosecute the fathers of illegitimate children in English spiritual courts in order to elicit support payments (actual success rates varied widely), her case takes the concept of "Platonic love" to its logical and ludicrous extreme, blatantly mocking the late vogue for Platonism at the royal court. Cavendish thus juxtaposes realism and fantasy within the dramatic form here to maximize the satiric power of her work.

The stereotypical expectations of romantic comedy are also thoroughly undermined through the course of Mistress Prudence's scenes with her many suitors, which are carefully interspersed throughout the play as a reminder to us that as difficult

as the trials of poor women might be, the tribulations of wealthy
young women on the same marriage market are equally taxing.
On the fantastic side of this plot, Prudence is given carte blanche
by her father to choose her spouse herself (an unheard-of concept
for most wealthy heiresses); however, this freedom does not prevent her from having to endure the importunities of virtually
every impecunious single male in the vicinity (a situation all too
likely for wealthy single women immediately after the Interregnum). The wooers who come to plead their cases run the gamut
from romantic idealism (one man offers Prudence nothing but
"Love") to sheer opportunism (one Monsieur Vanity declares that
"I being vain, and you rich, 'twould be very convenient we two
should joyn as Man and Wife, that one might maintain the
other"[33]); not surprisingly, the witty Prudence turns them all
down. Finally, an "ancient Man" comes to call and proves his love
by claiming: "I'le not require any Portion with you, since I am
Rich enough without; Nay, I will not only take you without a
Portion, but make you Mistress of all my Wealth, in so much that
I will freely give you all I am Worth; and I wish I were worth
Millions for your sake."[34] In the postwar environment Cavendish
depicts here, such a profession is the perfect romantic declaration
of true love, and Prudence gladly accepts his hand in marriage.

But the play provides one final twist to the tails of audience
expectations, for the young suitors, outraged at the news of Prudence's choice of an old man over their youth and physical attrac-
tions, demand that she answer for herself in a public forum. Just
as the spectators of a conventional comedy might object to the
resolution of this play, the wooers indignantly "declare the In-
justice and Injury this young Lady has done [them], and her self,
by refusing [they] that are young, handsome, healthy and strong,
for an old, infirm, weak, and decayed Man."[35] In her reply, however, Prudence slams the door defiantly upon their claims to her
affections:

I'le rather chuse an old Man that buys me with his Wealth, then a
young one, whom I must purchase with my Wealth; who, after he has
wasted my Estate, may sell me to Misery and Poverty. Wherefore, our
Sex may well pray, From Young Mens ignorance and follies, from
their pride, vanity and prodigality, their gaming, quarelling, drink-

ing and whoring, their pocky and diseased bodies, their Mortgages, Debts and Serjeants, their Whores and Bastards, and from all such sorts of Vices and Miseries that are frequent amongst Young Men, Good Lord deliver Us.[36]

Only in employing the framework of romantic comedy can Cavendish skewer it so neatly; only in taking advantage of the room for playfulness and apparent illogic in structure that drama provides can she portray and comment upon the real world of her surroundings so effectively. The Duchess's appropriation and manipulation of the dramatic form and rejection of the stylistic manners and conventions of her time enabled her to make use of fragmentary, seemingly disjunctive pieces to craft a remarkably accurate picture of her culture.

Such perceptive portraits of her environment can be found throughout her plays: to give only a few other examples, *The Female Academy* (1662) stages several debates and orations on the intellectual and political rights of women, *The Apocriphal Ladies* (1662) mocks the rise of class-transgressive upstarts at Court during a civil war, and *The Convent of Pleasure* (1668) is a complex depiction and debate over the tribulations of marriage for women.[37] In each case, as in the examples I have discussed here, the play makes use of a potent combination of fantasy and reality to suggest some avenues for female agency. Cavendish thus employs the more radical possibilities for mimetic transformation that drama provides, instead of remaining within the bounds inscribed by her predecessors and codified by later commentators. As she writes in one of her 1662 epistles, "as for the niceties of Rules, Forms, and Terms, I renounce, and protest, that if I did understand and know them strictly, as I do not, I would not follow them: and if any dislike my writings for want of those Rules, Forms, and Terms, let them not read them, for I had rather my writing should be unread than be read by such Pedantical Scholastical Persons."[38] Drama is not only a means for the author to depict the world around her, but, significantly, a way to enter into discourse with and affect that public world through her readers. For the readers posited by her plays are surprisingly specific: evidently wealthy enough to acquire folio books for their libraries (or well-connected enough to borrow a copy from a friend),[39] familiar with prewar plays, and sympathetic to postwar aristocratic concerns. Moreover, they are not only addressed as audience members, the "Spectators" appealed to in the verse prologues and epilogues frequently appended to specific plays, but as performers themselves.[40] Cavendish describes reading not as a solitary or silent activity, but as a form of public enactment: "Scenes," she writes, "must be read as if they were spoke or Acted . . . [W]hen as a Play is well and skillfully read, the very sound of the Voice that enters through the Ears, doth present the Actions to the Eyes of the Fancy as lively as if it were really Acted."[41] To read a play properly, in other words, is to bring it to life. For her pointedly addressed audience to bring her drama to life might thus unlock the individual possibilities for change that these plays so emphatically make apparent and set them free within the real world, unbound by the conventional safety net of theatrical practices. The Duchess herself reveled in her self-proclaimed "singularity;" her plays appropriate and adapt dramatic forms in order to model politically and socially singular conduct.

Margaret Cavendish's drama fulfills a crucial function in the history of women and the theater in England. By the time her first folio was published, the public theaters had been reopened for two years, and actresses had trod the boards professionally for the first time. It was possible to go to Lincoln's Inn Fields or Drury Lane and see women playing female parts, for instance, so the kinds of performativity set forth in her plays might seem to be passé. But her texts remain an important transition in this development, for her vision of readers acting and expanding their roles on the stages of their minds and on the stage of the world extended the powers of shaping self-representation to anyone who cared to read her plays and discover them. Far from fulfilling Virginia Woolf's vision of "those solitary great ladies who wrote without audience or criticism, for their delight alone,"[42] Margaret Cavendish emphasized the public nature and subjects of her personal and literary drama, at once destabilizing extant ideologies of decorum and providing examples of ways in which agency beyond the bounds of gender or class could be wrested from precarious, paradoxical circumstances. Rather than being at odds with the aesthetic values at the core of her chosen genre, then, Cavendish exploits the jarring, disjunctive mimetic possibilities that theater provides to depict and challenge the imaginative and actual worlds in which she lived.

NOTES

1. Elin Diamond, *Unmaking Mimesis* (New York: Routledge, 1997), iii.

2. Gweno Williams produced *The Convent of Pleasure* at the University College of Ripon and York St. John in 1995—see "'Why May Not a Lady Write a Good Play?': Plays by Early Modern Women Reassessed as Performance Texts," in *Readings in Renaissance Women's Drama,* ed. S. P. Cerasano and Marion Wynne-Davies (New York: Routledge, 1998), 95–107, for an account of some of her experiences. In addition, *The Sociable Companions* was performed under its secondary title (*The Female Wits*) for three weeks at the Canal Café Theater, Little Venice, London, in January 1995, and Williams is currently planning a future production of *Bell in Campo.*

3. Nancy Cotton, *Women Playwrights in England, c. 1363–1750* (Lewisburg, Pa.: Bucknell University Press, 1980), 46.

4. See Marvin Carlson, *Theories of the Theater: A Historical and Critical Survey, from the Greeks to the Present* (Ithaca: Cornell University Press, 1984), 24, for a detailed summary of these aesthetic propositions.

5. See Linda R. Payne, "Dramatic Dreamscape: Women's Dreams and Utopian Vision in the Works of Margaret Cavendish, Duchess of Newcastle," in *Curtain Calls: British and American Women and the Theater, 1660–1820,* ed. Mary Anne Schofield, and Cecilia Macheski (Columbus: Ohio State University Press, 1991), 18–33; Sophie Tomlinson, "'My Brain the Stage': Margaret Cavendish and the Fantasy of Female Performance," in *Women, Texts, and Histories 1575–1760,* ed. Clare Brant and Diane Purkiss (London: Routledge, 1992), 134–63; Susan Wiseman, "Gender and Status in Dramatic Discourse: Margaret Cavendish, Duchess of Newcastle," in *Women, Writing, History 1640–1740,* ed. Isobel Grundy and Susan Wiseman (Athens: University of Georgia Press, 1992). 159–230; Williams, "'Why May Not a Lady Write A Good Play?'," passim.

6. See Henry Ten Eyck Perry, *The First Duchess of Newcastle and her Husband as Figures in Literary History* (Boston: Ginn & Company, 1918), and Douglas Grant, *Margaret the First: A Biography of Margaret Cavendish Duchess of Newcastle* (London: Rupert Hart-Davis, 1957). Cavendish makes her own views of the deliberateness of this process clear elsewhere: *"Fancy,"* she proclaims in the prefatory epistle to *Poems and Fancies* (London, 1653), "goeth not so much by the *Rule, & Method,* as by *Choice;* and if I have chosen my *Silke* with *fresh colours,* and *matcht* them in *good Shadows,* although the *stitches* be not very true, yet it will please the Eye; so if my *Writing* please the *Readers,* though not the *Learned,* it wil satisfie me" (sig. A3). Spelling, punctuation, and capitalization in all quotations from Cavendish's works are taken from the originals.

7. Margaret Cavendish, *Playes Written by the Thrice Noble, Illustrious, and Excellent Princess, the Lady Marchioness of Newcastle* (London, 1662), sig. A7v.

8. Jonson's *Works* were first published in 1616, and reprinted in 1631, 1640, and 1641. Shakespeare's first folio appeared in print in 1623, and was reprinted in 1632, while the plays of Beaumont and Fletcher were published as a collection in 1648 and again in 1679. See W. W. Greg, *A Bibliography of the English Printed Drama to the Restoration* (Oxford: Clarendon Press, 1939–1959) for details.

9. Cavendish, *Playes* (1662), sig. A7v.

10. The idea that Cavendish's indicative names for her characters proves that she intends to write in a Jonsonian mode of "humors" is a curious assumption, for a great number of the playwrights of the Restoration, including Wycherley, Etherege, and Behn, did precisely the same thing in creating Horner, Mrs. Loveit, and Willmore, for instance (in *The Country Wife* [1675], *The Man of Mode* [1676], and *The Rover* [1677], respectively). In "'A Woman Write a Play!': Jonsonian Strategies and the Dramatic Writings of Margaret Cavendish; or, Did the Duchess Feel the Anxiety of Influence?," in *Readings in Renaissance Women's Drama*, 293–305, Julie Sanders provides a more complex and intriguing account of some of the interrelations between Cavendish's works and those of Jonson.

11. Cavendish, *Playes* (1662), sig. A4v.

12. This idea is firmly in keeping with neoclassic ideas such as Sidney's defense of poetry as setting out "all virtues, vices, and passions so in their own seats laid to the view, that we seem not to hear of them, but clearly to see through them." See "A Defence of Poetry," in *Miscellaneous Prose of Sir Philip Sidney,* ed. Katherine Duncan-Jones and Jan Van Dorsten (Oxford: Clarendon Press, 1973), 86. A number of Interregnum authors, including Christopher Wase, expressed similar purposes in the prefatory material of their printed plays.

13. Cavendish, *Playes* (1662), sig. A4.

14. Her commentary on Shakespeare in *CCXI Sociable Letters* notably privileges the "Course of Life" and the importance of writing "to the Life" as key elements in her approbation of his style and subject matter (1664, sigs. Hh2v–Hh3).

15. Cavendish, *Playes* (1662), sig. A4v.

16. Ibid., sig. A4, sig. A4v.

17. Payne, "Dramatic Dreamscape," 226.

18. Diamond, *Unmaking Mimesis,* xiv.

19. Cavendish, *Playes* (1662), sig. A7.

20. Erin Lang Bonin, "Margaret Cavendish's Dramatic Utopias and the Politics of Gender," *Studies in English Literature 1500–1900* 40.2 (Spring 2000): 343.

21. See my "Margaret Cavendish and the Theater of War," *In-between* 9 (2000): 263–73.

22. Cavendish, *Playes* (1662), 595.

23. Ibid., 599–600.

24. Ibid., 600.

25. Ibid., 610.

26. Ibid., 626–27.

27. Ibid., 631.

28. Wiseman, "Gender and Status," 174.

29. It is worth noting that Aphra Behn would use a very similar social setting for her comedy *The Rover* (1677); however, Cavendish's social commentary is infinitely more direct here.

30. Margaret Cavendish, *Playes Never Before Printed* (London, 1668), 5.

31. Ibid., 10.

32. Ibid., 65. In actuality, the child is a bastard son sired by Peg's brother, providing yet another pointed juxtaposition of fantasy and reality in this scene.

33. Ibid., 67.

34. Ibid., 69.

35. Ibid., 93.

36. Ibid., 95.

37. Anne Shaver provides detailed analysis and commentary on *The Convent of Pleasure* in both her article "Agency and Marriage in the fictions of Lady Mary Wroth and Margaret Cavendish, Duchess of Newcastle," in *Pilgrimage for Love: Essays in Early Modern Literature in honor of Josephine A. Roberts,* ed. Sigrid King (Tempe: Arizona Centre for Medieval and Renaissance Studies, 1999), 177–190, and her 1999 edition of the text in Margaret Cavendish, *The Convent of Pleasure and Other Plays,* ed. Anne Shaver (Baltimore: Johns Hopkins University Press, 1999).

38. Cavendish, *Playes* (1662), sig. A5v.

39. Though Samuel Pepys notably dismissed Cavendish's 1667 biography of her husband as "ridiculous," his diary shows that he stayed up all night to read a copy a friend had lent to his wife. See *The Diary of Samuel Pepys,* eds. Robert Latham and William Matthews, 11 vols. (London: G. Bell and Sons Ltd.,1974), 9:123.

40. Gweno Williams contends that the plays written by Cavendish and other early modern female dramatists are fully stageable and performable, arguing that "there is now an urgent need for more productions to unlock and realize the dramatic potential of these plays." See "'Why May Not a Lady Write a Good Play?,'" 105. I agree entirely, but wish to note here that the ways in which Cavendish uses the mimetic and mutable aspects of the genre already imply a kind of performativity when combined with early modern oral reading practices.

41. Cavendish, *Playes* (1662), sig. A6v.

42. Virginia Woolf, *A Room of One's Own* (London: Bloomsbury Classics, 1993), 102.

Playing Games with Gender and Genre: the Dramatic Self-Fashioning of Margaret Cavendish

SARA MENDELSON

UNTIL QUITE RECENTLY, THE PLAYS OF MARGARET CAVENDISH were dismissed both by her contemporaries and by modern critics as hopelessly unsuited for the stage. As far as we know, none of Cavendish's dramatic works ever received a single performance, public or private, during her own lifetime. Most modern scholars have echoed the negative judgment of Cavendish's contemporaries, concluding that her plays could not, should not, or (at best) were never intended to be performed.[1] Elaine Hobby, for example, has asserted that Cavendish's plays were not written for the public stage, but instead were meant to be "recited aloud by a reader in the privacy of her (or his) own home . . . a series of possible roles to try out for size."[2] Other scholars of the seventeenth-century stage have concurred, categorizing the bulk of Cavendish's dramatic oeuvre as a species of philosophical closet drama, with perhaps a few potential exceptions that might be adapted to performance if subjected to considerable alterations. Thus, Linda Payne, although reiterating the view that "most of Cavendish's plays were untheatrical," suggested in 1991 that three Cavendish plays—*Loves Adventures, Bell in Campo,* and *The Convent of Pleasure*—might contain the "dramatic elements and liveliness necessary to succeed on stage" with "extensive editing and rearranging of scenes."[3]

In the past few years, a handful of pioneers have begun a movement to reverse this negative assessment of the performance possibilities of Cavendish's dramatic oeuvre. Gweno Williams has analyzed a number of features of Cavendish's plays that indicate that she did indeed intend her plays as performance texts.[4]

Moreover, Williams has proved her case by putting it to the test.
After a successful staging of *The Convent of Pleasure* at the University College of Ripon and York St John in 1995, Williams has
gone on to film substantial parts of recent productions of *The
Lady Contemplation, The Female Academy,* and *Youths Glory
and Deaths Banquet.*[5]

EXPERIMENTS IN GENRE

Whether or not the consensus of scholarly opinion becomes converted to the view that Cavendish's plays were intended for the
public stage and can be adapted successfully to dramatic production, the very existence of such heated controversy over issues of
performance highlights a significant attribute of Cavendish's
dramatic works, her radical and often problematic attitude to
drama as a genre. In this respect, both detractors and admirers of
Cavendish's works are in agreement: her plays are unlike those
of other seventeenth-century authors. For the most part, critics
have focused their censures on the form rather than the substantive content of the plays. Indeed, Cavendish herself proclaimed
that her most blatant sin against contemporary aesthetic precepts was a formal or generic one, her disregard for the classical
unities of Aristotle's *Poetics.* Although Aristotle's authority in
scientific matters had declined considerably by the second half of
the seventeenth century, his *Poetics* was still regarded as the
standard treatise on the canons of literary composition. The *Poetics* strongly influenced neoclassical theorists, defining the
parameters of Restoration drama for those playwrights who
claimed any degree of artistic competence. Thus Dryden's first
major critical work, his essay *Of Dramatic Poesie* (published in
1668, the same year as Cavendish's second volume of plays), was
orthodox in its allegiance to Aristotelian principles of dramatic
structure.

Cavendish's rejection of the three classical unities was just one
aspect of her general penchant for breaking the rules that defined drama as a genre. To modern readers, perhaps even more
alien than her failure to follow Aristotelian canons is her habit of
constructing her plays from isolated plots and subplots that bear
little or no relation to each other within the play's frame of refer-

ence. In *Loves Adventures* (1662), for example, the main plot and subplots are juxtaposed in alternation without connecting links between the different plot elements: each thread is carried on by itself, as if it were alone in the play's universe. As Anne Shaver has commented, "to Cavendish's genre-bound contemporaries," the two subplots of *Loves Adventures* "may have seemed to belong in another play entirely."[6]

Critics have offered a number of explanations for the originality (or what contemporaries deemed the eccentricity) of the generic or structural features of Cavendish's dramatic oeuvre. Some scholars have suggested that the unconventional format of Cavendish's plays was influenced by their composition during the Interregnum, when public theaters in England were closed.[7] Yet while it is likely that Cavendish wrote many of her plays in Antwerp prior to her return to England in 1660, the two printed collections of her dramatic works were published in 1662 and 1668, while the Restoration theater was in full swing, with the exciting innovation of female actors playing female parts. Scholars have shown that Cavendish continually revised her own work, producing altered second editions of many of the texts she had composed during the 1650s.[8] She was also in the habit of collaborating with her husband to enhance the dramatic qualities of her plays.[9] There is no reason to assume she felt bound to publish her plays during the 1660s in what she judged to be an unperformable state.[10]

Others have suggested Cavendish's consciousness of her own lack of skill as an explanation for her disregard for conventional precepts of dramatic structure, citing Cavendish's own self-deprecating assessment of her abilities in her prefatory epistles.[11] For example, in an epistle "To the Readers" which precedes the 1662 *Playes,* Cavendish compares herself to a plain country cook who "cannot dress, or cook after the Fashions and Phancies . . . but as an honest, poor Servant, that rather wanted Art and Skill in my Works, than Will, or Indeavour to make, or dresse them to every Palate." Similarly, in her preface to *Plays Never Before Printed* (1668), Cavendish deprecates her own ability to compose her plays in conformity to the "ancient Rules":

When I call this new one, Plays, I do not believe to have given it a very proper Title: for it would be too great a fondness to my Works to think such Plays as these suitable to ancient Rules, in which I pretend no skill; or agreeable to the modern Humor, to which I dare acknowledg my aversion: But having pleased my Fancy in writing many Dialogues upon several Subjects, and having afterwards order'd them into Acts and Scenes, I will venture, in spight of the Criticks, to call them Plays.[12]

Yet it would be naive to interpret these epistles as artless confessions. Cavendish habitually used the topos of the self-deprecatory preface to emphasize her own originality, and was incensed when her modest protestations were taken at face value by her readers. In the preface to *Orations* (1662), she complained that "those Faults or Imperfections I accuse my self of in my Praefatory Epistles, they fling back with a double strength against my poor harmless Works, which shewes their malice and my truth."[13] Her apparent avowals of her lack of skill should be seen as a rhetorical ploy that enabled her to occupy the moral high ground in her debate with the "carping critics" in her audience.[14] Moreover, a significant function of her prefatory epistles is to inform her readers that she is well acquainted with the "ancient Rules." Thus the prefaces deny what they appear to assert, for they betray a keen and constant awareness of genre on Cavendish's part. Her prefatory matter implies that she has rejected the canons of genre, not because she lacks the knowledge or skill to follow the "ancient Rules," but because she refuses to be constrained by their artificial limitations.

It is worth noting that generic rule-breaking was not limited to Cavendish's plays, but was a feature of her entire literary oeuvre. Throughout her works there are numerous examples of a flexible and unconventional attitude to genre, of sudden shifts from one genre to another or mixtures of different genres within the same work. In her first published book, *Poems and Fancies* (1653), Cavendish explained that she had composed her scientific speculations in verse form because "Errours might better passe there, then in Prose, since Poets write most Fiction, and Fiction is not given for Truth, but Pastime."[15] Similarly, the preface to *CCXI Sociable Letters* flaunts a contemptuous disregard for generic boundaries. Cavendish would have written more plays, she tells her readers, but wanted to give them a change of pace: they should think of her letters as scenes from a play not bound by plot.[16]

Many of Cavendish's nondramatic works contain theatrical elements, such as the masque-like scenes in *The Blazing World*.[17] Even those plays that come closest to traditional ideas of a cohesive plot structure are apt to contain fractal elements that subvert the concept of genre from within. *The Convent of Pleasure* contains both a series of plays-within-the-play (presented as a succession of masque-like scenes) and a full-scale masque incorporated into the play, leading the viewer into a kind of generic maze.[18] Indeed, the more experienced Cavendish became as a writer, the more freely she experimented with genre. Whereas her earliest printed works show traces of sixteenth and early seventeenth-century stock literary conventions,[19] in later works, notably *The Blazing World,* Cavendish confidently broke free from the seventeenth-century mold to create entirely new literary forms.

THEATER AS A MEDIUM FOR EDUCATION

Why did Cavendish disregard the canons of genre in her dramatic works? No doubt she felt impelled to create her own unique form of theater for the same reason she insisted on inventing her own fashions, "not taking that pleasure in such fashions as was invented by others . . . for I always took delight in a singularity."[20] Moreover, Cavendish must have enjoyed playing the "disorderly woman" who defies the repressive manifestations of male authority, whether the intellectual ascendancy of Aristotle or that of his neoclassical disciples.[21] Yet Cavendish also had substantive reasons—philosophical, literary, and psychological—for subverting the generic conventions of her time.

First, Cavendish insisted that her works for the theater were written not merely as entertainment, but to fulfill a moral and educational role.[22] In the preface to her 1662 *Playes,* she suggested that the practice of acting in plays might facilitate the instruction of noble youth, who could thereby perfect their rhetorical skills and acquire more graceful deportment.[23] And in *The Blazing World,* her alter ego the Duchess of Newcastle clarifies for the Emperor and Empress the true moral purpose of the theater. The Duchess proclaims her contempt for those modish plays "made so Methodically and Artificially" by her 1660s contemporaries, whose effect on their auditors is to serve as a "Nursery of

Whining Lovers." Her own plays, in contrast, are intended as an "Academy or School for Wise, Witty, Noble and well-behaved men." The Emperor replies that he will have only "such a Theatre as may make wise men" with "such Descriptions as are Natural, not Artificial." The Duchess then promises to present her own plays on her next visit to the Blazing World.[24]

While Cavendish's theatrical intentions can certainly be construed as educational, many of her plays diverge from her own stated ideal in two significant respects. First, the lengthy moral and philosophical discourses that are scattered throughout her plays appear to be aimed at producing wise and witty *women* rather than men. (Indeed, the male sex en masse is generally depicted in the plays as violently opposed to women's educational aspirations, as in *The Female Academy,* in which the men try to drown out female oratory by blowing on trumpets.) Secondly, the virtuoso rhetorical performances delivered by Cavendish's female characters are the very reverse of the "natural descriptions" that she claimed were a special feature of her plays. These intellectual discourses represent the interpolation into her dramatic works of an alien genre, the formal oration, a scholastic exercise with which Cavendish experimented at length in her book of *Orations of Divers Sorts* (1662).

In her comedy *The Female Academy,* the orations delivered by the young female academicians demonstrate the crucial importance of the pedagogical process, at the same time that they validate the feminist educational goals affirmed throughout the play.[25] As Williams has commented, the Academy is itself a protected space where young women may "articulate their education in . . . elegant public philosophical discourses . . ." which are "increasingly fluent and creative," drawing ever larger audiences and thus "illustrating women's empowerment through education."[26] For this reason, Cavendish chose to include academic orations in her female characters' dialogue even though she was aware she risked such detrimental effects as the deflation of dramatic tension. Thus she signaled to readers that the expression of her philosophical and educational ideas was a higher priority than the popular appeal of her plays to Restoration audiences. As she remarked in the preface to her 1668 collection, the lack of appreciation by her contemporaries could not hinder her from writing, "nor from Printing what I write, since I regard not so much the present as future Ages, for which I intend all my Books."[27]

THEATER AS AUTOBIOGRAPHICAL SELF-FASHIONING

Another reason Cavendish chose to disregard traditional canons of drama as a genre is connected with her use of the theater as a medium for constructing a series of autobiographical or imagined selves. Even as a child, Cavendish had been attracted to the practice of what we now term "Renaissance self-fashioning" in her dress and behavior.[28] As an adult, she continued to experiment with modes of self-fashioning, both in her lifestyle and through her writings. In the plays, self-fashioning runs the gamut from thinly disguised autobiography to sheer fantasy, including dreamlike inversions of Cavendish's own life experiences which we might characterize as "anti-autobiography."

At the autobiographical end of the spectrum, Cavendish portrayed episodes in her life history which are clearly recognizable as adaptations for the stage of portions of her 1656 memoir, *A True Relation of my Birth, Breeding, and Life.*[29] The clearest example of this amalgam of autobiography and theater is *The Presence,* one of whose plots dramatizes those sections of *A True Relation* that depict Cavendish's experiences as a maid of honor at the exiled court of the queen, and of Cavendish's courtship there by the Marquis of Newcastle in 1645. Other plays also contain verbal and emotional echoes of *A True Relation.* In *The Public Wooing,* Lady Mute declares, "I had rather be thought ignorantly simple for being silent, than to express folly by too much speaking" (III, xxii), a paraphrase of Cavendish's explanation for her extreme bashfulness at the court of Henrietta Maria in *A True Relation.*[30]

These theatrical depictions of parts of Cavendish's life history bear a significant relationship to her autobiographical memoir. Appended to the end of *Natures Pictures* (1656), *A True Relation* was published long before Cavendish's two volumes of plays appeared in print, and more than a decade before she produced her biography of her husband, *The Life of . . . William Cavendishe,* in 1667. In accord with the generic conventions of the personal memoir, *A True Relation* places great rhetorical emphasis on the accuracy of its factual details. Cavendish introduces her narrative by proclaiming it to be a *"true* relation" in contrast to the fictional tales of *Natures Pictures* which have preceded it. She repeats the words "true," "truly" or "truth" no less than twenty-three times in her brief memoir, concluding with the observation that her account was composed "not to please the fancy, but to tell the truth, lest after-Ages should mistake, in not knowing I was daughter to one Master Lucas of St. John's neer Colchester in Essex."[31]

In some ways *A True Relation* is indeed a remarkably candid account, revealing aspects of Cavendish's personality that did not contribute to a noble and heroic image: her cowardice and excessive bashfulness, her violent temper, her self-confessed egotism and extraordinary ambition, "for I think it no crime to wish my self the exactest of Natures works, my thred of life the longest, my Chain of Destinie the strongest, my minde the peaceablest; my life the pleasantest, my death the easiest . . . also to do my endeavour, so far as honour and honesty doth allow of, to be the highest on Fortunes Wheele, and to hold the wheele from turning, if I can."[32] When Cavendish does distort the facts in *A True Relation,* it is primarily by strategic selection and omission rather than outright prevarication, for example in her failure to mention her eldest brother's illegitimate birth.

When she turned to biography in 1667, Cavendish claimed to have applied even more stringent standards of objective truth to her *Life* of her husband William Cavendish, now Duke of Newcastle. Her Thucydidean rhetorical stance—that of telling the truth for the benefit of future ages, whatever the cost to the author in current popularity—was only partly restrained (as she reports) by the duke's request that she repress her desire to air her grudges in public.[33] In the epic expanse of the *Life* of the duke, her own autobiography was reduced to a minuscule part of the whole, narrated virtually as a third-person appendage.

As Williams has pointed out, one of the great enigmas of Cavendish's publishing career is her omission of *A True Relation* from the revised second edition of *Natures Pictures* in 1671.[34] In effect, she suppressed her prose memoir without supplying a new version to take its place, for her 1667 *Life* of the duke contains hardly any material about Cavendish herself. Having defined the parameters of conventional life-writing within such a narrow compass, Cavendish was left with very little scope within her self-imposed generic constraints to indulge in autobiographical self-fashioning, or even to express the alien subjectivity of a female voice. We can begin to understand why she may have felt impelled to abandon autobiography as a well-defined genre during the 1660s, subsequently omitting *A True Relation* from the revised 1671 edition of *Natures Pictures*.

Whatever the reason for her decision to suppress her 1656 memoir, life-writing for Cavendish during the Restoration was henceforth split into two radically different modes. On the one hand, she proclaimed the rhetoric of "truth" or Thucydidean objectivity for her historical writing, reserving this rigidly controlled style for her *Life* of the duke. Like Thucydides, she declared that the only truly objective historian was the biographer who could claim eyewitness or personal knowledge of the events and individuals to be described and interpreted: "Historians are various, writing according to their opinions, judgement, and belief, not often to the Truth . . . wherefore no History should be esteemed but what was written by the Authors themselves, as such as write their own History of their lives, actions, and fortunes, and the several accidents that befell in their time."[35] In the Preface to her biography of her husband, Cavendish emphasized her use of simple unadorned prose, having been "forced by his Graces Commands, to write this History in my own plain Style, without elegant Flourishings, or exquisit Method, relying intirely upon Truth . . ."[36]

On the other hand, Cavendish stopped trying to establish a linear narrative of the events of her own life. Instead, she explored the autobiographical possibilities of other formats to construct a series of parallel selves whose attributes were not restricted by the limitations of autobiography as a genre. In her plays and other literary modes—including *CCXI Sociable Letters, The Blazing World,* and the *Orations,* as well as innumerable prefaces and epistles—she found virtually unlimited scope for experiments in autobiographical self-fashioning, employing a variable mixture of genres to rewrite her own past, present, and imagined future.

From both a literary and personal point of view, the value of using the theatre as a vehicle for autobiography was that it allowed Cavendish to probe the emotional meanings of past events.

Some of these psychological aperçus can be discerned in *A True Relation,* but apparently Cavendish later decided that intimate revelations were inappropriate for a conventional memoir. In her plays, however, the dramatic in every sense of the word could never be out of place. *The Presence* thus offers a deeply felt recollection of past events, as emotionally charged as a vivid and revealing dream. By dramatizing her memories, Cavendish was able to articulate her own youthful emotions and thereby purge them in the process.

AUTOBIOGRAPHICAL SELF-FASHIONING AND THE SUBVERSION OF GENRE

One drawback of the autobiographical mode as Cavendish adapted it to the theater was that it tended to undermine her attempts to conform to generic conventions. As she herself remarked, a program of life-writing would inevitably force the playwright to break generic rules, since life as it was lived could never be contained within the artificial "unities" of neoclassical drama. The formal elements of her plots and subplots, Cavendish explained, were liable to appear dissociated or structurally fragmented, because she was attempting to represent what she considered more probable and "lifelike" behavior:

> I would have my Playes to be like the Natural course of all things in the World, as some dye sooner, some live longer, and some are newly born, when some are newly dead, and not all to continue to the last day of Judgment; so my scenes, some last longer than other some, and some are ended when others are begun; likewise some of my Scenes have no acquaintance or relation to the rest of the Scenes.[37]

Again *The Presence* provides the best example of autobiographically based materials that could not be contained within the classical unities. The play became so long and so fragmented that Cavendish was unable to arrange it in two sequential parts, as she did with other lengthy dramatic compositions like *Loves Adventures* or *Bell in Campo.* In order to maintain a performable length, Cavendish cut out large segments of the play and published them as disconnected "Scenes." *The Presence* along with its disjointed *Scenes* thus illustrates the conflict between two contradictory aspirations, Cavendish's goal of constructing a stage-worthy performance text and her desire to sustain an auto-biographical narrative beyond the bounds of genre.

We can identify similar tendencies toward generic fragmenta-tion in Cavendish's comedies which feature characters based on neo-Jonsonian humors. In their comedic mode, heroines such as Lady Bashful, Lady Mute, and Lady Contemplation are intended as parodies of Cavendish's own exaggerated personality traits or "humours." In these semi-autobiographical creations, Cavendish combines self-mockery with self-justification, since her supposed faults are reinterpreted in the course of each play as virtues in disguise. At their best, these neo-Jonsonian comedies succeed in realizing the true comic potential of their heroines. In the figure of Lady Contemplation, Cavendish achieves a wonderful multi-layered irony as she simultaneously dramatizes and parodies herself as fantasist, for Lady Contemplation's eccentric behavior mirrors her own role as author of equally vivid and compelling fantasies, including the figure of Lady Contemplation herself. For Lady Contemplation, as for Cavendish, daydreams and imaginary creations are far more real than reality. Yet this ab-sorption in fantasy tends to have an isolating effect in drama as well as in real life. Some of Cavendish's mock-autobiographical heroines appear to operate as detached fragments of her own personality; their one-dimensional humoral traits make it diffi-cult to integrate their conversation and plot lines with that of other equally detached fragments.

Another form of autobiographical self-fashioning featured throughout Cavendish's dramatic oeuvre is that of the epic hero-ine who gives concrete shape to a series of imagined selves. These chronicles of heroic female figures have been compared to dream-like visions or waking fantasies.[38] Yet these fantasies are more closely related to Cavendish's autobiographical project than mere utopian dreamscapes, for many of them represent what we might call "anti-autobiography," imaginary scenarios rooted in an inversion of Cavendish's own life history. Thus Lady Sans-pareille in *Youths Glory Deaths Banquet* plays out the fantasy of what might have happened had Thomas Lucas lived long enough to direct his daughter Margaret's education. As Cavendish tells us in *A True Relation,* her father died when she was only two years old, and her mother subsequently oversaw the lax and defective female education deemed appropriate to her daughters' sex and class. Cavendish was supplied with tutors in music and needlework who were kept "rather for formalitie than benefit, for my Mother cared not so much for our dancing and fidling, singing and prating of severall languages; as that we should be bred virtuously, modestly, civilly, honorably, and on honest principles."[39]

In *Youths Glory and Deaths Banquet,* Cavendish is able to reverse all these parameters in the upbringing of her heroine Lady Sanspareille. Father Love is still alive to overrule Mother Love's mistaken notions about women's education, which he dismisses as "fools breeding up fools." Instead, he guides his daughter through a rigorous academic regime with obsessive and almost incestuous concern for her intellectual development. Once Sanspareille has become a prodigy, it is she rather than her father who dies, and the playwright can experience the vicarious pleasure of being present at her own alter ego's apotheosis in a magnificent funeral.[40]

At the same time, Sanspareille's brief but glorious career and premature death serve to dramatize Cavendish's own anxieties about what were believed to be the injurious effects of a compulsive preoccupation with intellectual matters. When newly married and trying to conceive a child, Cavendish and her husband were warned by their physician, Sir Theodore Mayerne, that her self-imposed writing regime was likely to be detrimental to her health.[41] The same notion was voiced by Cavendish herself in *A True Relation,* as she incorporated the medical concept of "melancholia" into her autobiographical self-fashioning. She had diagnosed herself as of a "contemplative melancholy" humor, although this intellectual disposition was usually regarded as a male rather than a female attribute, since melancholy as a bodily humor was identified with intense intellectual activity, especially in the fields of mathematics and natural philosophy, as in Dürer's figure of Melancholia.[42] The melancholy humor was also associated with a weak bodily constitution, even for males. The health risks of an overly studious disposition would have been exacerbated for females, whose bodies were already dominated by the passive cold and wet humors and were consequently more vulnerable to disease.[43]

The dangers associated with the life of the mind were thought to be most acute in the case of the child prodigy. In early modern society, it was widely believed that prodigies were particularly liable to die young. Cavendish could have cited a famous instance among her close friends the Evelyns, whose young son Richard died in 1658. As John Evelyn wrote in his diary, his son had succumbed after six fits of a quartan ague at the age of "5 years and 3 days only, but at that tender age a prodigy for wit and understanding; for beauty of body, a very angel; for endowment of mind, of incredible hopes," having under his father's tutelage mastered English, Latin, and French, as well as showing a "strong passion" for Greek. Evelyn's diary entry concludes, "[h]ere ends the joy of my life, and for which I go even mourning to the grave."[44]

Evelyn was zealously involved in the education of his entire family, including his wife and children of both sexes. Although he blamed his son's death on the "women and maids" who had "covered him too hot as he lay in a cradle," Evelyn himself was thought to be at least partly culpable for forcing his infant son's intellectual growth like a hothouse flower. In this social and intellectual context it was reasonable for Cavendish to imagine that if she had received an intensive scholarly education, guided by a father like John Evelyn instead of a mother like Elizabeth Lucas, then she too might have developed into a remarkable prodigy, a blazing star who was fated to die young at the height of her powers.

Like Lady Sanspareille, other female dramatic characters similarly transcend the life circumstances and the "effeminate" personality traits that Cavendish apparently would have liked to overcome in herself. The young students of *The Female Academy* effortlessly produce elegant orations brimming with wit and learning; moreover they are not in the least shy before large mixed audiences of strangers. These articulate heroines represent the very reverse of Cavendish's own tongue-tied bashfulness, an attribute she characterized in *A True Relation* as a "natural defect" that she found impossible to cure. Several of Cavendish's heroines show remarkable courage and prowess in military affairs, in complete contrast to Cavendish herself, who confessed in her autobiographical memoir that she was "naturally a coward," being frightened at the noise of a mere popgun, or afraid of a sword held against her "although but in jest."[45] Affectionata of *Loves Adventures* achieves a brilliant military career in which she vanquishes the Turks in battle and saves the life of her patron Lord Singularity. Later in a council of war with the Venetians, Affectionata displays an astute grasp of military strategy as well as a mastery of the arts of rhetoric. In *Bell in Campo,* Lady Victoria with her band of "heroickesses" manages to outdo her husband in the field of battle and win back territory he has lost to the enemy. Thus her heroines act out Cavendish's anti-autobiographical fantasy of overcoming her "effeminate" defects and of "entering the male world of heroic action and honour."[46]

Genre and Gender

In these and other examples of her anti-autobiographical creations for the theater, Cavendish betrays an underlying preoccupation with gender. The female paragons depicted in her plays are prodigies, not just of their own sex, but of *both* sexes. Cavendish's heroines eclipse men as much as they surpass other women, as they perform incredible feats at which the male sex is normally presumed to excel. At the same time, these early modern superwomen display all the exemplary virtues of their own sex. By endowing her female characters with these "hermaphroditical" attributes, Cavendish challenged contemporary assumptions about the nature of gender differences and the "natural" proclivities and capacities of each sex. In so doing, she destabilized the hierarchical worldview that defined the gender order in the comedies of sexual reversal of her Jacobean predecessors. Yet in the context of Cavendish's anti-autobiographical dreamscapes, questions about gender are posed implicitly rather than explicitly. Sometimes Cavendish gives us the impression that she has not fully suspended her own disbelief in her heroines' extraordinary abilities, at least in terms of their dramatic portrayal. In *Loves Adventures,* for example, although the main plot includes many striking action scenes that could have been staged with spectacular effect, most of Affectionata's masculine exploits are simply narrated as third-person descriptions, almost as if Cavendish were not quite ready to confront the radical implications for gender of her vicarious fantasies.

Cavendish's theatrical gender games form a wide spectrum, in which her exploration of the Other entails a journey to the far side of the psychological and cultural boundary between the two sexes. Many of her plays feature female characters who take on male roles or display masculine attributes. There are debates in dialogue form about the innate capacities and proper social roles of the two sexes. Both men and women manage to disguise themselves successfully as members of the opposite sex, with subversive consequences for readers' assumptions about the unknown potentialities of each sex. Whether they prove to be stageworthy or not, all such theatrical depictions of the "performative quality" of gender are worthy of our attention, for they are instances of what Judith Butler has characterized as the "serious play" required by feminism.[47]

It is probably no accident that Cavendish's most successful plays in terms of modern audience appreciation are those in which gender takes center stage as the dominant issue. *The Convent of Pleasure,* which has recently established its popularity as a modern performance text, is unified by its constant focus on gender. All the issues presented for debate are gender issues, and nearly all are framed as women's issues: is heterosexual love and marriage a good or a bad thing for women? Is it desirable or even possible for women to avoid marriage? Can women be happier and more successful living among their own sex, in communities which exclude men? Is love and even sexual attraction between women a possible mode of behavior? Is any man capable of masquerading as a woman so perfectly as to infiltrate the inner sanctum of women's private culture? Because the range of gender issues imposes a conceptual unity on the disparate themes and their complex interrelationships, the audience experiences an overall sense of cohesion even when Cavendish experiments with departures from generic form, as in the plays-within-the-play in act 3 and the masque of sea-creatures in act 4. Within the terms of reference of the play's primary focus on gender, these disparate generic elements are perceived as enriching rather than weakening the play's formal structure.[48]

At times it may appear to the reader that Cavendish's multiple purposes of philosophical discourse and autobiographical self-fashioning put so much centrifugal pressure on the structure of her dramatic works that the genre becomes strained almost to the breaking point, or at least to the point at which her contemporaries of the 1660s rejected her plays as unplayable. Yet from a modern perspective, we can view the structural tensions generated by the impulse to play gender games as a creative force that impelled Cavendish to experiment with genre and extend its boundaries to new dramatic possibilities that modern audiences can appreciate and enjoy.

NOTES

1. Hilda Smith, *Reason's Disciples* (Urbana: University of Illinois Press, 1982), 76–77; Jacqueline Pearson, "'Women May Discourse . . . as Well as Men': Speaking and Silent Women in the Plays of Margaret Cavendish, Duchess of Newcastle," *Tulsa Studies in Women's Literature* 4 (1985): 33–45; Kathleen Jones, *A Glorious Fame: The Life of Margaret Cavendish, Duchess of Newcastle 1623–1673* (London: Bloomsbury, 1988), 130.

2. Elaine Hobby, *Virtue of Necessity: English Women's Writing 1649–88* (Ann Arbor: University of Michigan Press, 1989), 105.

3. Linda Payne, "Dramatic Dreamscape: Women's Dreams and Utopian Vision in the Works of Margaret Cavendish, Duchess of Newcastle," in *Curtain Calls: British and American Women and the Theater, 1660–1830,* ed. Mary Anne Schofield and Cecilia Macheski (Athens, Ohio: Ohio University Press, 1991), 30.

4. Gweno Williams, "'Why May Not a Lady Write a Good Play?' Plays by Early Modern Women Reassessed as Performance Texts," in *Readings in Renaissance Women's Drama: Criticism, History and Performance 1594–1998,* ed. S. P. Cerasano and M. Wynne-Davies (London: Routledge, 1998): 95–107; Alison Findlay, Stephanie Hodgson-Wright, and Gweno Williams, *Women and Dramatic Production 1550–1700* (London: Longman, 2000); Gweno Williams, "'The Play is Ready to be Acted': Women and Dramatic Production, 1570–1670" (co-authors Alison Findlay and Stephanie Hodgson-Wright), in *Women's Writing: The Elizabethan to Victorian Period* 6.1 (1999): 129–48; see also Susan Wiseman, "Gender and Status in Dramatic Discourse: Margaret Cavendish, Duchess of Newcastle," in *Women, Writing, History: 1640–1740,* ed. Isobel Grundy and Susan Wiseman (London: B. T. Batsford, 1992), 164; Sophie Tomlinson, "'My Brain the Stage': Margaret Cavendish and the Fantasy of Female Performance," in *Women, Texts and Histories, 1575–1760,* ed. Clare Brant and Diane Purkiss (London: Routledge, 1992): 137–40.

5. Gweno Williams, performance video (co-authors Alison Findlay, and Stephanie Hodgson-Wright), *Women Dramatists 1550–1670: Plays in Performance* (Lancaster: Women and Dramatic Production in Association with Lancaster University Television, 1999); performance video, *Margaret Cavendish, Duchess of Newcastle: Plays in Performance 1* (York: Margaret Cavendish Performance Project in Association with Women and Dramatic Production, 2002).

6. Anne Shaver, ed., "Introduction" to Margaret Cavendish, *The Convent of Pleasure and Other Plays* (Baltimore: Johns Hopkins University Press, 1999): 10.

7. Payne, "Dramatic Dreamscape," 30.

8. James Fitzmaurice, "Margaret Cavendish on Her Own Writing: Evidence from Revision and Handmade Correction," *Papers of the Bibliographical Society of America* 85 (September 1991): 297–307; "Problems with Editing Margaret Cavendish," *Renaissance English Text Society Publications* (January 1991): 1–17; Gweno Williams, "'No Silent Woman': The Plays of M. Cavendish, Duchess of Newcastle," in *Women and Dramatic Production*, 95–122.

9. Jeffrey Masten, *Textual Intercourse: Collaboration, Authorship, and Sexualities in Renaissance Drama* (Cambridge: Cambridge University Press, 1997); Williams, "'No Silent Woman'," 100–116.

10. Tomlinson, "'My Brain the Stage.'"

11. Laura Rosenthal, "'Authoress of a Whole World': The Duchess of Newcastle and Imaginary Property," in *Playwrights and Plagiarists in Early Modern England: Gender, Authorship, Literary Property* (Ithaca: Cornell University Press, 1996): 60.

12. Margaret Cavendish, *Playes* (London, 1662), prefatory matter; *Plays Never Before Printed* (London, 1668), prefatory matter.

13. Margaret Cavendish, *Orations of Divers Sorts* (London, 1662); prefatory matter; Sara Mendelson, *The Mental World of Stuart Women: Three Studies* (Brighton: Harvester, 1987): 36.

14. Rosenthal, "'Authoress of a Whole World'," 69; Masten, *Textual Intercourse*, 159–62; for a nuanced analysis of Cavendish's intentions see Tomlinson, "'My Brain the Stage.'"

15. Cavendish, *Poems and Fancies* (London, 1653), prefatory matter; See Mendelson, *Mental World*, 37.

16. James Fitzmaurice, "Introduction," to Margaret Cavendish, *The Sociable Letters*, ed. J. Fitzmaurice (New York: Garland, 1997): xii.

17. Sylvia Bowerbank and Sara Mendelson, eds., *Paper Bodies: A Margaret Cavendish Reader* (Peterborough, Ontario: Broadview Press, 2000): 236–43.

18. Ibid., 19–20.

19. H. M. Cocking, "Originality and Influence in the Works of Margaret Cavendish, Duchess of Newcastle," M. Phil. thesis, Reading University, 1972.

20. Bowerbank and Mendelson, *Paper Bodies*, 60.

21. Andrew Hiscock, "'Here's no design, no plot, nor any ground': the drama of Margaret Cavendish and the disorderly woman," *Women's Writing* 4.3 (1997): 404–7; Bowerbank and Mendelson, *Paper Bodies*, 247.

22. Annette Kramer, "'Thus by the Musick of a Ladyes Tongue': Margaret Cavendish's Dramatic Innovations in Women's Education," *Women's History Review* 2 (1993): 72–73.

23. Tomlinson, "'My Brain the Stage,'" 141.

24. Bowerbank and Mendelson, *Paper Bodies*, 247–8; see also Wiseman, "Gender and Status in Dramatic Discourse," 159–77.

25. Hiscock, "'Here's No Design,'" 410–12.

26. Williams, *Women and Dramatic Production*, 98.

27. *Plays,* 1668, "To the Readers," sig. A2.

28. Stephen Greenblatt, *Renaissance Self-Fashioning: From More to Shakespeare* (Chicago: University of Chicago Press, 1980).

29. *A True Relation* was originally appended to *Natures Pictures drawn by Fancies Pencil to the Life* (London, 1656); it is reprinted in Bowerbank and Mendelson, *Paper Bodies,* 41–63.

30. Bowerbank and Mendelson, *Paper Bodies,* 46.

31. Ibid., 63.

32. Ibid., 61–62.

33. *The Life of. . . William Cavendishe, Duke, Marquess, and Earl of Newcastle...* (London, 1667), sig. f2.

34. Gweno Williams, "Margaret Cavendish's *A True Relation of my Birth, Breeding and Life,*" in *A Companion to Early Modern Women's Writing,* ed. Anita Pacheco (Oxford: Basil Blackwell, 2002), 165–76.

35. *Natures Pictures,* 245; compare Thucydides' *History of the Peloponnesian War,* ed. M. I. Finley (Harmondsworth: Penguin Classics, 1972), 48.

36. Cavendish, *Life,* 3.

37. Cavendish, *Playes* (1662), Prefatory Epistle "To the Reader", sig. A4.

38. Payne, "Dramatic Dreamscape," 21–22.

39. Bowerbank and Mendelson, *Paper Bodies,* 43; for Cavendish's negative comments on women's conventional education, see her Sociable Letter number 26, quoted in Rosemary Kegl, "'The World I have made': Margaret Cavendish, feminism and *The Blazing World,*" in *Feminist Readings of Early Modern Culture: Emerging Subjects,* ed. Valerie Traub, M. Lindsay Kaplan, and Dympna Callaghan (Cambridge: Cambridge University Press, 1996): 124.

40. Gweno Williams, performance video, *Margaret Cavendish, Duchess of Newcastle: Plays in Performance 1.*

41. Theodore Mayerne, "A Boke, Wherein is Contained Rare Minerall Receipts . . . ," Portland MSS, PwV 90 (unfoliated), University of Nottingham Library; it is significant that Cavendish often expressed in her works the belief that she had been forced to choose between producing children of the body or of the mind.

42. Raymond Klibansky, Erwin Panofsky, and Fritz Saxl, *Saturn and Melancholy* (New York: Basic Books, 1964).

43. Sara Mendelson and Patricia Crawford, *Women in Early Modern England 1550–1720* (Oxford: Clarendon Press, 1998), 19–20.

44. John Evelyn, *Diary and Correspondence of John Evelyn, F. R. S,* ed. William Bray, 4 vols. (London: 1857), entry for 27 January 1657/8.

45. Bowerbank and Mendelson, *Paper Bodies,* 62.

46. Tomlinson, "'My Brain the Stage'", 147; Alexandra Bennett, ed., *Bell in Campo and The Sociable Companions* (Peterborough, Ontario: Broadview Press, 2002), 12–16.

47. Judith Butler, *Gender Trouble: Feminism and the Subversion of Identity* (New York: Routledge, 1990), 24–25.

48. For further discussion of this point see Williams, "'Why May Not a Lady . . .'"; Bowerbank and Mendelson, *Paper Bodies,* 19–21.

Margaret Cavendish's Drama: An Aesthetic of Fragmentation

GISÈLE VENET

THE PROLOGUE TO MARGARET CAVENDISH'S *THE SOCIABLE COMpanions; or, The Female Wits* pretends to anticipate the failure of the play: "Noble Spectators, Our Authoress doth say,/She doth believe you will condemn her play."[1] The explanation she offers for this possibly frustrating outcome shows her to be fully aware of what might appear as most discrediting shortcomings for a stage play, the absence of a "plot" and an overall "design" that would lay the "foundation" to any work of art and "keep out censure":

> Here's no design, no plot, nor any ground,
> Foundation none, nor any to be found,
> But like the World's Globe, it hath no support,
> But hangs by Geometry: nor hath it fort
> To make it strong, nor walls to keep out censure.
>
> (9)

Incidentally, she also gives us all the necessary clues to reinterpret her work along new lines, for her fragmentary modes of thought and writing are not to be read in terms of a failure to produce well-made plays sustained by conventional logic or a well-organized succession of theatrical moments. Her entirely new creative approaches *require* fragmentation as a means of breaking away from conventions and of staging new attitudes towards others or a new conception of the self. In fact, this aesthetics of fragmentation corresponds to new needs and allows her to come to terms with modern issues, especially that of the female self claiming to be her own "monarch."

Long before Margaret Cavendish's apparent wariness of the

verdict of critics and audiences (and yet acting as her own most severe censor), Ben Jonson had staged different opinions of the relation between audience and author and the latent antagonism that was to develop into a critical genre of its own and culminate with the Restoration: in *Every Man Out of His Humour* (1598), his new-styled Prologue used satirical polemics as an approach to the criticism of drama. Ben Jonson relies on his alter ego, Acer, to speak an extempore "prologue" before becoming the character Macilente. In this play, the comedian who was to play the part of the official Prologue is late: his traditional function would have been to placate the audience and fend off the potential booing and shouting so that the play could start. The poor tardy actor, arriving with "the third sounding" that signals the beginning of the play, is in fact only too glad to be thus muted and spared the "venomous hiss" from the audience. He offers his place to two characters, Mitis and Cordatus, after Acer has expressly chosen them as the only dramatic critics allowed to stay:

> I leave you two, as censors, to sit here:
> Observe what I present, and liberally
> Speak your opinions upon every scene,
> As it shall pass the view of these spectators.[2]

In fact, they are placed there "to espy" the audience as if Acer/Jonson was prepared to pounce upon the first "gallant of this mark," the critic, that would dare to disagree: Acer/Jonson wishes to appear only intent on pleasing "attentive auditors"— "such as will join their profit with their pleasure"—and let their eyes "flow with distilled laughter" at his "new conceits" and "invention." If he dismisses criticism in advance, it is because he feels confident that failure to please can only be due to shortcomings in others, not in himself or his work:

> . . . [I]f we fail
> We must impute it to this only chance,
> Art hath an enemy call'd ignorance.[3]

Acer/Jonson seems to address the audience as so many half-wits to be taught better by the author, who knows all there is to know about rules, design, and censure. And indeed, the *extempore* speech ends with the appreciation by Mitis and Cordatus of the new rules paradoxically derived from *Vetus Comœdia,* the old comedy, and defiantly applied as new to the play. Cordatus, however, also has misgivings about the result: "how it will answer the general expectation, I know not." A scholarly (if pedantic) exposition of what a play should be like follows, mentioning "equal division of it into acts and scenes, according to the Terentian manner," and "the whole argument fall[ing] within compass of a day's business." Yet in spite of this provocative dogmatic statement, the two "censors" finally conclude on the happy "license, or free power to illustrate and heighten our invention" retained by Jonson from the classics themselves, "not to be tied to those strict and regular forms which the niceness of a few, who are nothing but form, would thrust upon us."[4] We feel relieved, and at the same time almost agree with Mitis; when asked earlier how he likes Acer/Jonson's spirit, he answers: "I should like him much better, if he were less confident."[5]

The feeling at this stage is that the dramatist's view of drama rests on a mutually bellicose confrontation of audience and author, with the author as master of the one-sided meaning. Jonson stands worlds apart from the sense of shared involvement and creation of meaning expected from his audience by the nondogmatic Shakespeare—worlds apart, too, from the use Margaret Cavendish would make of a Prologue. Rereading Cavendish's Prologue to *The Female Wits* with Jonson's arrogance (feigned or real) in mind, we grow even more sensitive to the difference in tone and image, and to the revelation of the attitudes to art and self a prologue could comprise. In spite of the distance in years and mood, and incidentally in gender, Cavendish writes an *ars poetica* of her own, although instead of turning against others as a threat to the self (like Jonson) or remaining self-effacing (like Shakespeare), she seems to imply that the threat comes from inside, from some sort of ontological vulnerability, and that it might well be the price one has to pay to reach both an awareness of the self and self-acknowledgement.

Cavendish's Prologue shows her fully aware that she could be no other than fragmentary in her approach to plots and dramatic construction, implying some sort of "negative capability" of her own, to borrow Keats's description of Shakespeare's creative manner. "No design, no plot"—indeed, her plays are easier to remember for some of their striking themes than for the organization of events or sequences of dialogue: we retain memorable fragments rather than a sense of wholeness. Moreover, she might include fragments of other hands, like her husband's,[6] or shifts from plot to plot, leaving the reader or audience unprepared for such quick changes of scenes or characters. This fragmentary mode may appear at its worst as a caricature of intentions. *The Unnatural Tragedy* (1662), for example, is a disconcerting fragmentary utopia of three "Sociable Virgins" opposed to marriage and determined to "sit and rail against men."[7] The main plot alternates with other plots, like the "unnatural tragedy" of incest between Monsieur Frère and Madam Sœur, whose final outcome is rape and violent death. In spite of the audacity of the subject, the tragedy of incest fails to equal the far more challenging and far-reaching play by John Ford, *'Tis Pity She is a Whore* (1633), with its full acknowledgment of a natural philosophy that allows permissiveness and leads to transgression.[8]

But more constructive meaning may be derived from the very lack of structure in plays like *The Lady Contemplation,* or *The Convent of Pleasure,* or *Bell in Campo.* Cavendish has a clear perception of the workings of her imagination, and this is corroborated by her "baseless fabric of a vision," her amazing prose fiction, *The Blazing World.* Her allusion (still in the Prologue) to "the World's Globe" that has "no support" hints at a lack of foundation in mimetic reality that entails a specific approach to creation: no *effet de réel* is to hinder her creative impulse in perpetual motion, no restrictive link with the reality of the world outside. The allusion could be reminiscent of Donne's celebrated outcry of mental and cosmic disorganization—"all coherence gone"[9]—when faced with the new epistemological approaches to Science—"And new Philosophy calls all in doubt"[10]—which appear in his "anatomy of the world" in the earlier years of the seventeenth century. This same world, according to Cavendish, "hangs by Geometry," jeopardized in its own physicality, and therefore, as she seems to suggest, it may find its truer foundation in abstract, mathematical principles akin to Descartes'. A new coherence is to be found in constructions of the mind rather than on the unreliable perception of the senses, and many works of art or literature of the period staged this questioning of sense experience: Calderon's play, *La Vida es un Sueño [Life is a Dream]*—staged in 1635 and published in 1636, one year before

Descartes published his *Discours de la Méthode* (1637)—encapsulated all these obsessions of the Baroque age. As the philosopher "methodically" brought himself to "call all in doubt," even the very evidence of his senses, he discovered that doubt required thought, the foundation of the modern self: "Cogito, ergo sum." For Cavendish, the world might well be truer for being fictional, as in her own Blazing World, or for relying more on important moments—fragments—in her plays than on the continuity of plot or a coherence produced by trivially true-to-life effects or characters.

Her Prologue again insists on a sense of exposure, an awareness of essential, existential vulnerability—"no fort to make it strong"—and hints at the value of the repeated metaphor or utopia of the warlike female for claiming equal rights for the female sex or a vindication of a right to exist as an individual. Just as she acknowledges her vulnerability, she also insists in the last line of the prologue that "she will valiantly stand the adventure," and the two key words "valiantly" and "adventure" shed light on her conception of a militant writing. Braving confrontation, the audacious writer as articulate adventurer goes to war against the commonplaces of "the weaker vessel"—against the silence imposed on women as a condition of their feminine attractiveness and a mark of their difference with men: Shakespeare's Coriolanus, a quintessential male warrior returning from a victorious battle, thus symptomatically greets his wife as "my gracious silence."[11] Cavendish presents her challenge to maiming cultural conventions as "adventure," and this also calls to mind the moving and equally audacious figure of the Duchess of Malfi, in Webster's play, who, as prologue to her tragedy, rebels against her brothers' imposing restrictions on her choice of a new husband:

> I am going into a wilderness
> Where I shall find no path, nor friendly clue
> To be my guide.[12]

We must keep in mind this sense of an essential vulnerability combined with audacity as a background to interpretation. Another salient characteristic is the recurrent metaphor of her work as a world, so characteristic of her apprehension of her own creative mental space. It is best expressed in a short version of her

Blazing World featuring in *The Lady Contemplation* (1662), a few years before Cavendish sees herself as the Empress of her imaginary world: as early as in scene 1 of act I, in the first part of the twofold play, Lady Contemplation objects to Lady Visitant's trivial praise of "the pleasures of the World" that, according to the latter, should not to be abandoned "for the sake of dull contemplation." Lady Contemplation has contrary views:

> Why, the greatest pleasures that can be in Fruition, I take in Imagination: for whatsoever the sence enjoyes from outward objects, they may enjoy in inward thoughts. For the mind takes as much pleasure in creating Fancies, as Nature to create and dissolve, and create Creatures anew. For Fancy is the Minds creature, & *imaginations* are as several worlds, wherein those Creatures are bred and born, live and dye; thus the mind is like infinite Nature.[13]

The fragmented structure of Cavendish's plays should not therefore be disparaged as a failure to create coherent wholes, but as having a positive aesthetic value and possibly epistemological import as well.

Her plays are indeed replete with echoes of those "fractures and disjunctures" described by Susan Wiseman,[14] which are due to political circumstances as well as to a desire to oppose an oppressive gender ideology. Echoes of a disruptive armed conflict that brought chaos to so many households like her own are recurrent in the plays, forming a thematic obsession of disruption. In *The Sociable Companions; or, The Female Wits,* wealth is transferred from the aristocracy to "Usurers, Lawyers and Physicians": "for the Civil War hath made all sorts of men like as Vultures, after a Battle, that feed on the Dead, or dying Corps."[15] The general tone of the scene is Jonsonian, and the names remain descriptive of the characters, in keeping with the satirical tradition inherited from Jacobean or Caroline stage practice: the usurer is inevitably named M. Get-all, the lawyer Sergeant Plead-all, the physician Dr. Cure-all. But corruption is no longer merely moral or humoral, as in Jonson or Marston; it is given a bodily reality, although the metaphorical sense is still implicit: "Men and Women's bodies are corrupted and weakened . . . Their bodies are full of the Scurvy."[16] Ben Jonson's Comedy of gulls has turned sour: in *The Sociable Companions; or, The Female Wits,* Peg explains to the usurer tricked into a trial for getting a woman with child that: "this child which is laid to your charge is none of mine, but a bastard of my brother's, Captain Valour; but by reason my brother was ruined in the Civil Wars, . . . I had not means to maintain him" (55). In *The Lady Contemplation,* Lady Poor Virtue epitomizes the evils that plague royalist families after the Wars: first she grieves for a father killed "in the defence of his King and Country."[17] But the loss entails complete disruption of her former life, so much so that this noble lady finds herself eventually working for a farmer (191), not as an idle if weary Rosalind in the Forest of Arden, but as a rustic, hardworking shepherdess, antinomic of the refined character of the pastoral tradition that had prevailed in European literature throughout the sixteenth and seventeenth centuries. A biting satire of idleness conflicts with the comic mood: Lord Title has barely time to venture forth an idyllic topos about her life—"But most commonly Shepherds and Shepherdesses sit and sing to pass away the time" (206)—that she answers with a prosaic description of her real, hard chores. In spite of her stoic attitude in the face of hardships, as when she refuses to mourn for the loss of her estate—"I cannot mourn for anything that is in Fortune's power to take away" (185)—she becomes the very symbol of the victimized aristocrat. Fragmented purpose and structure accompany the disruptive mood: the echoes from a tragic reality, inserted into the plays, do not bring coherence to the mood or themes, but seem to be only occasionally used as a basis for pathetic episodes, themselves discontinuous. Lady Poor Virtue easily switches back from the character of a hardworking rustic farmhand to the conventional Perdita-like shepherdess courted by the same aristocrat Lord Title, this time under "a hedge overhanging like a bower," and the discontinuity in the mood provides—restores?—a continuity with the pastoral tradition of the Shakespearean heritage: as she is questioned about the refinement of speech that makes her "so learnedly judicious," she answers that "Fire, Air, Water, and Earth, Animals, Vegetables and Minerals, are Volumes large enough to express Nature" (209), echoing this time the banished Duke of the winter pastoral in the Forest of Arden who would find "books in brooks."[18]

This satire of pastoral style is built on the discrepancy between the outer appearances of a girl with a sheep hook and Lord Title's false ideas of a pastoral, sophisticated simplicity, but there is also a significant discrepancy between her appearance and her speech. On their first meeting (act 4, part I), Lord Title wishes her to be his shepherd, as in any conventional Arcadia. She declines his offer, becoming this time the standard bluestocking with her selection of emblematic borrowings from classical literature to support her moral refusal: "I glory more in being chast, than Hellen of her beauty, or Athens of their learning" (196). She thus refers repeatedly to the Greeks, the Lacedemonians, the Persians, the Romans, who are praised for their respective virtues, and Lord Title, amazed, inevitably exclaims: "and yet a cottager" (197). But what here is meant to bind the characters together through the common cultural heritage shared by a homogenous elite (in spite of their appearances) can elsewhere highlight the "disjunctures" produced by cultural references that have ceased to be a social cement.

The beginning of *The Sociable Companions; or, The Female Wits* (act 1, scene 1) stages a further debunking of cultural models: when Harry Sensible meets his friend William Fullwit who, sitting with books and "studying to be a wiseman" (17), quotes Plutarch, Machiavelli, Lucan, and Caesar's *Commentaries,* he points out the inadequacy of Ancient authors as a basis to explain the present: "Why such books, since you are neither Greek nor Roman? Those historians . . . will not benefit thee nor thy Native Country" (17). In *The Unnatural Tragedy,* the three "Sociable Virgins" question the validity of historians as sources of truth.[19] In keeping with Cavalier or Caroline contempt of highbrow attitudes to letters, the satire in *The Sociable Companions; or, The Female Wits* also applies to poetry: Fullwit has made "a copy of verses," but the Captain objects to them—"I cannot endure verses"—and claims he would vomit even to a "drunken song."[20] Verse to him is like *Crocus Metallorum,* whose foul taste and poisonous effect make him flee. He thus develops a physiology of poetry that proves alien to his physiology of trivial life and good wine.

The discrepancy emphasized in cultural models also applies elsewhere in the play to gendered social behaviors. In the first part of *The Sociable Companions; or, The Female Wits,* the stage appears as a vacant space where idle men, wasting good money in taverns, prove unable to resist drinking and wenching, whereas the women, their sisters left penniless at home, devise makeshift ways to make money. These "female wits" of the play's title busy themselves in what will become the main theme of Restoration plays and eighteenth-century novels: matrimony, or rather the "matrimoney" of the marriage market. Their financial activities also provide the play with a multiplicity of intrigues and plots within plot, proving creative both in meaning and form; male characters, on the contrary, remain ineffectual, not even rising to the creative inventiveness of Falstaff and his companions in tavern scenes.

The dissociation of sensibility that T. S. Eliot had detected in early Jacobean playwrights is still at work, taking the "fracture" a degree further. Nature and culture have parted for good. Such a disruption occurs when Lady Contemplation, for instance, refuses to enter into dialogue with Lady Visitant, or with Lady Conversation later, on the ground that conversation debases thoughts.[21] Lady Visitant gives her own definition of what "tongue" means: it is an organ of language, the social and cultural means to convey inner thoughts. For her, speech moves from inside towards outside. She is contradicted by Lady Contemplation for whom it is merely a natural organ, meant by nature for taste, and allowing contact with concrete natural reality—food. For the latter, speech allows ingestion or incorporation in a movement from outside to inside.

In a similar approach to cultural models, the conventional discourse that hyperbolically idealized men, as when Ophelia describes her lover as "the courtier, soldier, scholar," collapses, and the dividing line between male and female becomes a shifting frontier. A play like Bell in Campo (1662) again proves representative of a "fracture" or "disjuncture," not least because two dramatic modes collide (or at least fail to coincide). Victoria, the warlike leader of a female regiment, who turns a besieged fort and garrison into a blazing victory, is opposed to Madam Jantil (for Gentle?) who prefers building an ostentatious monument to her dead husband and conceives it as a closed space with several rooms for her to live in. In this play, once more, the world of men as men—fighting battles, waging wars—turns out to be a failure and this compels them to accept submission or necessarily undergo collapse and loss. This is so pronounced that epic values, the tactics and strategies of the war, and the final victory are all taken over by women under the leadership of Victoria—and this even though they had initially set out to follow their husbands purely out of marital love. In *The Convent of Pleasure,* the men are even reduced to herd swine, a probable allusion to the Circe myth. As a final debasement of the glorious male image, they must cross-dress as country wenches, but even this proves ineffectual, as they are unable to walk about in petticoats (228).

Even when men finally recover their function as dignified lovers at the denouement of the play, they have shown themselves despicable wooers all the way through. For example, in *The Lady Contemplation,* Sir Golden Riches leaves Lady Poor Virtue whom he has failed to woo and is only too happy to give gold and gifts to Mall Mean-Bred to get her cheap love. In *The Convent of Pleasure,* the miseries of married women are staged in brief successive scenes as so many plays-within-the-play, in sharp antithesis to the Masque of love between the "Princess" and Lady Happy, which is framed as idealized pastorals (224–34).

An awareness of the failure to reach completion seems to emerge, shared by men and women alike and emblematized by Lady Ward in *The Lady Contemplation,* when she complains, "I am like a house which Time hath not fully furnished, nor Education thoroughly finished" (209). Pulling asunder the former unified world of male and female culture, these two plays, *The Convent of Pleasure* and *Lady Contemplation,* could be read as two paroxystic responses to the challenge of generalized failure or two paradoxical answers, both again antithetical to each other and yet pointing in the same direction. Both plays display worlds of seclusion and exclusion; they are Cavendish's most striking expression of fractures and disjunctures with their plurality of satellite scenes and fragmented episodes loosely gathering around two major figures, Lady Happy and Lady Contemplation. In *The Convent of Pleasure,* Lady Happy refuses to love men, as their love spells enslavement (220). Being very rich, she turns her estate into a "Convent," subverting the traditional image of the *Hortus conclusus*—the mystical enclosed garden of love inherited from medieval tradition—into a garden of timeless pastoral, the Golden Age restored: "My cloister not a place of restraint, but a place of freedom, not to vex the senses but to please them" (220). Such had been Rabelais's fictional "Abbaye de

Thélème," whose motto was "Fais ce que voudras" ("As you like it").

Seclusion, however, also implies severing all ties, as much as it entails exclusion: all men are forbidden entrance.[22] The answer to the fragmented vision is here given in terms of gender ideologies. Besides, Lady Happy's creed is not religious devotion, but a cult of Nature, which implies a criticism of age-old religious praise for suffering and restraint. She is "not a Votress to the gods but to Nature," and her estate is described as the ideal Country House, with "Gardens, Orchards, Walks, Groves, Bowers, Arbours, Ponds, Springs" (223). Cross-dressing is accepted in *The Convent of Pleasure,* but only as a mock-male disguise: a "Princess," recently admitted within the secluded place, is allowed to go "in Masculine Habits," and a pastoral idyllic relation, unisexual if sexless, takes place: "More innocent lovers never can there be, than my most Princely lover, that's a She" (229). Yet, in the pastoral mood of the Convent, innocence goes with experience, however equivocal. The Princess, known as such by Lady Happy "as they hold each other in their Arms," declares: "These my Imbraces though of Female kind, / May be as fervent as a Masculine mind" (229).

The inhabitants of the convent while away the time in a series of masques and plays-within-the-play emblematically illustrating the freedom so specific to the Arcadian world where no necessity of time—nor of gender, at this stage—commands. In act 4 in particular, the diversity of styles and effects is structurally justified by the May games: while these traditionally express the freedom of the youth and celebrate the return of Spring, the fertility rites are here ironically subverted, as carnal love between man and woman is forbidden: Lady Happy prays to both Nature and the Gods in act 5 not to "suffer [her] . . . to fall in love" (239), when at last she discovers her dear "She" is a "He." These Midsummer Night's games nevertheless give her and the "Princess" scope to disguise themselves as shepherds and shepherdesses, as is quite in keeping with the festive rituals of either the Twelve Nights after Christmas Day or the Midsummer Nights after May Day—the only periods when the supreme transgression for women, cross-dressing, was allowed: Jessica thus dresses like a torchbearer for her escape during Carnival days in *The*

Merchant of Venice, and Viola goes dressed as the boy Cesario in the play aptly entitled *Twelfth Night.* But in *The Convent of Pleasure* cross-dressing implies a restoration of gender differences, as the wolf is in the sheepcote and the "Princess" turns from a female shepherd into a male Prince, just as Prince Pyrocles, in Sidney's *Arcadia,* finally discloses his true identity after long concealment in female dress. But before the fatal disclosure takes place and thus puts an end to the utopia of the all-woman Convent, Cavendish takes this secluded world away from the trivial world of ordinary gender division to create a "world-within-a-world" effect, a vision-within-a-vision of what the world should be like. Idealization is conveyed through the discourse of compliment in the masque of Shepherds of act 4, when the "Princess" in "Masculine Shepherd's Clothes" praises the all-encompassing "Wit" of Lady Happy: "My Shepherdess, your Wit flies high."[23] It is an opportunity to display, in a sort of "blazing" vision, a pastoral version of Donne's *Anatomy of the World,* this time without the disquieting aspects of the "new Philosophy," seen as a kind of Faustian journey to the confines of the universe that allows the Shepherd to draw the list of earthly and cosmic phenomena that the heroine's "Wit" is able to interpret and master: "Thus doth your Wit reveal / What Nature would conceal."[24]

Lady Happy's answer to the Shepherd's compliment is "Your wit doth search Mankind," and it takes in its turn the shape of an "Anatomy," this time of the mind, that is based on a treatise of the passions, which implies an interrelation of humors, fancies, and appetites,[25] but also praises reason as "The Center of the Mind."[26] This particular instance resembles Prospero becoming master of the revels to create the masque of Ceres and Iris, to Ferdinand's amazement in act 4 of Shakespeare's *The Tempest:* the He-Princess, so to speak, takes in hand the really creative masque, that of Neptune, before being exposed as the Prince in hiding. Is Cavendish paying here an indirect compliment, unexpected in this context, to gender discrimination and to the husband who had written lines for this specific scene (as he wrote many scenes and so many prologues for his wife's plays)? The play ends in typically Shakespearean denial—"Words are nothing"[27]—and evokes Feste's statement in *Twelfth Night:* "Nothing that is so is so," as if to dispel the equivocation of the earlier utopia of an all-female world. Or maybe we are invited to forget

about the conventional ending, however "happy," with the wed-
ding of Lady Happy and the "Princess" turned Prince? Whatever
the ultimate meaning to give to "words" that are "nothing," fragments of signification survive the utopia: in act 2, scene 3,
Madam Mediator describes life in the Convent as better than
being "Emperess of the Whole World" since "every Lady there
enjoyeth as much Pleasure as any absolute Monarch can do,
without the Troubles and Cares, that attend on Royalty."[28] In the
closed world of the walled-in Convent, monarchs have turned
monads, self-sufficient and with no communication with the
outer world—thus evoking Leibniz's description of the new modern self in his *Monadology* (1714).

In *The Lady Contemplation,* a similar sense of seclusion within
a world of one's own takes place, as Lady Contemplation excludes
others by avoiding all speech intercourse. More pleased with her
contemplation than with devotion, she again creates a world of
self-rule, in which "the whole race of Mankind can become Em-
perours."[29] The mind is a "deity," complete by itself "for it entertains itself with itself," which again provides the best definition
of the monarchical self as monad. Outside this blazing world of
the self, external reality is a debased sphere and man can only be
perceived through a riddle that lacks the nobility of the oedipal
riddle. In her sarcastic and pessimistic answer to Sir Humphrey
Interruption, who is curious about her "conceptions," Lady Contemplation adopts an anti-humanist stance to describe man:

> I had a conception of a Monster, as a Creature that had a rational
> Soul yet was a Fool: It had had a beautiful and perfect shape, yet was
> deformed and ill-favoured; It had clear distinguishing senses, and
> yet was sencelesse; It was produced from the Gods, but had the na-
> ture of a Devil; It had an eternal life, yet dyed as a Beast; It had a
> body, and no body. (198)

In such a passage, she anticipates both Pascal's views of the
absolute dereliction of man in *Les Pensées* and Swift's dystopian
Yahoo in *Gulliver's Travels,* just as much as she echoes Hamlet's
celebrated words—"What piece of work is a man . . . the beauty
of the world, the paragon of animals—and yet, to me, what is this
quintessence of dust?"[30] In *The Lady Contemplation,* culture and
nature are opposed through different schemes, as if culture be-

longed to the outer and rejected world and nature to the world of the imagination. In the process of reversal and dissociation, the *discordia concors* of the Baroque age, the paradoxical unity of contraries found in the relationship between Prospero and Caliban, seems then to have come to an end. New aesthetics appear here that will have their heyday during the Restoration period: they could be called aesthetics of antithesis, with the impossibility ever to reconcile opposites or recover the *coincidentia oppositorum* of the former age. Contrary to the idealization of the pastoral that takes place in *The Convent of Pleasure,* it is a satire of the genre that is shown in *The Lady Contemplation,* where the tradition is in fact undermined. Significantly, the antithesis is here constituted through two separate plays: the opposites do not combine and coexist in the same work, as they do in *As You Like It,* a typically Baroque play in that the pastoral and its parody finally contribute to a unified denouement.

Yet, strangely enough, within this antithetical mode, one further turn of the screw is given to the constitution of the self as a monad. In the world of Lady Contemplation, the world of the lover and the world of the beloved come from the same brain: it is on the same mental stage that a narcissistic, monadic self-love projects its fantasies, as in *The Blazing World.* There too, the female regiments and the seizure of a fort, also present in *Bell in Campo,* with their connotations both of adventure and reassuring safety, find their way into the imaginary world, this time with Pallas (another "Victoria") as the idealized figure of the female epic.

This treatment of the stage as place both of seclusion and exclusion allows for the vindication of the right of a woman to speak for herself, whatever the "design," "plot," "fort to make it strong," and "walls to keep out censure" chosen as so many bulwarks by Cavendish, who has a knack of turning her own shortcomings into creative versatility. But her drama is also the place where a modern conception of the individual expresses itself. Earlier than Defoe's emblematic figures of the modern self or the insular individual, whether Robinson Crusoe secluded on his island or Moll Flanders isolated in the overcrowded streets of London, Cavendish created her own version of the insular self. She adopted an anti-mundane attitude, characterized by a rejection of the real world, but not as central as in the movement of sensibility that had led to Vanity painting or preaching: Lady Happy and Lady

Contemplation have this in common that they do not turn away from the world either to escape the vanity of self-love or to turn to the contemplation of the hidden God, the *Deus absconditus* of Augustinian faith: if they do so, it is primarily to contemplate their own selves as newfound lands. For Lady Contemplation, "the Mind's a Commonwealth, and the thoughts are the citizens therein, and Reason rules as a King," with passions as "the unruly Rout,"[31] a commonplace metaphor if we remember the similar image Brutus uses in Shakespeare's *Julius Caesar* to express his state of mental disorder:

> . . . The state of man
> Like to a little kingdom suffers then
> The nature of an insurrection.[32]

But Contemplation makes clear at the same time that "the world is in my mind though my mind is not in the world," since the world is pure subjectivity: "My mind draws the World,/That Landscape in my brain."[33]

Cavendish's plays all stage a polemic of gender that leads to awareness and celebration of the self. Significantly enough, Defoe's Roxana, the monadic self-reliant, self-contained individual, achieves her insular self precisely by identifying herself, like a Cavendish heroine, as "Masculine-Feminine." But what finally emerges more fundamentally from Cavendish's dramatic aesthetics of fragmentation is epistemological. Relying on an episodic structure, the better to set apart some of her characters in epiphanic moments of poetic invention, Margaret Cavendish finally renders manifest the rise of modern subjectivity through the emancipation of imagination. "Contemplation" is being and, thus, becomes another way of asserting the creed of the modern self: "Cogito, ergo sum"—"I contemplate, therefore I am."

NOTES

1. Margaret Cavendish, *Playes* (London,1668), 9.
2. Ben Jonson, *Every Man Out of His Humour,* in *Ben Jonson's Plays,* ed. Felix E. Schelling, vol. 1 (London: J. M. Dent & Sons, 1910), 63.
3. Ibid., 64.
4. Ibid., 65.
5. Ibid., 64.

6. In act 4 of *The Convent of Pleasure, in* Margaret Cavendish, *The Convent of Pleasure and Other Plays,* ed. Anne Shaver (Baltimore and London: Johns Hopkins University Press, 1999), for example 238–39.

7. *The Unnatural Tragedy,* in Margaret Cavendish, *Playes* (London, 1662), act I, scene 7, 330.

8. The whole debate between Giovanni and Friar Bonaventure, at the opening of the play, revolves around the Epicurean atheism that the young man derives from his study of natural philosophy at university. The Friar clearly foresees the trespassing of all moral barriers as a result, incest being then considered as the worst of all possible transgressions. See Gisèle Venet, "Préface," in John Ford, *Dommage que ce soit une putain,* trans. Jean-Michel Déprats, ed. G. Venet (Paris: Gallimard, 1998).

9. John Donne, *The First Anniversary,* in *John Donne: Poésie,* ed. Robert Ellrodt (Paris: Imprimerie nationale, 1993), 312.

10. Ibid.

11. *Coriolanus,* in William Shakespeare, *The Complete Works,* ed. Stanley Wells and Gary Taylor (Oxford: Clarendon Press, 1988), 2.1. 171.

12. John Webster, *The Duchess of Malfi,* ed. Elizabeth M. Brennan (London: Benn, 1964) 1.1. 358–61.

13. Cavendish, *Playes,* 184.

14. Susan Wiseman, "Gender and Status in Dramatic Discourse: Margaret Cavendish, Duchess of Newcastle," in *Women, Writing, History: 1640–1740,* ed. Isobel Grundy and Susan Wiseman (London: B. T. Batsford, 1992): 161–77.

15. Margaret Cavendish, *The Sociable Companions, or, The Female Wits,* ed. Amanda Holton (Oxford: The Seventeenth Century Press, 1996), 34.

16. Ibid.

17. Cavendish, *Playes,* 184.

18. *As You Like It,* in Shakespeare, *The Complete Works,* 2.1. 12.

19. Cavendish, *Playes,* 335–36.

20. Ibid., 31.

21. Ibid., 209.

22. In Shakespeare's *Love's Labours Lost,* male characters try to keep the women outside the realm of Navarre, although as wooers, they are compelled to transgress their own rules.

23. Cavendish, *The Convent of Pleasure,* 235.

24. Ibid., 237.

25. Robert Burton, in his *Anatomy of Melancholy* (London, 1621) is equally intent on writing a treatise of passions as he observes this interrelation at length.

26. Cavendish, *The Convent of Pleasure,* 237.

27. Ibid., 245.

28. Ibid., 226.

29. Cavendish, *Playes,* 183.

30. *Hamlet,* in Shakespeare, *The Complete Works,* 2.2. 303–8.

31. Cavendish, *Playes,* 229.

32. *Julius Caesar,* in *The Complete Works,* 1.1. 366–68.

33. Cavendish, *Playes,* 229.

Notes on Contributors

ALEXANDRA BENNETT is Assistant Professor of English at Northern Illinois University. She has published articles on Elizabeth Cary, Margaret Cavendish, and women's drama, and is currently working on an extended study of early modern women's drama, performativity, and agency.

HERO CHALMERS is a member of the Faculty of English at Cambridge University. She has published articles on Mary Carleton and Margaret Cavendish and has recently completed a monograph entitled *Royalist Women Writers (1650–89)*.

LINE COTTEGNIES teaches English literature at the University of Paris 8—Saint-Denis (France). She is the author of *L'Eclipse du regard: la poésie anglaise du baroque au classicisme (1625–1660)* (1997). She has published articles on various aspects of seventeenth-century literature, including on Margaret Cavendish. She also published a French translation of her *Blazing World (Le Monde glorieux,* with a postface and illustrations) in 1999. She is currently working on epicureanism in the literature of the period.

JAMES FITZMAURICE is Professor and Coordinator of Graduate Studies in English at Northern Arizona University. He has been a postdoctoral fellow at Yale University and a senior visiting research fellow at Gonville and Caius College, Cambridge. He has published essays on Aphra Behn, Thomas Carew, Margaret Cavendish, Ben Jonson, Dorothy Osborne, and Jane Barker. He is general editor for *Major Women Writers of Seventeenth-Cen-*

tury England (1997), and he edited *Margaret Cavendish: The Sociable Letters* (1997) as well as Newcastle's *The Humorous Lovers* (1997).

SARAH HUTTON is Reader in Renaissance and Seventeenth-Century Studies at Middlesex University. Her publications include *Platonism and the English Imagination,* edited with Anna Baldwin (1994), *Women Science and Medicine 1550–1700,* edited with Lynette Hunter (1997), a new edition of Ralph Cudworth, *Treatise Concerning Eternal and Immutable Morality* (1996) and a revised edition of *The Conway Letters,* ed. M. H. Nicolson (1992). She is a consultant to the Feminism and Enlightenment research project organized by Barbara Taylor and research associate on the Newton Papers Project. She is also Director of *International Archives in the History of Ideas.*

SARA MENDELSON is Associate Professor in the Arts and Science Programme at McMaster University, and a Fellow of the Royal Historical Society. She is the author of *The Mental World of Stuart Women: Three Studies* (1987), *Women in Early Modern England 1550–1720* (1998) (with Patricia Crawford), and *Paper Bodies: A Margaret Cavendish Reader* (2000) (with Sylvia Bowerbank), as well as articles on Stuart women's diaries, early modern sexual identities (with Patricia Crawford), women's work, female civility in seventeenth-century England, popular perceptions of Elizabeth I, and nine entries for the *New Dictionary of Biography.*

EMMA L. E. REES is Senior Lecturer in English Literature at University College, Chester. She has worked on Margaret Cavendish for ten years, and is currently finishing a book to be published shortly. The main focus of her research is the body of work Cavendish produced while in exile in the 1650s.

LISA T. SARASOHN is Professor of History at Oregon State University. Her most recent publications are *Gassendi's Ethics: Freedom in a Mechanistic Universe* (1996), "Thomas Hobbes and the Duke of Newcastle: A Study in the Mutuality of Patronage," *Isis* 90 (1999), and "Was *Leviathan* Patronage Artifact?," *History of Political Thought* 21 (2000). She is currently working on a book on Margaret Cavendish and the Newcastle Circle.

BRANDIE R. SIEGFRIED is an Associate Professor of English Renaissance Literature at Brigham Young University. Her recent publications include articles for *Early Modern Literary Studies, Shakespeare Yearbook, George Herbert Journal,* and the *IASIL Annual.* She has completed the manuscript of her first book, *The Women's Line: Literary Conquest in the Wake of Elizabeth Tudor,* and is currently working on a second book, *The Literary History of Gráinne Ní Mháille.*

GISÈLE VENET, Professor at the University of Paris 3—Sorbonne Nouvelle, is the author of *Temps et vision tragique dans le théâtre de Shakespeare et de ses contemporains* (1985, reprinted 2002). She is currently editing Burton's *Anatomy of Melancholy* in French. She has edited a parallel-text edition of Shakespeare for Gallimard—Bibliothèque de la Pléiade (*The Tragedies,* two volumes, 2002; forthcoming, *The Histories* and *The Comedies*). She has also published Webster's *The Duchess of Malfi* with French translation (1992), as well as John Ford's *'Tis Pity She's a Whore* (1998), Shakespeare's *King Lear, All's Well that Ends Well* (1996), and *Henry V* (1999), in French translation. She is also the author of *Lectures d'Henry V* (2000). She has published widely on sixteenth and seventeenth-century drama and the links between England and dominant aesthetics in contemporary Europe.

NANCY WEITZ is a researcher in Learning Technologies and member of the English Faculty at the University of Oxford. She has published articles and essays on Milton's *Comus,* Vives's *Instruction of a Christian Woman,* and Bathsua Makin's *Essay to Revive the Antient Education of Gentlewomen.* Her current work includes plans for an online edition of regicide texts (with Diane Purkiss). She is a founding member and first President of the Margaret Cavendish Society.

Index

233